CIMA Exam Practice Kit

Management Accounting Financial Strategy

CIMA Exam Practice Kit

Management Accounting Financial Strategy

Tony Graham

Amsterdam • Boston • Heidelberg • London • New York • Oxford
Paris • San Diego • San Francisco • Singapore • Sydney • Tokyo

CIMA Publishing
An imprint of Elsevier
Linacre House, Jordan Hill, Oxford OX2 8DP
30 Corporate Drive, Burlington, MA 01803

First published 2007

Copyright © 2007, Elsevier Ltd. All rights reserved

No part of this publication may be reproduced in any material form (including
photocopying or storing in any medium by electronic means and whether
or not transiently or incidentally to some other use of this publication) without
the written permission of the copyright holder except in accordance with the provisions
of the Copyright, Designs and Patents Act 1988 or under the terms of a licence issued by the
Copyright Licensing Agency Ltd, 90 Tottenham Court Road, London, England
W1T 4LP. Applications for the copyright holder's written permission to reproduce any part of
this publication should be addressed to the publisher

Permissions may be sought directly from Elsevier's Science and Technology Rights
Department in Oxford, UK: phone: (+44) (0) 1865 843830; fax: (+44) (0) 1865 853333;
e-mail: permissions@elsevier.com. You may also complete your request on-line via
the Elsevier homepage (http://www.elsevier.com), by selecting 'Customer Support' and
then 'Obtaining Permissions'

Notice
No responsibility is assumed by the publisher for any injury and/or damage to persons
or property as a matter of products liability, negligence or otherwise, or from any use
or operation of any methods, products, instructions or ideas contained in the material
herein.

British Library Cataloguing in Publication Data
A catalogue record for this book is available from the British Library

Library of Congress Cataloguing in Publication Data
A catalogue record for this book is available from the Library of Congress

ISBN–10: 0 7506 8390 2
ISBN–13: 978 07506 8390 6

For information on all CIMA Publishing Publications
visit our website at www.cimapublishing.com

Typeset by Integra Software Services Pvt. Ltd, Pondicherry, India
www.integra-india.com
Printed and bound in The Netherlands

Working together to grow
libraries in developing countries

www.elsevier.com | www.bookaid.org | www.sabre.org

ELSEVIER   BOOK AID International   Sabre Foundation

Contents

Syllabus Guidance, Learning Objectives and Verbs	xii
Learning Outcomes, Syllabus Content and Examination Format	xv
Examination Techniques	xx

Part 1 Formulation of Financial Strategy — 1

1 Objectives of Organisations — 3
- Primary objective — 3
- Practical problems — 3
- Other stakeholders — 4
- Questions — 5
  - Question 1 – Objectives — 5
  - Question 2 – Educational — 5
  - Question 3 – Police — 6
  - Question 4 – Healthcare — 7
  - Question 5 – Financial Objectives — 8
- Answers — 9
  - Question 1 – Objectives — 9
  - Question 2 – Educational — 10
  - Question 3 – Police — 12
  - Question 4 – Healthcare — 13
  - Question 5 – Financial Objectives — 15

2 Assessment — 17
- Stakeholders — 17
- Profitability ratios — 17
- Investor ratios — 18
- Liquidity ratios — 18
- Gearing ratios — 18
- Treasury appraisal — 19
- Non-financial measures — 19
- Not-for-profit organisations — 19
- Questions — 21
  - Question 1 – Drugsco (Practice Question) — 21
  - Question 2 – Snowdome (Practice Question) — 22

	Question 3 – Hotel (Practice Question)	23
	Question 4 – ML	23
	Question 5 – XYZ training	24
Answers		26
	Question 1 – Drugsco	26
	Question 2 – Snowdome	27
	Question 3 – Hotel	27
	Question 4 – ML	27
	Question 5 – XYZ training	29

3 Dividend Policy — 31

Dividend irrelevancy theory — 31
Empirical research — 31
Implications and other practical points — 32
Alternatives to dividends — 32
Questions — 33
    Question 1 – PDQ dividends — 33
    Question 2 – RG plc — 34
Answers — 35
    Question 1 – PDQ dividends — 35
    Question 2 – RG plc — 36

Part 2 Financial Management — 39

4 Sources of Finance — 41

Factors to consider in choosing a source of finance — 41
Issue of shares to new shareholders — 41
Rights issues — 42
Pricing a rights issue — 42
Debt — 42
Considerations when issuing debt — 42
Lease vs buy — 42
SME funding problems — 43
Questions — 44
    Question 1 – X rights (Practice Question) — 44
    Question 2 – Mr Y (Practice Question) — 44
    Question 3 – EPS after project (Practice Question) — 44
    Question 4 – Lease or buy (Practice Question) — 44
    Question 5 – PJH — 45
    Question 6 – VID — 46
    Question 7 – Rump — 47
    Question 8 – RZ — 48
Answers — 49
    Question 1 – X rights — 49
    Question 2 – Mr Y — 49
    Question 3 – EPS after project — 49
    Question 4 – Lease or buy — 50
    Question 5 – PJH — 50
    Question 6 – VID — 52
    Question 7 – Rump — 53
    Question 8 – RZ — 55

5 Stock Market Efficiency

Principle
Weak form efficiency
Semi-strong form efficiency
Strong form efficiency
Summary
Implications for managers
Questions
    Question 1 – Investment (Practice Question)
    Question 2 – Newspaper (Practice Question)
    Question 3 – Founder
    Question 4 – COE
Answers
    Question 1 – Investment
    Question 2 – Newspaper
    Question 3 – Founder
    Question 4 – COE

6 Cost of Capital

Cost of equity
Capital asset pricing model (CAPM)
Cost of debt
Weighted average cost of capital (WACC)
Assumptions and use of the cost of capital
Questions
    Question 1 – Equity (Practice Question)
    Question 2 – Growth (Practice Question)
    Question 3 – CAPM (Practice Question)
    Question 4 – Debt (Practice Question)
    Question 5 – Loan stock (Practice Question)
    Question 6 – WACC (Practice Question)
    Question 7 – LS
    Question 8 – CAP
    Question 9 – WEB
    Question 10 – Deaton
Answers
    Question 1 – Equity
    Question 2 – Growth
    Question 3 – CAPM
    Question 4 – Debt
    Question 5 – Loan stock
    Question 6 – WACC
    Question 7 – LS
    Question 8 – CAP
    Question 9 – WEB
    Question 10 – Deaton

7 Adjustments to WACC

Financial risk and the cost of capital
Business risk and the cost of capital

viii Contents

Questions — 84
- Question 1 – Gearing change (Practice Question) — 84
- Question 2 – New values (Practice Question) — 84
- Question 3 – APV (Practice Question) — 84
- Question 4 – Beta (Practice Question) — 84
- Question 5 – Degearing (Practice Question) — 84
- Question 6 – REM — 84
- Question 7 – ZX APV — 86
- Question 8 – DEB — 86
- Question 9 – Imlico — 87

Answers — 89
- Question 1 – Gearing change — 89
- Question 2 – New values — 89
- Question 3 – APV — 89
- Question 4 – Beta — 90
- Question 5 – Degearing — 90
- Question 6 – REM — 90
- Question 7 – ZX APV — 92
- Question 8 – DEB — 92
- Question 9 – Imlico — 93

8 Impact of Financing — 95

Questions — 96
- Question 1 – ZX Inc. — 96
- Question 2 – UR — 97
- Question 3 – ABC services — 98
- Question 4 – AEF — 99

Answers — 101
- Question 1 – ZX Inc. — 101
- Question 2 – UR — 102
- Question 3 – ABC services — 104
- Question 4 – AEF — 105

Part 3 Business Valuations and Acquisitions — 107

9 Business Valuations — 109

Present value of future cash flows — 109
Price/earnings ratio — 109
Dividend valuation model — 110
Dividend yield — 110
Asset valuations — 110
Intellectual capital — 110
General comments — 110

Questions — 111
- Question 1 – Target (Practice Question) — 111
- Question 2 – CD — 111
- Question 3 – PDQ software — 112
- Question 4 – EQU — 113
- Question 5 – MediCons plc — 115
- Question 6 – BiOs — 116

Contents   ix

Answers		118
Question 1 – Target		118
Question 2 – CD		118
Question 3 – PDQ software		120
Question 4 – EQU		122
Question 5 – MediCons		123
Question 6 – BiOs		125

10 Mergers and Acquisitions — 129

Synergy — 129
Consideration for purchase — 130
Hostile bids and defence strategies — 130
City code and company law — 131
Management buyout (MBO) — 131
Questions — 132
    Question 1 – Company A (Practice Question) — 132
    Question 2 – PR — 132
    Question 3 – AB plc — 133
    Question 4 – TDC — 134
    Question 5 – RD — 135
    Question 6 – PCO plc — 136
Answers — 139
    Question 1 – Company A — 139
    Question 2 – PR — 139
    Question 3 – AB plc — 140
    Question 4 – TDC — 141
    Question 5 – RD — 143
    Question 6 – PCO plc — 144

Part 4 Investment Decisions and Project Control — 147

11 Investment Appraisal — 149

Appraisal methods — 149
Relevant costs in a net present value — 150
Asset replacement — 151
Capital rationing — 151
Questions — 153
    Question 1 – Machine (Practice Question) — 153
    Question 2 – IRR (Practice Question) — 153
    Question 3 – Labour (Practice Question) — 153
    Question 4 – RBS (Practice Question) — 153
    Question 5 – Money (Practice Question) — 154
    Question 6 – Taxation (Practice Question) — 154
    Question 7 – Cycle (Practice Question) — 154
    Question 8 – Rationing (Practice Question) — 154
    Question 9 – Indivisible (Practice Question) — 155
    Question 10 – ZX Rationing — 155
    Question 11 – TFC — 155
    Question 12 – Expansion — 156

Answers — 158
- Question 1 – Machine — 158
- Question 2 – IRR — 158
- Question 3 – Labour — 159
- Question 4 – RBS — 159
- Question 5 – Money — 159
- Question 6 – Taxation — 159
- Question 7 – Cycle — 160
- Question 8 – Rationing — 160
- Question 9 – Indivisible — 160
- Question 10 – ZX rationing — 161
- Question 11 – TFC — 161
- Question 12 – Expansion — 163

12 Risk in Investment Appraisal — 165
- Uncertainty — 165
- Real options — 166
- Post-implementation audits — 166
- Questions — 167
  - Question 1 – Rock (Practice Question) — 167
  - Question 2 – X training — 167
  - Question 3 – HS and IT — 169
  - Question 4 – SS — 169
- Answers — 171
  - Question 1 – Rock — 171
  - Question 2 – X training — 171
  - Question 3 – HS and IT — 173
  - Question 4 – SS — 174

13 Overseas Investments — 177
- Questions — 178
  - Question 1 – GH — 178
  - Question 2 – KH — 179
  - Question 3 – TMC — 180
  - Question 4 – AB overseas — 181
- Answers — 182
  - Question 1 – GH — 182
  - Question 2 – KH — 183
  - Question 3 – TMC — 184
  - Question 4 – AB overseas — 185

Part 5 Case Studies and Exam Papers — 189

14 Case Study Questions — 191
- Questions — 192
  - Question 1 – KL Group — 192
  - Question 2 – Dobbs — 195
  - Question 3 – C&C — 197
  - Question 4 – Hi-Clean — 200
  - Question 5 – JHC Group — 203

	Answers	207
	Question 1 – KL Group	207
	Question 2 – Dobbs	210
	Question 3 – C&C Airlines	213
	Question 4 – Hi-Clean	215
	Question 5 – JHC Group	219
15	**May 2006 Questions and Answers**	**223**
16	**Nov 2006 Questions and Answers**	**259**

Syllabus Guidance, Learning Objectives and Verbs

A The syllabus

The syllabus for the CIMA Professional Chartered Management Accounting qualification 2005 comprises three learning pillars:

- Management Accounting pillar
- Business Management pillar
- Financial Management pillar.

Within each learning pillar there are three syllabus subjects. Two of these subjects are set at the lower 'Managerial' level, with the third subject positioned at the higher 'Strategic' level. All subject examinations have a duration of three hours and the pass mark is 50%.

Note: In addition to these nine examinations, students are required to gain three years relevant practical experience and successfully sit the Test of Professional Competence in Management Accounting (TOPCIMA).

B Aims of the syllabus

The aims of the syllabus are:

- To provide for the Institute, together with the practical experience requirements, an adequate basis for assuring society that those admitted to membership are competent to act as management accountants for entities, whether in manufacturing, commercial or service organisations, in the public or private sectors of the economy.
- To enable the Institute to examine whether prospective members have an adequate knowledge, understanding and mastery of the stated body of knowledge and skills.
- To complement the Institute's practical experience and skills development requirements.

C Study weightings

A percentage weighting is shown against each topic in the syllabus. This is intended as a guide to the proportion of study time each topic requires.

All topics in the syllabus must be studied, since any single examination question may examine more than one topic, or carry a higher proportion of marks than the percentage study time suggested.

The weightings *do not* specify the number of marks that will be allocated to topics in the examination.

D Learning outcomes

Each topic within the syllabus contains a list of learning outcomes which should be read in conjunction with the knowledge content for the syllabus. A learning outcome has two main purposes:

1 to define the skill or ability that a well-prepared candidate should be able to exhibit in the examination;
2 to demonstrate the approach likely to be taken by examiners in examination questions.

The learning outcomes are part of a hierarchy of learning objectives. The verbs used at the beginning of each learning outcome relate to a specific learning objective, for example evaluate alternative approaches to budgeting.

The verb 'evaluate' indicates a high-level learning objective. As learning objectives are hierarchical, it is expected that at this level, students will have knowledge of different budgeting systems and methodologies and be able to apply them.

A list of the learning objectives and the verbs that appear in the syllabus, learning outcomes and examinations follows:

Learning objectives	Verbs used	Definition
1 Knowledge		
What you are expected to know	List	Make a list of
	State	Express, fully or clearly, the details of/facts of
	Define	Give the exact meaning of
2 Comprehension		
What you are expected to understand	Describe	Communicate the key features of
	Distinguish	Highlight the differences between
	Explain	Make clear or intelligible/State the meaning of
	Identify	Recognise, establish or select after consideration
	Illustrate	Use an example to describe or explain something

3 Application

How you are expected to apply your knowledge

Apply	To put to practical use
Calculate/compute	To ascertain or reckon mathematically
Demonstrate	To prove with certainty or to exhibit by practical means
Prepare	To make or get ready for use
Reconcile	To make or prove consistent/compatible
Solve	Find an answer to
Tabulate	Arrange in a table

4 Analysis

How you are expected to analyse the detail of what you have learned

Analyse	Examine in detail the structure of
Categorise	Place into a defined class or division
Compare and contrast	Show the similarities and/or differences between
Construct	To build up or compile
Discuss	To examine in detail by argument
Interpret	To translate into intelligible or familiar terms
Produce	To create or bring into existence

5 Evaluation

How you are expected to use your learning to evaluate, make decisions or recommendations

Advise	To counsel, inform or notify
Evaluate	To appraise or assess the value of
Recommend	To advise on a course of action

Key to Icons

- Exam focus
- Key points
- Questions
- Answers

Learning Outcomes, Syllabus Content and Examination Format

Syllabus outline

The syllabus comprises:

Topic and study weighting

A	Formulation of Financial Strategy	20%
B	Financial Management	30%
C	Business Valuations and Acquisitions	25%
D	Investment Decisions and Project Control	25%

Learning aims

Students should be able to:

- understand and apply contemporary thinking on strategic financial management;
- understand and utilise appropriate tools for strategic financial management;
- evaluate strategic financial management options in the light of the needs of management and the policy of the enterprise;
- characterise and describe the enterprise's financial strategy and use that characterisation to develop optimal financial strategy for all stages of the life-cycle; and
- assess and evaluate proposed strategies.

Assessment strategy

There will be a written examination paper of three hours, with the following sections.

Section A – 50 marks

A maximum of four compulsory questions, totalling 50 marks, all relating to a single scenario.

Section B – 50 marks

Two questions, from a choice of four, each worth 25 marks. Short scenarios will be given, to which some or all questions relate.

A – Formulation of financial strategy – 20%

Learning outcomes

On completion of their studies students should be able to:

(i) identify an organisation's objectives in financial terms and evaluate their attainment;
(ii) discuss the interrelationships between decisions concerning investment, financing and dividends;
(iii) identify and analyse the impact of internal and external constraints on financial strategy (e.g. funding, regulatory bodies, investor relations, strategy and economic factors);
(iv) evaluate current performance, taking account of potential variations in economic and business factors;
(v) recommend alternative financial strategies for an organisation.

Syllabus content

- The financial and non-financial objectives of different organisations (for example value for money, maximising shareholder wealth, providing a surplus).
- The three key decisions of financial management (by which we mean investment, financing, dividend) and their links.
- Benefits of matching characteristics of investment and financing, for example in cross-border investment.
- Identifying the financial objectives of an organisation and the economic forces affecting its financial plans, for example interest, inflation and exchange rates.
- Assessing attainment of financial objectives.
- Developing financial strategy in the context of regulatory requirements (e.g. price and service controls exercised by industry regulators) and international operations.
- Modelling and forecasting cash flows and financial statements based on expected values for economic variables (e.g. interest rates) and business variables (e.g. volume and margins) over a number of years.
- Analysis of sensitivity to changes in expected values in the above models and forecasts.
- Identifying financing requirements (both in respect of domestic and international operations) and the impacts of different types of finance on the above models and forecasts.
- Assessing the implications for shareholder value of alternative financial strategies, including dividend policy. *Note*: Modigliani and Miller's theory of dividend irrelevancy will be tested in broad terms. The mathematical proof of the model will not be required, but some understanding of the graphical method is expected.
- Current and emerging issues in financial reporting (e.g. proposals to amend or introduce new accounting standards) and in other forms of external reporting (e.g. environmental accounting).

B – Financial management – 30%

Learning outcomes

On completion of their studies students should be able to:

(i) identify and evaluate optimal strategies for the management of working capital and satisfaction of longer-term financing requirements;

(ii) identify and evaluate key success factors in the management of the finance function and its relationship with other parts of the organisation and, where necessary, with external parties;

(iii) discuss the role and management of the treasury function.

Syllabus content

- Working capital management strategies. (*Note*: No detailed testing of cash and stock management models will be set since these are covered at the Managerial level.)
- Types and features of domestic and international long-term finance: share capital (ordinary and preference shares, warrants), long-term debt (bank borrowing and forms of securitised debt, e.g. convertibles) and finance lease, and methods of issuing securities.
- The lender's assessment of creditworthiness.
- The lease or buy decision (with both operating and finance leases).
- The operation of stock exchanges (e.g. how share prices are determined, what causes share prices to rise or fall and the efficient market hypothesis). (*Note*: No detailed knowledge of any specific country's stock exchange will be tested.)
- The capital asset pricing model (CAPM): calculation of the cost of equity using the dividend growth model (knowledge of methods of calculating and estimating dividend growth will be expected), the ability to gear and ungear betas and comparison to the arbitrage pricing model.
- The ideas of diversifiable risk (unsystematic risk) and systematic risk (*Note*: Use of the two-asset portfolio formula will not be tested.)
- The cost of redeemable and irredeemable debt, including the tax shield on debt (numerical questions on the cost of convertible debt will not be tested).
- The weighted average cost of capital (WACC): calculation, interpretation and uses.
- Criteria for selecting sources of finance, including finance for international investments.
- The effect of financing decisions on balance sheet structure and on ratios of interest to investors and other financiers (gearing, earnings per share, price–earnings ratio, dividend yield, dividend cover gearing, interest cover).
- Management of the finance function and relationships with professional advisors (accounting, tax and legal), auditors and financial stakeholders (investors and financiers).
- The role of the treasury function in terms of setting corporate objectives, liquidity management, funding management and currency management.
- The advantages and disadvantages of establishing treasury departments as profit centres or cost centres, and their control.

C – Business valuations and acquisitions – 25%

Learning outcomes

On completion of their studies students should be able to:

(i) calculate values of organisations of different types, for example service, capital intensive;
(ii) identify and calculate the value of intangible assets (including intellectual property);
(iii) identify and evaluate the financial and strategic implications of proposals for mergers, acquisitions, demergers and divestments;
(iv) compare and recommend alternative forms of consideration for, and terms of, acquisitions;
(v) calculate post-merger or post-acquisition values of companies;

(vi) identify and evaluate post-merger or post-acquisition value enhancement strategies;
(vii) discuss and illustrate the impact of regulation on business combinations;
(viii) evaluate exit strategies.

Syllabus content

- Valuation bases for assets (e.g. historic cost, replacement cost and realisable value), earnings (e.g. price/earnings multiples and earnings yield) and cash flows (e.g. discounted cash flow, dividend yield and the dividend growth model).
- The strengths and weaknesses of each valuation method and when each is most suitable.
- Recognition of the interests of different stakeholder groups in mergers, acquisitions and company valuations.
- Application of the efficient market hypothesis to business valuations.
- Selection of an appropriate cost of capital for use in valuation. The impact of changing capital structure on the market value of a company. (*Note*: An understanding of Modigliani and Miller's theory of gearing, with and without taxes, will be expected, but proof of their theory will not be examined.)
- Forms of intellectual property and methods of valuation.
- The reasons for merger or acquisition (e.g. synergistic benefits). Forms of consideration and terms for acquisitions (e.g. cash, shares, convertibles and earn-out arrangements), and their financial effects.
- The post-merger or post-acquisition integration process (e.g. management transfer and merger of systems).
- The implications of regulation for business combinations. (*Note*: Detailed knowledge of the City Code and EU competition rules will not be tested.)
- The function/role of management buyouts, venture capitalists. Types of exit strategy and their implications.

D – Investment decisions and project control – 25%

Learning outcomes

On completion of their studies students should be able to:

(i) analyse relevant costs, benefits and risks of an investment project;
(ii) evaluate investment projects (domestic and international) taking account of potential variations in business and economic factors;
(iii) recommend methods of funding investments, taking account of basic tax considerations;
(iv) evaluate procedures for the implementation and control of investment projects;
(v) recommend investment decisions when capital is rationed.

Syllabus content

- Identification of a project's relevant costs (e.g. infrastructure, marketing and human resource development needs), benefits (including incremental effects on other activities as well as direct cash flows) and risks (i.e. financial and non-financial).
- Linking investments with customer requirements and product/service design.
- Linking investment in IS/IT with strategic, operational and control needs (particularly where risks and benefits are difficult to quantify).
- Calculation of a project's net present value and internal rate of return, including techniques for dealing with cash flows denominated in a foreign currency and use of the weighted average cost of capital.

- The modified internal rate of return based on a project's 'terminal value' (reflecting an assumed reinvestment rate). The effects of taxation (including foreign direct and withholding taxes) and potential restrictions on remittances on these calculations.
- Recognising risk using the certainty equivalent method (when given a risk free rate and certainty equivalent values).
- Adjusted present value. (*Note*: The two step method may be tested for debt introduced permanently and debt in place for the duration of the project.)
- Capital investment real options (i.e. to make follow-on investment, abandon or wait).
- Project implementation and control in the conceptual stage, the development stage, the construction stage and initial manufacturing/operating stage.
- Post completion audit of investment projects.
- Single period for capital rationing for divisible and non-divisible projects. (*Note*: Multi-period rationing will not be tested.)

Examination Techniques

Essay questions

Your essay should have a clear structure, i.e. an introduction, a middle and an end. Think in terms of 1 mark for each relevant point made.

Numerical questions

It is essential to show workings in your answer. If you come up with the wrong answer and no workings, the examiner cannot award any marks. However, if you get the wrong answer but apply the correct technique then you will be given some marks.

Reports and memorandum

Where you are asked to produce an answer in a report type format you will be given easy marks for style and presentation.

- A *report* is a document from an individual or group in one organisation sent to an individual or group in another.
- A *memorandum* is an informal report going from one individual or group to another individual or group in the same organisation.

You should start a report as follows:

    To: J. SMITH, CEO, ABC plc

    From: M ACCOUNTANT

    Date: 31st December 200X

    Terms of Reference: Financial Strategy of ABC plc

Part 1

Formulation of Financial Strategy

Objectives of Organisations

✎ Exam focus

You should understand the primary objective of companies, the assumption of which underlies the rest of the syllabus. You should also be able to discuss other stakeholders and their objectives, particularly in the context of corporate governance.

🔑 Key points

Primary objective

In financial management we will assume that the primary aim of the organisation is to maximise shareholders' wealth. As shareholders own shares, this is accomplished by maximising the share price. In theory, the share price should be, depending on the efficiency of the market, the present value of the cash flows paid to the shareholders.

Practical problems

In practice the information shareholders have is limited, and many of the estimates will be very rough approximations. Traditionally, managers were rewarded for producing strong profits, but this often led to short-term behaviour and did not necessarily result in a high share price.

Shareholder value analysis (SVA) tried to reward managers for improving the share price by identifying seven factors under the control of the management which influenced the share price:

- sales growth
- profit margin
- marginal cash tax-rate
- investment needed in fixed assets
- investment needed in working capital
- cost of capital (to reflect risk)
- the competitive advantage period.

Various performance models have been developed to set objectives and reward managers accordingly.

Other stakeholders

The theoretical approach ignores other stakeholders, such as employees, society, customers, suppliers and lenders.

Different countries build in the concerns of other stakeholders to a greater or lesser extent, depending on their culture and/or legislation.

In the UK, corporate governance is a mixture of legislation and voluntary codes. It mostly deals with the way in which companies are controlled and run, and as such tends to protect the shareholders' interests and to some extent that of the lenders and suppliers.

There are moves, however, to a wider social awareness and some companies are now producing environmental and social performance reports with objectives and achievements in numerous areas.

Questions

Question 1 – Objectives

This question concerns two organisations, one in the private sector and one in the public sector.

Organisation 1
This is a listed company in the electronics industry. Its stated financial objectives are:

- to increase earnings per share year on year by 10% per annum; and
- to achieve a 25% per annum return on capital employed.

This company has an equity market capitalisation of £600 million. It also has a variety of debt instruments trading at a total value of £150 million.

Organisation 2
This organisation is a newly established purchaser and provider of healthcare services in the public sector. The organisation's legal status is a trust. Its total income for the current year will be almost £100 million. It is considering funding the building of a new healthcare centre via the Private Finance Initiative (PFI). The total debt will be £15 million. Capital and interest will be repaid over 15 years at a variable rate of interest, currently 9% each year. The trust's sole financial objective states simply 'to achieve financial balance during the year'. Its other objectives are concerned with qualitative factors such as 'providing high quality healthcare'.

Requirements

(a) Discuss

 (i) the reasons for the differences in the financial objectives of the two types of organisation given above; and
 (ii) the main differences in the business risks involved in the achievement of their financial objectives and how these risks might be managed.

 Use the scenario details given above to assist your answer wherever possible.

 (18 marks)

(b) Explain how the financial risks introduced into the public sector organisation by the use of PFI might affect the achievement of its objectives and comment on how these risks might be managed.

 (7 marks)

Note: Candidates from outside the UK may use examples of private financing of public sector schemes in their own country in answering part (b) of this question if they wish.

(Total = 25 marks)

Question 2 – Educational

(a) You are a newly appointed Finance Manager of an Educational Institution that is mainly government funded, having moved from a similar post in a service company in the private sector. The objective, or mission statement, of this Institution is shown in its publicity material as:

 To achieve recognised standards of excellence in the provision of teaching and research.

The only financial performance measure evaluated by the government is that the Institution has to remain within cash limits. The cash allocation each year is determined by a range of non-financial measures such as the number of research publications the Institution's staff have achieved and official ratings for teaching quality.

However, almost 20% of total cash generated by the Institution is now from the provision of courses and seminars to private sector companies, using either its own or its customers' facilities. These customers are largely unconcerned about research ratings and teaching quality as they relate more to academic awards such as degrees.

The Head of the Institution aims to increase the percentage of income coming from the private sector to 50% over the next five years. She has asked you to advise on how the management team can evaluate progress towards achieving this aim as well as meeting the objective set by government for the activities it funds.

Requirement

Discuss the main issues that an institution such as this has to consider when setting objectives.

Advise on

- whether a financial objective, or objectives, could or should be determined; and
- whether such objective(s) should be made public.

(9 marks)

(b) The following is a list of financial and non-financial performance measures that were in use in your previous company:

Financial	Non-financial
Value added	Customer satisfaction
Profitability	Competitive position
Return on investment	Market share

Requirement

Choose two of each type of measure, explain their purpose and advise on how they could be used by the Educational Institution over the next five years to assess how it is meeting the Head of the Institution's aims.

(16 marks)

Note: A report format is NOT required in answering this question.

(Total = 25 marks)

Question 3 – Police

A regional police force has the following corporate objectives:

- to reduce crime and disorder;
- to promote community safety;
- to contribute to delivering justice and maintaining public confidence in the law.

The force aims to achieve these objectives by continuously improving its resources management to meet the needs of its stakeholders. It has no stated financial objective other than to stay within its funding limits.

The force is mainly public-funded but, like other regional forces, it has some commercial operations, for example policing football matches when the football clubs pay a fee to the police force for its officers working overtime. The police force uses this money to supplement the funding it receives from the government. The national government is proposing to privatise (i.e. sell off) these commercial operations and has already been in preliminary discussions with an international security company. This company's stated financial objectives are:

- to increase earnings per share year on year by 5% per annum; and
- to achieve a 20% per annum return on capital employed.

Arguments put forward by government in favour of privatisation focus on the conflict of objectives between mainstream operations and commercial activities, and savings to the taxpayer. However, the proposals have met with strong opposition from most of the force's stakeholders.

Requirements

(a) Discuss the reasons for the differences in the objectives of the two types of organisation given above. Use the scenario details given above to assist your answer wherever possible.

(12 marks)

(b) Discuss the influence the commercial operations might currently have on the police force's ability to meet its stated objectives. Include in your discussion an evaluation of the possible effects on mainstream services and the various stakeholder groups if the commercial operations were to be privatised.

(13 marks)
(Total = 25 marks)

Question 4 – Healthcare

Two senior executives have recently met on a course where they were being taught about setting financial objectives and the three key policy decisions listed below:

1. the investment decision;
2. the financing decision;
3. the dividend decision.

One of the executives works for a large healthcare company listed on the stock exchange, the other works in the public sector health service where all services are provided free of charge to users at the point of delivery. The public sector health service is financed through an annual cash budget funded entirely by taxes and government borrowing and has no treasury department.

The following extracts are from their conversation after the course:

Healthcare company executive
  Life must be so much easier for you. We have to raise finance from various sources to fund any new investment. We also have to ensure that we pay a dividend that keeps our shareholders happy.

Public sector health service executive
  I don't think you would find a cash-constrained life, as we experience it, very easy. I would like to be able to raise money on the stock market to fund our business requirements. I would also much prefer to have my own treasury department to go to at any time rather than having to wait and see what we have been allocated in our annual budget.

Requirements:

(a) Identify in which of the three key policy decisions listed above the public sector health service would have **least** involvement, and explain why. Additionally, identify in which of the three key policy decisions listed above a treasury department would have **most** involvement, and explain why.

(8 marks)

(b) Describe each of the three key policy decisions listed and discuss the importance of each of them to the shareholders in the healthcare company.

(9 marks)

(c) Describe the main methods of raising new equity finance and recommend the most appropriate method for the healthcare company to raise equity finance on the stock market.

(8 marks)
(Total = 25 marks)

Question 5 – Financial Objectives

When determining the financial objectives of a company, it is necessary to take three types of policy decision into account: investment policy, financing policy and dividend policy.

Requirements

(a) Discuss the nature of these three types of decision, commenting on how they are inter-related and how they might affect the value of the firm (that is the present value of projected cash flows).

(12 marks)

(b) Describe the different functions of the treasury and financial control departments of an organisation and comment on the relative contributions of these two departments to policy determination and the setting and achievement of financial objectives.

(13 marks)
(Total marks = 25)

✓ Answers

Question 1 – Objectives

(a) (i) **Differences in financial objectives**

Objectives in the private and public sectors have come closer together in recent years, as private companies appreciate the needs of other stakeholders apart from shareholder, and the public sector concentrates more on value for money and the best use of the financial resources.

However, the financial objectives remain the key areas for the private sector, whose primary responsibility is to their shareholders, and the public sector's primary objectives are the provision of a quality service.

In addition, the private sector will generally set their objectives, by reference to the needs of their stakeholders, while the public sector organisation will have many of its objectives imposed by the government.

EPS
Earnings per share are used by shareholders to judge the growth achieved. While it can be misleading, it gives an idea of the profits generated in the year. The public sector generally does not have such a financial measure but concentrates more on the service provided.

ROCE
The private sector company has to give a sufficient return to its investors for the risk they perceive in the investment. This can be approximated by tracking the return on capital employed.

In the public sector, to convince the 'investors', usually the government, to release funds and not to withdraw resources, the organisation needs to persuade them that the activities represent value for money. This is often politically driven rather than being based on long-term financial analysis.

Cash limits
The public sector has a major objective to achieve financial balance during the year, as it is unable to raise more during the year. The private sector charges customers and can raise more revenue by selling more.

(ii) **Business risks and management**

A major difference between the two is how risk in the organisation is built into the objective. A private sector company has the risk that it may fail to attract any customers and hence any revenue. Hence the objectives are focused around the revenues and profits generated.

In the trust, the 'customers' have little choice in the healthcare in the area, so there is little risk to the trust in terms of the quantity of service required dropping. However, there is a major risk in terms of the quality of service delivered, so the main objectives relate to this. This is bound to be more difficult to measure, so a number of targets have been developed by government to assess progress in these areas.

Generally, we could say the main risk to a private sector organisation is that demand for the product falls, while for a public sector one, demand for the service increases beyond what can be managed within its resources.

The private sector company could manage its major commercial risk by:

- maintaining and monitoring its quality
- analysing customers and competitors
- ensuring against risks where possible.

The public sector trust has to manage the risk that it fails to give a service of sufficient quality within its financial constraints, by:

- monitoring value for money of the services provided, both internally and externally
- ensuring that services bought are the most effective
- using private finance where possible to ease financial constraints.

(b) **Financial risks**

The original aim of PFI was to allow services to be expanded and quality enhanced without increasing the public funds provided. This was done by private sector providing assets such as the new centre for relatively low financial rates; this is possible because there is much less risk of default on payments and the private sector company is therefore happy with a lower return than normal.

The main risks to the trust's financial objective from this PFI debt are:

- interest rates might rise and not be matched by government finance
- income falls but interest and capital still have to be paid.

However, annual payments will be £15 million/8.06 = £1.86 million which is less than 2% of annual income, so it is unlikely that this will be a problem for the trust. If it does materialise, the trust may be able to negotiate longer terms (15 years is shorter than the usual PFI).

Question 2 – Educational

(a) **Setting objectives**

The main issues to consider in setting objectives are:

- deciding who the main stakeholders are
- assessing and estimating the level of financial resources which are likely
- whether one objective can meet all the needs of the various stakeholders
- can the objective be measured
- should the objectives and performance be made public.

A financial objective is fairly easy to measure against progress, and performance can also be compared to other similar educational institutions. However, one objective is probably not sufficient, given the different nature of the two markets.

However, other educational institutions may not have the same political influences. In addition, the results of the two areas will be affected by the apportionment of costs between them. Lastly, the institution may not be in full control of its policies in areas such as fees and selection, so that it may be misleading to draw conclusions from its performance, particularly in comparison with others.

(b) **Performance measures**

Financial measures were traditionally those used by management, but there has been an increasing focus on non-financial areas as well in order to judge success in terms of meeting objectives. These will tend to pick up objectives relating to the needs of different stakeholders.

Financial measures

(i) Value added

This measure looks at the performance of an organisation by trying to identify the value added to the service by the organisation's own efforts. It is more common in the private sector, but has been introduced in some areas of the public sector to allow better comparisons to be made. A school with an intake from a wealthy intelligent background would be expected to produce better results than one with a poor deprived intake, but the second school might have added more value in terms of improving the level which the children attained between entering and leaving the school.

The institution could try to look at the background of students and assess the improvement made, compared with competitors or against expected performance based on their prior attainment. This would be complicated to undertake and an approximation might look at the student body for each year as a whole, comparing the average intake background and attainment to the average results on leaving. An even cruder measure would be to look at the average degree class or the percentage of firsts and 2.1s.

This measure is included under financial measures as the private sector often use (Sales value – Cost of purchases and services) to measure it. The public sector is less likely to use financial terms to measure it, as seen above.

(ii) Profitability

This measure looks at the profits generated per unit of input (such as per staff member), but does not look at the *quality* of those profits. It can therefore lead to short-term focus, as the risk to longer-term profits is not considered. In the context of the institution, this might mean putting a very large number of students in one lecture room in order to decrease cost per student or increase revenue per lecturer.

However, in the long term, results and hence the reputation and recruitment might suffer, leading to lower profits.

Used in conjunction with other measures, it can give useful information on how the institute compares to others.

This measure does not connect directly to the stated mission statement of the institute, so it may need to rethink its objectives as discussed in part (a) before introducing this measure.

Non-financial measures

(i) Customer satisfaction

This is an important measure because if customers are not satisfied, they could go elsewhere and other potential customers could be discouraged. In the context of the institution, the two sets of 'customers' are government-funded students and companies. Although the first group have limited ability to seek redress if not satisfied, poor performance in exams could reduce government funding, as could a high percentage of student drop-out, and reduce applications for courses. The second group could show their disappointment much more quickly by not booking further courses or seminars and having an immediate impact on income.

Measuring customer satisfaction can be difficult, but course assessments at the end of every course, quality audits by regulatory bodies, company discussions and peer reviews could help.

(ii) Competitive position

In a competitive marketplace, an organisation needs to be aware of its position in that market. The institution needs to be aware of how it is doing compared with its competitors. Government funding now partly relies on the level and quality of research, and as this is externally assessed it will make comparisons in this area easier. The amount of revenue generated by company work for competitors will be less easy to ascertain. Student courses can be easily compared against competitors as the number on particular courses are publicly available, and absolute numbers and trends can be compared for all the courses offered.

Question 3 – Police

(a) **Differences in objectives**

Objectives in the public and private sectors have been coming closer together, as the public sector has become more aware of the need to give value for money, and the private sector has started to recognise other stakeholders apart from shareholders.

Despite this, the private company's primary responsibility is to their shareholders within the constraints imposed by society and government. Public bodies generally have their objectives imposed by government rather than setting their own.

EPS
Earnings per share are used by shareholders to judge performance by looking at the growth achieved. While it can be misleading, it gives an idea of the profits generated in the year. The public sector generally does not have such a financial measure but concentrates more on the service provided. Indeed, some public sector organisations would consider it a failure to have not spent all the revenue received (i.e. to have achieved a 'nil profit' position).

ROCE
The private sector company has to give a sufficient return to its investors for the risk they perceive in the investment. This can be approximated by tracking the return on capital employed.

In the public sector, to convince the 'investors', usually the government, to release funds and not to withdraw resources, the organisation needs to persuade them that the activities represent value for money. This is often politically driven rather than being based on long-term financial analysis.

Cash limits
The public sector has a major objective to stay within its cash resources, as it is unable to raise more during the year. The private sector charges customers and can raise more revenue by selling more.

Risk

A major difference between the two is how risk in the organisation is built into the objectives. A private sector company has the risk that it may fail to attract any customers and hence any revenue. Hence the objectives are focused around the revenues and profits generated.

In the police force, the 'customers' have little choice in the police services in the area, so there is little risk to the police operations in terms of the quantity of the service required falling. However, there is a major risk in terms of the quality of service delivered, so the main objectives relate to this. This is bound to be more difficult to measure, so a number of targets have been developed by government to assess progress in these areas.

Generally, we could say the main risk to a private sector organisation is that demand for the service falls, while for a public sector one its demand for the service increases beyond what can be managed within its resources.

(b) **Influence of commercial operations**

The government has argued that there is a conflict of objectives, as they feel that senior police officers may divert resources to activities such as football matches, which will have a negative impact on the resources available for other mainstream operations, in order to ease financial constraints.

However, it could be argued that a visible police presence at football matches will help to maintain public confidence in the law and reduce crime and disorder on the streets.

Additional finance raised could also help the force to meet its other objectives by providing more resources.

The impact on the various stakeholder groups is likely to be:

- Senior police officers will probably fear a reduction in the financial resources and hence a reduction in mainstream activities, unless the government make up the shortfall.
- Police officers will lose a major opportunity to earn overtime and is likely to be an unpopular move.
- Football clubs and other organisations that have the police force may be concerned that the quality of service will deteriorate. The police have wide experience of managing crowds at matches and have wider powers than a private company if there are problems in surrounding streets.
- The local community is likely to be concerned in a similar way that trouble in the area on football match days will not be dealt with effectively.
- The government will receive cash for selling the service.

Question 4 – Healthcare

(a) **Key policy decisions**

The public sector health service will have little involvement in a dividend decision. This determines how much of the surplus cash is returned to shareholders. As the public sector health service does not have shareholders, this is not relevant; surplus cash is used to provide additional services.

A treasury department in a private sector company is likely to have most involvement in the financing decision. Although the department may be involved in the dividend decision and, to some extent, assessing investment opportunities, this is to the extent that they impinge on their primary role. This is to ensure that funds are available when needed and that surplus funds are put to good use.

(b) **Importance to shareholders**

The investment decision considers the benefits of investing cash, either in projects or in working capital, or even in high yield deposit accounts. This is important to shareholders, as it will determine the cash flows which are generated by the company and will ultimately affect the dividends paid and the share price. Assessing projects in the healthcare industry can be difficult as large investments are often required which promise the possibility of returns over many years, making the cash flows hard to estimate. Shareholders will also be concerned to compare the risk as well as the return between profits, as a higher risk investment should carry a higher return to compensate.

The financing decision considers the source of the finance required for the business operations. This will be a mixture of equity and long-term debt finance; companies need to balance the benefits to their shareholders – debt is a cheaper form of finance as the returns required are lower (due to lower risk) and the debt interest is tax allowable, but excessive gearing can increase the risk to the company, and hence the shareholders, dramatically.

The dividend decision looks at how much of the surplus cash generated should be paid out to the shareholders, and how much retained for future investments. Companies often make two payments a year, and shareholders generally prefer a predictable, steadily rising, dividend rather than one, which follows the fluctuations of the profits. A dividend policy is often declared for a number of years to give this predictability. A company which then delivers what it promised will generally be regarded as less risky, and hence more valuable, by shareholders.

(c) **Raising equity finance**

Equity can be raised via a placing, an offer for sale or a public offer.

A placing is when shares are offered to a small number of investors, usually institutions. The costs are likely to be lower but will concentrate ownership.

An offer for sale allots shares to an issuing house which then offers them to the public. Issuing costs are higher, but it will create a wider share base.

In a public offer, the company itself offers them to the public. This will involve high issue costs to cover publicity and underwriting.

The healthcare company is already listed on the stock exchange; it is likely that a rights issue, in which existing shareholders are given the right to subscribe for more shares, will be the method used. The shareholders buy them at a price below the market price, but can sell these rights if they cannot afford to subscribe. Theoretically, although the proportional shareholdings may change, an investor should be no worse off or better off whether they take up or sell the rights.

Question 5 – Financial Objectives

(a) **Investing, financing and dividend policies**

The investment decision considers the benefits of investing cash either in projects or in working capital or even in high yield deposit accounts. This is important to shareholders as it will determine the cashflows which are generated by the company and will ultimately affect the dividends paid and the share price. Assessing projects can sometimes be difficult as the returns may be spread over many years making the cashflows harder to estimate. Shareholders will also be concerned to compare the risk as well as the return between profits, as a higher risk investment should carry a higher return to compensate.

The financing decision considers the source of the finance required for the business operations. This will be a mixture of equity and long-term debt finance; companies need to balance the benefits to their shareholders – debt is a cheaper form of finance as the returns required are lower (due to lower risk) and the debt interest is tax allowable, but excessive gearing can increase the risk to the company, and hence the shareholders, dramatically.

The dividend decision looks at how much of the surplus cash generated should be paid out to the shareholders, and how much retained for future investments. Companies often make two payments a year, and shareholders generally prefer a predictable, steadily rising, dividend rather than one which follows the fluctuations of the profits. A dividend policy is often declared for a number of years to give this predictability. A company which then delivers what it promises will generally be regarded as less risky, and hence more valuable, by shareholders.

The three decisions are, therefore, interrelated as the finance needed for viable projects will come from both internal funds, which have not been paid out as dividends, and externally raised finance. The mixture of funds raised and used will then affect the cost of capital, which in turn will affect the viability of investments.

(b) **Treasury and Financial Control Departments**

A treasurer will be responsible for ensuring that funds are available (at a reasonable cost) when required and that surplus funds are reinvested to gain the maximum benefit to the company.

A financial controller is responsible for accounting, reporting and controlling those funds.

Therefore, in a large company, the treasury function might include

- Establishing corporate finance objectives
- Managing liquid assets
- Determining policies and identifying sources of funding
- Currency and interest rate hedging.

The financial control function will more concerned with the recording and reporting of financial information, such as:

- Preparing financial statements
- Preparing budgets
- Monitoring performance against budget.

While the treasury department sets the objectives and policies in this area, and the financial control department implements and monitors these, the relationship is more complex. The treasury has responsibility for the financing decision discussed in (a) above, whilst the financial control has responsibility for the investment decision. They are thus inter-related in that the financial control will specify the funds required for treasury to access, but the cost of those funds raised by treasury will then affect the viability of the projects assessed by financial control.

In smaller companies, the two functions may be combined and individual responsibilities may be less clear cut.

Assessment 2

✏️ Exam focus

You need to be able to analyse a set of financial statements with supporting information. This analysis will be primarily based on ratios, but may also look at non-financial information. In each case, it is important to interpret your findings rather than just presenting a list of calculations. Look for connections between ratios and remember that it is virtually impossible to make a comment about a ratio unless you are comparing it to another result calculated on the same basis.

✏️ Key points

Stakeholders

A number of stakeholder groups are interested in the financial performance of an organisation. These include the management, investors, lenders and potential investors and lenders. A number of others, such as society, government, suppliers, customers and employees may be interested in specific areas as well.

Profitability ratios

(a) Return on capital employed (ROCE) = $\dfrac{\text{Profit before interest + tax (PBIT)}}{\text{Long-term debt + equity}}$

(b) Operating profit margin = $\dfrac{\text{PBIT}}{\text{Sales revenue}}$

(c) Asset turnover = $\dfrac{\text{Sales revenue}}{\text{Capital employed}}$

(d) Return on equity = $\dfrac{\text{Profit after interest and tax}}{\text{Shareholders' funds}}$

(e) Expense ratio = $\dfrac{\text{Expense}}{\text{Sales revenue}}$

Investor ratios

(a) Earnings per share (EPS) = $\dfrac{\text{Distributable profit for the year}}{\text{Number of shares in issue}}$

(b) P/E ratio = $\dfrac{\text{Share price}}{\text{EPS}}$

(c) Dividend yield = $\dfrac{\text{Dividend}}{\text{Share price}}$

(d) Payout ratio = $\dfrac{\text{Dividend}}{\text{Distributable profit for the year}}$

(e) Dividend cover = $\dfrac{\text{Distributable profit for the year}}{\text{Dividend}}$

Liquidity ratios

(a) Receivables collection period = $\dfrac{\text{Average trade receivables}}{\text{Annual credit sales}} \times 365 \text{ days}$

(b) Payables payment period = $\dfrac{\text{Average trade payables}}{\text{Annual purchases}} \times 365 \text{ days}$

(c) Inventory holding period = $\dfrac{\text{Average inventory}}{\text{Annual cost of sales}} \times 365 \text{ days}$

(d) Current ratio (liquidity ratio) = $\dfrac{\text{Current assets}}{\text{Current liabilities}}$

(e) Quick ratio (Acid test) = $\dfrac{\text{Current assets excluding inventory}}{\text{Current liabilities}}$

Gearing ratios

(a) Gearing ratio = $\dfrac{\text{Long-term debt}}{\text{Long-term debt + shareholders' funds}}$

(b) Interest cover = $\dfrac{\text{PBIT}}{\text{Interest}}$

Many of the above ratios (such as ROCE and Gearing) have several different definitions. This does not matter as long as the result is compared to a ratio calculated in the same way.

It is important to realise that a ratio on its own tells you very little and no absolute targets can be set without reference to the circumstances of a particular organisation. To make informed comments we need to make comparisons. These can be with:

- the previous year
- the budget
- an investor's expectations
- a competitor
- the industry average.

Treasury appraisal

Treasury can be treated as a cost centre or a profit centre. A profit centre might mean charging business units a market rate for services and encouraging an effective service, but may tempt the treasury department to speculate as well as involve additional administration time and costs.

Non-financial measures

Non-financial measures may also be important to the long-term success of the company. Areas which these measures might look at include:

- customer satisfaction
- employee motivation and welfare
- management motivation and welfare
- environmental issues.

There can be a tendency for managers to become overwhelmed by the number of measures. There needs to be a balance between having enough to control the most important aspects of the business without having too many to be sensibly managed.

Not-for-profit organisations

A not-for-profit organisation is likely to have a large number of stakeholders. It is not that easy to reduce them down to a few key stakeholders, but even then they are likely to have very different, possibly with conflicting views on what the organisation's key objectives should be.

The three 'E's of economy, effectiveness and efficiency look at:

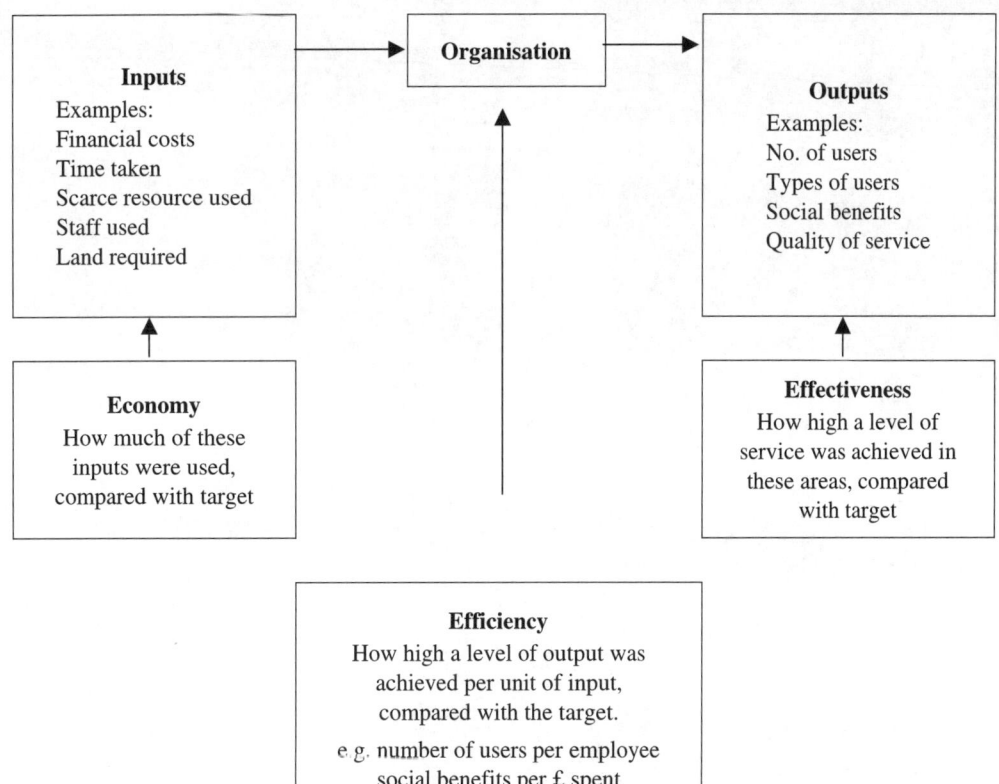

Many not-for-profit organisations, especially those in the public sector, have targets set or conditions imposed by the government. These often involve the publication of certain key indicators and include:

- local councils' performance in numerous areas
- schools' exam results and absentee rates
- hospitals' waiting times
- level of service and prices for railways and utilities.

Questions

Question 1 – Drugsco (Practice Question)

Analyse and comment on the results of a large listed pharmaceuticals company, Drugsco plc:

	2001 £m	2002 £m
Revenue	8,341	9,000
Cost of sales	(5,209)	(6,178)
	3,132	2,822
Finance costs	(206)	(136)
	2,926	2,686
Taxation	(933)	(819)
	1,933	1,867
Dividends declared were £1,202 m for 2001 and £1,249 m for 2002.		
Non-current assets	4,312	4,188
Current assets		
Inventory	804	855
Trade receivables	2,302	2,285
Investments	1,001	1,447
Cash	261	215
	4,368	4,802
Current liabilities		
Trade payables	2,608	2,705
	1,760	2,097
	6,072	6,285
Loan stock	(4,439)	(3,842)
	1,633	2,443
Share capital (25p shares)	886	894
Additional paid in capital	621	805
Other reserves	126	744
	1,633	2,443
Share price at year end	£5.45	£4.18

The company has a policy of writing off all development expenditure as incurred. The patent on a revolutionary drug expired at the end of 2001; 2002 saw many competitors producing similar products. As a result there has been some fierce competition on price on what was in 2001 one of the company's strongest products.

Note: Assume Purchases approximates to Cost of Sales in both years.

Question 2 – Snowdome (Practice Question)

Snowdome plc

Income statement for the year ending 31 December 2002

	£'000
Sales revenue	105,430
Cost of sales	(73,801)
Gross profit	31,629
Operating expenses	(29,654)
Profit before interest and tax	1,975
Finance costs	(1,613)
	362
Tax	(131)
Profit after tax	231

Dividends were declared of £143,000.

Balance sheet as at 31 December 2002

Non-current assets	15,964
Current assets	
Inventory	12,932
Receivables	15,574
Cash	130
	28,636
Creditors due within one year	
Trade payables	10,943
Total assets less current liabilities (15,964 + 28,636 − 10,943)	33,657
Share capital	1,100
Reserves	16,427
	7,527
10% debentures	16,130
	33,657

Using the data above, calculate the following ratios:

Return on capital employed
Operating profit margin
Asset turnover
Return on equity
Earnings per share
Price earnings ratio
Dividend per share
Dividend cover
Dividend yield (assume Snowdome shares are currently trading at 260p)
Interest cover
Gearing (based on book values)
Current ratio
Quick ratio

Question 3 – Hotel (Practice Question)

A family run hotel has 60 rooms and a dining room and is located in Edinburgh. Suggest four ways in which they could attempt to measure customer satisfaction.

Question 4 – ML

ML plc is a large company that is listed on a major international stock exchange. Its shares are held mainly by large financial institutions which have, in general, favoured a generous dividend payout policy.

ML plc manufactures consumer electrical goods. This is a rapidly changing industry that requires significant new investment in developing new products every few years. Failure to make such investment is likely to result in reduced competitiveness. The following data are relevant to the company for each of the years ended 30 September:

	2000	2001	2002	2003
£1 ordinary shares (million)	300	300	300	450
Dividend (£ million)	50	55	55	70
Retained profit for year (£ million)	200	250	100	300
Total debt (£ million)	1,000	1,100	1,350	850
Share price at 30 September (£)	4	5	6	5
New investment in fixed assets (£ million)	190	260	100	290

The company made a rights issue on 1 October 2002 of 1 for 2 at an issue price of £4 per share. All debt carries interest at 10% per annum and any new debt is taken on at the end of each year. Prior to the year 2000, debt had stood at £1,000 million for some years.

The company has not made any takeovers and there has been no significant divestment of fixed assets.

Requirements

(a) Suggest possible explanations as to why the share price has

- risen in the year to 30 September 2002 despite a loss being made;
- fallen in the year to 30 September 2003 despite a profit being made.

(4 marks)

(b) Using the information available in the table, calculate the following ratios for ML plc for both the year to 30 September 2000 and the year to 30 September 2003:

- Earnings per share;
- Price earnings ratio (using the share price at 30 September);
- Dividend cover.

Briefly explain each of the three types of ratio, commenting on any changes in the ratios you have calculated for ML plc.

(11 marks)

(c) Analyse the investment, financing and dividend decisions of ML plc and discuss how they interrelate. Refer to the table provided and use supporting calculations where appropriate.

(10 marks)

Ignore taxation.

(Total = 25 marks)

Question 5 – XYZ training

XYZ is a financial publishing and training company that helps to prepare students for professional exams. Its activities are concentrated in North America and Europe and include classroom tuition and book publishing. It has recently expanded its publishing activities into e-learning (mainly CD ROMs). Customers include professional firms, self-paying students, college lecturers and bookshops throughout America and Europe, with growing export sales to the Far East. XYZ is carefully reviewing all aspects of its business and is currently focusing on working capital management in its publishing division. Recent data shows the following:

	XYZ Publishing	Publishing	Industry average of publishing companies	Industry average of publishing companies
Year	2002 $m	2003 $m	2002	2003
Sales	30	31	10% growth in 2002	8% growth in 2003
Cost of sales	20*	22*	70% of sales	70% of sales
Average inventory	18**	19**	75 days based on cost of sales	70 days based on cost of sales
Average receivables	10	11	62 days	61 days
Average payables	3	3	70 days	73 days
Bad debts	1	1.5	0.5% of sales	0.5% of sales
Inventory write-off	3	4	13% of sales	13% of sales

* 50% of the cost of sales relates to print costs and cost of sales excludes any inventory write-off cost or bad debt cost. ** If on-demand printing were introduced, physical inventories would be expected to fall by 80% from their current level.

(On-demand printing is where books are only printed when orders are received. The current method is to print for the estimated demand over the following 12 months.) The cost of capital is 5%.

At a recent Board Meeting the following comments were made on how to maximise the use of working capital:

Director of Publishing:
Inventory control has been a big problem. We have been particularly badly hit in 2003 by a large number of changes in syllabi for the various professional bodies. This has made it difficult to predict demand when setting print quantities. Changing syllabi has also resulted in a large number of books needing to be re-printed at higher

per unit costs while other books were substantially overprinted, requiring large quantities of books to be thrown away. On-demand printing, while costing 20% more to print compared with current printing, may be worth considering. To manage the information needs of on-demand printing an upgraded computer system would be needed costing $0.5 million per annum.

Sales Director:

I think our receivables position needs some attention. I would recommend extra staffing in credit control to reduce receivable days and the use of aggressive legal action in an attempt to reduce our bad debt levels. The extra staffing we would need to reduce the receivable days would cost $250,000 per annum. By putting this resource in place, I estimate that our receivable days would fall to the 2003 industry average. Estimating the cost of taking legal action is more difficult, but current estimates show that an investment of about $200,000 per annum would reduce bad debts to 0.4% of sales.

The Finance Director has asked you to produce a draft response to the following memorandum received from the Chief Executive.

MEMORANDUM

To: Finance Director
From: Chief Executive
Date: 25 May 2004
Subject: Working capital

Approximate number of marks available for the points raised by the Chief Executive

I need your guidance on how to manage our working capital. I would like a report on the following:

(a) Compare the inventory control, receivable control and gross margin record for our Publishing Division with the industry average and interpret your results.

(9 marks)
[5 marks of which are for calculations]

(b) Advise on whether we would have been better off in 2003 to have printed using on-demand printing.

(9 marks)
[6 marks of which are for calculations]

(c) Evaluate the recommendations of the Sales Director. (Use 2003 data and assume that all sales are on credit.)

(7 marks)
[4 marks of which are for calculations]

Requirement

Prepare a draft response to the Chief Executive's memorandum.

(Total = 25 marks)

Answers

Question 1 – Drugsco

(Workings are for X1)

		X1	X2
ROCE	= 3,132/6,072	= 52%	45%
Op profit margin	= 3,132/8,341	= 38%	31%
Asset turnover	= 8,341/6,072	= 1.4 times	1.4 times
Return on equity	= 1,933/1,633	= 120%	76%
EPS	= 1,933/3,544	= 54.5p	52.2p
P/E ratio	= 545/54.5	= 10	8
Dividend yield	= 1,202/3,544 ÷ 5.45	= 6.2%	8.3%
Payout ratio	= 1,202/1,933	= 62%	67%
Dividend cover	= 1,933/1,202	= 1.6	1.5
Receivables coll period	= 2,302/8,341 × 365	= 101 days	100 days
Inventory holding days	= 804/5,209 × 365	= 56 days	61 days
Payables days (assume cost = purchases)	= 2,608/5,209 × 365	= 183 days	160 days
Current ratio	= 4,368/2,608	= 1.7	1.8
Quick ratio	= 3,564/2,608	= 1.4	1.5
Gearing ratio	= 4,439/6,072	= 73%	61%
Interest cover	= 3,132/206	= 15.2	20.8

Comments

As the intangible development costs are written-off, the net assets look low compared with the sales generated. The ROCE has dropped from 52 to 45% although the company is managing to generate the same value of sales per £ of net asset. The problem has arisen because of a fall in the profit margin from 38 to 31%. This is probably connected with the increase in competition on one of the company's main products, in that the company had to lower its prices. Given the high total sales value, the company must have worked hard to increase the volume and this may be connected to the slightly higher inventory holding days (up by 9%).

The company appears to be paying payables more quickly than it was – and we would need to check against industry averages to see if this was more in line with competitors or being overly generous.

The gearing has been reduced through a repayment of debt, increasing the interest cover. However, the reduced profits (from the drop in the profit margin) have hit return on equity hard (120–76%) and the company has increased its dividend payout ratio to give a small increase in the dividend.

Although current EPS is fairly similar to last year, investors have marked the stock down by 25%, reflecting a less favourable view of the future and the company's ability to develop a replacement for its revolutionary drug. The price earnings ratio has similarly dropped by 25%.

Question 2 – Snowdome

ROCE	$=$	$\dfrac{\text{PBIT}}{\text{Capital employed}}$	$\dfrac{1{,}975}{33{,}657}$	5.9%
Operating margin	$=$	$\dfrac{\text{PBIT}}{\text{Sales}}$	$\dfrac{1{,}975}{105{,}430}$	1.87%
Asset turnover	$=$	$\dfrac{\text{Sales}}{\text{Capital employed}}$	$\dfrac{105{,}430}{33{,}657}$	3.13 times
ROE	$=$	$\dfrac{\text{PAT}}{\text{Equity}}$	$\dfrac{231}{17{,}527} = 0.013$	1.3%
EPS	$=$	$\dfrac{\text{Earnings avail to SH}}{\text{No. of equity shares}}$	$\dfrac{231}{2{,}200}$	10.5p
PE ratio	$=$	$\dfrac{\text{Current share price}}{\text{EPS}}$	$\dfrac{260}{10.5}$	25
DPS	$=$	$\dfrac{143}{2200}$	0.065	6.5 pence per share
Dividend cover	$=$	$\dfrac{\text{EPS}}{\text{DPS}}$	$\dfrac{0.105}{0.065}$	1.6 times
Dividend yield	$=$	$\dfrac{\text{DPS}}{\text{Current share price}}$	$\dfrac{6.5\text{p}}{260\text{p}} \times 100$	2.5%
Interest cover	$=$	$\dfrac{\text{PBIT}}{\text{Interest}}$	$\dfrac{1{,}975}{1{,}613}$	1.2 (dangerously low)
Gearing	$=$	$\dfrac{\text{Total debt}}{\text{Total equity}}$	$\dfrac{16{,}130}{17{,}527}$	92% (dangerously high)
Current ratio	$=$	$\dfrac{\text{Current assets}}{\text{Current liabilities}}$	$\dfrac{28{,}636}{10{,}943}$	2.6
Quick ratio	$=$	$\dfrac{\text{CA} - \text{inventory}}{\text{Current liabilities}}$	$\dfrac{28{,}636 - 2{,}932}{10{,}943}$	2.3

Question 3 – Hotel

Ways in which customer satisfaction could be measured include:

- feedback forms with scoring on a scale 1–5
- percentage of guests who return
- percentage of hotel rooms occupied
- number of bookings for next 6 months
- percentage of guests eating in the hotel.

Question 4 – ML

(a) **Share price movements**

The stock market seems in practice to be closest to the semi-strong form of efficiency which states that the share price reflects all publicly available information.

2002 price rise

Although the company made a loss in the year to 30 September 2002, the share price reflects public information which impacts on expectations for the future. Thus it appears to feel profits will recover (as they did). Additionally, the market may have already built in the expectation of a loss, and a smaller loss than expected had a favourable impact on the price.

2003 price drop

As there has been a rights issue, there are more shares representing the overall market value. We would expect a price ex-rights of:

$$\frac{[(2 \times 6) + (1 \times 4)]}{3} = £5.33$$

The current price of £5 is slightly lower, possibly reflecting a lower profit than had been expected, which affected the market's view of future prospects.

(b) **Ratios**

	2000	2003
EPS	250/300 = 83.3p	370/400 = 82.2p
P/E ratio	400/83.3 = 4.8	500/82.2 = 6.1
Dividend cover	250/50 = 5	370/70 = 5.3

EPS looks at the profits available for distribution generated per share. The results are only comparable if the number of shares is constant; in this case the rights issue means that a holder of 2 shares in 2000 would now hold 3 shares in 2003.

The P/E ratio gives the multiple linking the share price to the earnings per share. This gives an indication of future expectations, and incorporates growth estimates and an allowance for risk. A higher ratio suggests higher expectations compared with current performance. This may mean the market expects higher growth or lower risk than envisaged in 2000, but may also mean that current earnings are not as good as the long-term trend expected.

Dividend cover indicates the ease with which dividends can be covered by profits generated in the year. This will tend to fluctuate, as profits are more volatile than the steady dividend policies usually followed, and therefore needs to be analysed as a long-term trend. A cover of 5 is fairly safe, but does not mean that the company will always have the cash available to maintain the dividend.

(c) **Investment, financing and dividend decisions**

Investment in positive NPV projects will increase the present value of cash for the company, which will lead ultimately to an increase in the present value of the cash paid to shareholders. This in turn, assuming a relatively efficient market, will increase the share price and hence shareholders' wealth.

In order to finance these investments, cash will be needed and this can be from raising new finance or by using cash the company already has. The former is more expensive in that it will incur issue costs, while the latter reduces the cash available for dividends. In most markets, information is less than perfect and a reduction in dividends may cause the market to reduce its future expectations, and hence the share price, unless it understands the future benefits to be obtained by withholding the cash. There is therefore a compromise to be reached between the dividend policy and the financing decision.

In ML, there appears to have been investments and funding as follows:

In £m	2000	2001	2002	2003
Investment	190	260	100	290
Funding				
Cash retained	NA	160	–	190
New equity	NA	–	–	600
New debt	NA	100	250	(500)
Dividends	50	55	55	70

It would therefore appear that the dividends are kept in place and steady growth allowed, while issuing new debt annually when needed to make up the cash required for investment. This accesses outside finance in the cheapest way, but ML reduces the risk to shareholders engendered in a high gearing level by periodically raising more equity to lower the debt level. This has higher issue costs and is unlikely to be popular with shareholders on an annual basis, so is kept to a larger issue every few years.

Question 5 – XYZ training

DRAFT REPORT

To: Chief Executive
From: Finance Director
Date: 25 May 2004

Management of working capital

This report will consider the performance of the Publishing Division, advise on whether we would have been better using on-demand printing and evaluate the recommendations of the Sales Director.

1 *Publishing division performance*

	Division		Industry	
Year	2002	2003	2002	2003
Inventory days	328 days	315 days	75 days	70 days
Inventory write-offs	10%	12.9%	13%	13%
Receivables days	122 days	130 days	62 days	61 days
Bad debts	3.3%	4.8%	0.5%	0.5%
Gross margin	33%	29%	30%	30%

Inventory write-offs have increased to industry levels, probably due to the change in syllabuses. The division holds a much higher level of inventory than the industry average, probably because they print to meet the whole year's estimated demand. This may well lead to further write-offs if demand turns out to be lower than expected. It is also possible that growing overseas sales have led to inventories being held overseas as well.

Receivables days are twice the industry average and rising. In addition bad debts are now nearly ten times the industry level and have risen from last year. The receivables collection and bad debts need urgent attention. It is possible these are linked to the expansion overseas, but care needs to be taken before offering credit. It is possible that the results have been distorted by a major customer going into liquidation.

The gross margin has fallen from its position above the industry average to below it. This has been caused in part by the printing costs associated with the change in syllabuses.

2 *On-demand printing*

Based on 2003, the current system compared with on-demand printing shows the following:

	Current $m	On-demand $m
Print costs	11.00	13.20
Inventory write-offs	4.00	0.00
Computer	0.00	0.50
Finance cost of stock		
5% × $19m	0.95	
5% × $19m × 1.20 × 0.20		0.23
	15.95	13.93

The financial analysis shows an annual cost saving of $2.02 million in moving to on-demand printing. In addition, the lower inventories may mean a saving in storage costs, which have not been quantified. However, it will need careful management to ensure that large orders can be met on time and that peak demand periods can be managed. Despite these concerns, the financial case for moving to on-demand printing is compelling.

3 *Sales Director's recommendations*

Based on 2003 data, the current position compared with the Sales Director's suggestions shows the following:

	Current $m	Suggested $m
Extra staffing		
Current receivables	11	
New receivables = $31m × 31/365		5.18
Finance cost at 5%	0.55	0.26
Salaries		0.25
	$0.55m	$0.51m
Legal action		
Bad debts	1.50	0.12
Legal action		0.20
	$1.50m	$0.32m

These show that based on the financial estimates, we would save $40,000 from introducing extra staffing in credit control and $1.16 million by taking more aggressive legal action. While this suggests we should implement both, it is important to consider other alternatives such as factoring our debts, undertaking stricter credit checks before granting credit and reviewing our terms of trade. It is also important to consider the impact on our relationship with customers if we tighten our credit periods or pursue aggressive legal action.

It is likely that this analysis would benefit from looking at each type of receivable, by nature of business and location, separately so that the key areas of concern can be highlighted and appropriate action taken.

Dividend Policy

3

📝 Exam focus

The dividend is one of the three key decisions for a company. In an exam, you need to be able to explain and discuss the different views on dividend policy, and the practical consequences of each.

🔑 Key points

Dividend irrelevancy theory

Modigliani and Miller based their argument on the assumption of a perfect capital market:

> Market value = PV of future dividends

In other words, the pattern of dividends is irrelevant – investors will be indifferent between a series of annual dividends and a single large dividend many years in the future, as long as their present values were the same.

This means that management should not worry about dividend policy but concern themselves with finding positive NPV investments which will increase the present value of the cash that can ultimately be paid out.

The dividend paid should be any cash left over when all available positive NPV projects have been undertaken. This is sometimes known as a residual dividend policy.

Empirical research

Empirical research seems to suggest that dividend policy does affect the market value, and so in the context of dividends the assumption of a perfect capital market seems less appropriate.

In particular:

- The dividend is taken as an important signal of how the company is doing. A low or nil dividend will tend to suggest a struggling company as investors will not have full information about the projects the company has decided to undertake instead.

- The theory assumes that investors who need cash will be able to sell shares at the higher value and will be no worse off in total (cash in hand + value of shares held). However, transaction costs mean investors are not indifferent between income and capital gain.
- Similarly, distorting taxes (tax applied in different ways at different rates) on capital gains and dividends will mean investors are not indifferent.

Implications and other practical points

- Ideally, a company should set a dividend policy that suits its own shareholders. This will depend partly on the investors' personal tax position. However, as its 'clientele' are likely to want different things, it might be easier to broadcast widely a policy of high or low dividends and let the shareholder mix change to those that like the stated policy.
- Shareholders like a degree of certainty as it reduces the risk of investment (and makes the shares more valuable). A stated long-term policy, which is adhered to, is therefore beneficial. The balancing act for the managers is to give an attractive enough dividend without running the risk of having to default on their stated policy in later years.
- Raising new finance involves issue costs, so it is probably unwise to pay out very high dividends if the company is likely to need finance in the future.
- Loan covenants may restrict the level of dividends that can be paid.

Alternatives to dividends

Instead of paying a dividend, surplus cash could be used to repurchase some of the shares. It has the advantage that a large cash dividend one year may mislead investors into thinking that this is the start of a much higher dividend stream for the foreseeable future. A share buy back is clearly a one-off and is unlikely to be misinterpreted.

Alternatively, a scrip dividend gives shareholders the choice between a cash dividend and more shares (which would increase the capital value of their holding). However, the company does not know what shareholders will choose, which therefore makes budgeting difficult. In addition, there may be personal tax consequences for investors taking up the shares.

Questions

Question 1 – PDQ dividends

PDQ plc is a medium-sized listed company. The results to 31 December 2004 have just been announced. Earnings per share (EPS) and declared dividends per share (DPS) for the last five years are shown below:

	2004	2003	2002	2001	2000
EPS (pence)	140	136	131	127	122
DPS (pence)	82	81	79	78	77

Dividends are paid on 31 December each year and the dividend shown as declared in a particular year would have been or will be paid on 31 December the following year. If the current dividend policy is maintained, the directors of PDQ plc estimate that annual growth in earnings and dividends will be no better than the average growth in earnings over the past four years.

PDQ plc is reluctant to take on debt at the present time to finance growth. The company is therefore considering a change in its dividend policy and total investment programme to allow 50% of its earnings to be retained for identified capital investment projects which are estimated to have an average post-tax return of 15%. The market risk premium is expected to be 4% over the risk free rate of 6%. The company's beta is currently quoted at 1.5 and is not expected to change for the foreseeable future.

Requirements

(a) Calculate the share price which might be expected by the market:

  (i) if the company does not announce a change in dividend policy
  (ii) if the company does announce a change in dividend policy using whatever model(s) you think appropriate.

(10 marks)

(b) (i) Comment on the limitations of the model(s) you have used in your answer to part (a).
  (ii) Discuss the reasons why the share price might react differently from the market's expectations.

(15 marks)
(Total = 25 marks)

34 Exam Practice Kit: Management Accounting Financial Strategy

Question 2 – RG plc

The following financial data relate to RG plc:

Year	Earnings per share (pence)	Net dividend per share (pence)	Share price (pence)
2001	42	17	252
2002	46	18	184
2003	51	20	255
2004	55	22	275
2005	62	25	372

A firm of market analysts which specialises in the industry in which RG plc operates has recently re-evaluated the company's future prospects. The analysts estimate that RG plc's earnings and dividends will grow at 25% for the next two years. Thereafter, earnings are likely to increase at a lower annual rate of 10%. If this reduction in earnings growth occurs, the analysts consider that the dividend payout ratio will be increased to 50%.

RG plc is all-equity financed and has one million ordinary shares in issue. The tax rate of 33% is not expected to change in the foreseeable future.

You are required:

(a) to calculate the estimated share price and P/E ratio which the analysts now expect for RG plc, using the dividend valuation model, and comment briefly on the method of valuation you have just used. Assume a constant post-tax cost of capital of 18%.

(10 marks)

(b) to comment on whether the dividend policy being considered by the analysts would be appropriate for the company in the following two sets of circumstances

   (i) the company's shareholders are mainly financial institutions
   (ii) the company's shareholders are mainly small private investors.

(8 marks)

(c) to describe briefly three other dividend policies which RG plc could consider.

(7 marks)
(Total = 25 marks)

✅ Answers

Question 1 – PDQ dividends

(a) **Share price calculation**

(i) *No change in dividend*

Past growth, g, given by $\quad 122(1+g)^4 = 140$
$$g = 0.035$$

Using CAPM, $K_e = 6\% + (4\% \times 1.5) = 12\%$

Share price $= \dfrac{D_1}{K_e - g} = \dfrac{(82 \times 1.035)}{(0.12 - 0.035)} = £9.98$

(ii) *50% retention*

g estimated by $b \times r = 0.50 \times 0.15 = 0.075$

Share price $= \dfrac{(140 \times 1.075 \times 0.50)}{(0.12 - 0.075)} = £16.72$

(b) (i) *Limitations*

The model used was the same in both cases although the future growth rate was derived in a different way. Particular limitations of the calculations are:

- CAPM was used to derive the cost of equity. This assumes rational well-diversified investors in an efficient market, which is a reasonable approximation for PDQ which is a listed company. It also assumes that beta will stay the same but it will change gradually over time as the risk of the company perceived by the shareholders changes.
- The dividend valuation model used assumes that growth continues at the same rate forever. Clearly, this has not happened in the past and is unlikely to be the case into the indefinite future. A high growth rate, such as in (ii), will have a higher impact than it possibly should, as it assumes indefinite growth of 7.5% per annum.

(ii) *Market price*

The market price may not react in the way predicted as it has only looked at the information provided by the company in terms of its dividend intentions, in isolation. Even if we assume that the market understands and believes the growth prospects arising from the changed dividend policy, it takes no account of external factors. Thus, there may be a sudden collapse or boom in the entire market, there may be a higher demand for the shares than can be supplied, pushing up the price, or investors may need cash for other investments and so liquidate their positions, pushing the price down. In the short term such factors can be a greater influence on the share price than the fundamental information about the company.

Question 2 – RG plc

(a) **Share price and P/E ratio**

Share price given by PV of future dividends (discounted at 18%):

$$\frac{(25 \times 1.25)}{1.18} + \frac{(25 \times 1.25)^2}{1.18^2} + \frac{(62 \times 1.25^2 \times 1.10 \times 0.5)/(0.18 - 0.10)}{1.18^2} = 533\text{p}$$

$$\text{P/E ratio (trailing or historical)} = \frac{533}{62} = 8.6$$

$$\text{P/E ratio (leading or prospective)} = \frac{533}{(62 \times 1.25)} = 6.9$$

The dividend valuation model is appropriate when an investor will only receive the dividend stream and has little chance of acquiring their share of the assets or altering the dividend policy. This is particularly relevant for minority shareholders, although it relies on being able to predict the long-term growth rate in dividends.

(b) **Appropriateness of policy**

(i) Generally financial institutions prefer large dividend payouts, as it is beneficial from a tax perspective. Tax on dividend income is not as high as for capital gains, when shares are sold, and for some organisations may be nil. In addition, selling shares will involve transaction costs.

Dividends here so far followed a steady upward trend, but have been maintained at roughly 40% of earnings so that the trend can be continued even if earnings dipped. Raising the payout ratio may mean that the company is unable to maintain this indefinitely and a year with low earnings may lead to a drip in the dividend. Although theory says this should not affect the share price, in practice institutions that were relying on the dividend will sell shares, causing the price to fall and the cost of equity to rise.

(ii) Small private investors will also look carefully at their tax position. Generally, they will be indifferent or prefer dividends to the company retaining the cash, increasing the share price and allowing investors to make a capital gain. The exception to this is an investor who has unused capital gains tax exemption (i.e. zero rates on gains) and is a higher rate taxpayer (higher rate on dividends); these investors would prefer a low payout and a consequent capital gain.

It is therefore difficult to say how small private investors would react as a group as they are likely to have different tax requirements. It might be reasonable to assume that they have been attracted to RG by its past dividend policy and that to change it dramatically might not be welcomed.

(c) **Other policies**

Pay out all profits as dividends
The company would have to retain some cash for day-to-day operations but would release the rest to the shareholders. It would then have to raise more finance, either debt or equity, if it wanted to undertake long-term investments.

Pay out no dividends
When a company needs to invest large amounts of cash, possibly in the early stage of its life, it may retain all profits and cash, as it is cheaper to use retained cash than raise additional finance with its associated issue costs. The shareholders would need to be aware of the policy and the benefits to them of following it.

Increase dividends by 10% per annum
The company appears to have approximately followed this over the past five years, as it allows shareholders to predict and rely on the annual dividend. The disadvantage is that it does not relate to the profits generated, so the starting point must be at a low enough level to ensure that the company will have adequate dividend cover in the subsequent years.

Part 2

Financial Management

Sources of Finance 4

📝 Exam focus

You need to be able to advise companies on the pros and cons of raising finance in different ways. Ensure that you understand the factors that should be taken into account and look for information about the company so that you can make appropriate comments about the options.

🔑 Key points

Factors to consider in choosing a source of finance

- Duration
- Amount
- Accessibility of the finance
- Administration costs
- Servicing costs – for example interest or dividends
- Gearing
- Dividend policy (if choosing between retained profits and equity issues)
- Pricing issues
- Security
- Tax implications.

Issue of shares to new shareholders

(a) Offer for sale by prospectus: shares are offered at a *fixed price* to the public and are presented in a prospectus.
(b) Offer for sale by tender: potential shareholders are asked the number of shares and the amount they are prepared to pay. The issuing house then ranks the bids to determine which applicants are at the top of the list, and who therefore become shareholders.
(c) A placing: shares are placed with a broker who sells the shares to its clients. This tends to be the cheapest way to issue new shares.
(d) Introduction: shares have already been issued, for example on an overseas stock exchange or already have a wide distribution, and are introduced to the marketplace.

Rights issues

This is an issue of shares to existing shareholders in proportion to their current holding, as required by Company Law and tends to be cheaper due to less advertising costs.

Pricing a rights issue

$$\text{Theoretical ex-rights price} = \frac{\begin{array}{c}\text{Current market value of company} \\ \text{(Market value of existing shares} \\ \text{pre-rights)}\end{array} + \begin{array}{c}\text{Proceeds of} \\ \text{rights} \\ \text{issue}\end{array}}{\text{Number of shares ex-rights}}$$

Debt

Short term

Bank overdrafts
Trade credit
Government grants
  and loans

Medium term

Bank loans
Leasing
HP
Government grants and loans

Long term

Bonds
Debentures
Preference shares
Convertible debentures

Considerations when issuing debt

Security – fixed and floating charge
Gearing and interest cover
Impact on EPS
Interest rates
Duration of the loan
Risk
Size of the loan
Yield curve

A financial manager must consider the likely movement in interest rates when choosing the type of finance, for example whether to borrow short or long term. It shows the market expectation of interest rates and should be reviewed before making large borrowing decisions.

Lease vs buy

In questions you may be asked to compare leasing to buying an asset:

Under leasing, consider lease payments and tax relief thereon
Under buying, consider the purchase cost and the tax effect of the capital allowances
Discount both at the opportunity cost of finance, which is the cost of the loan if the asset is purchased, and choose the lower cost option.

SME funding problems

SMEs (Small and Medium Enterprises) often find themselves with a funding gap. They are too small for a full stock market quotation but need to raise significant finance which proves very expensive/impossible through basic loans or increasing the overdraft.

The government has introduced a number of tax incentives to encourage investment in SMEs.

- The Enterprise Investment Scheme
- Venture Capital Trusts
- Share Incentive Schemes

Venture Capital companies, such as 3i, and some banks provide equity finance to SMEs. Venture Capitalists retain an interest in a company for a number of years, before looking for an exit route.

Venture Capitalists invest after assessing the viability of a company, credibility of its management, realistic forecasts of growth, retention and distribution of profits, prospects of a successful future listing and the proportion of shareholding on offer. However, as they are accepting a high level of risk, they will require a very high return. This is usually in the form of capital gain over 5–7 years.

Business Angels are often business people who provide small capital amounts (<£100,000) for an equity stake (sometimes called the informal venture capital market). They may also offer their management expertise.

Questions

Question 1 – X rights (Practice Question)

X plc has 1,000,000 shares with a current market price of £1.50 each. The company holds a rights issue of one new share for every two existing shares at a price of 75p. What is the ex-rights price?

Question 2 – Mr Y (Practice Question)

Using the data in Question 1, assume a shareholder Mr Y owns 1,000 shares in the company. Show Mr Y's position if he

takes up his rights
sells his rights
does nothing.

Question 3 – EPS after project (Practice Question)

A company is considering investing in a £4 million project. The project will increase profits each year by £1.8 million. The finance can be raised either by issuing new shares at £2 per share or new 10% debentures at par. Assume dividends per share remain constant.

The income statement and balance sheet extract for 2003 is as follows:

	£m
Profit before interest and tax	5.765
Finance costs	0.240
	5.525
Taxation @ 30%	1.658
Profit after tax	3.867
Dividends were declared of £1.25m.	
Share capital 5m shares @ 50p each	2.5
Reserves	3.8
	6.3
6% debentures	4.0

Calculate the EPS in 2003.
Calculate the EPS in 2004 if the project is financed by debt.
Calculate the EPS in 2004 if the project is financed by equity.
Calculate the immediate effect of the project on the book value of gearing, assuming the investment is made on 1 Jan. 2004.

Question 4 – Lease or buy (Practice Question)

A company is considering purchasing an asset costing £1 million. The asset will generate cost savings of £400k per annum for 4 years when it will be scrapped for £300k. The company will pay tax at 30% one year in arrears and obtain writing down allowances at 25%. The company pays tax at 30%.

The first WDA will be obtained immediately.

The company cost of capital is 10% and the firm intends to finance the new plant via a 4-year loan costing 6% per annum. Alternatively the company could lease the asset and a leasing company will lease the asset for £240k per annum in advance for 4 years. Should the company lease or buy the asset?

Question 5 – PJH

Assume you are the Management Accountant in PJH Limited. The company manufactures soft furnishings (such as curtains and drapes) for theatres, exhibitions and concert halls in the United Kingdom. It has been trading for 20 years. 55% of the shares are owned between 10 members of the founding family. There are also 25 other shareholders with holdings of various sizes.

Two years ago, the company received an offer of £25 million for its entire equity, which the Board of Directors rejected without conducting any serious evaluation. The company is forecasting pre-tax earnings of £4.5 million on turnover of £32 million for the current year. These sales and earnings levels are expected to continue unless new investment is undertaken. The Managing Director, Mrs Henry, who is also a major shareholder, is planning a major expansion programme that will require raising £5 million of new finance for capital investment. This investment yields a positive net present value (NPV) of £1.2 million when evaluated at the company's post-tax cost of capital of 9%.

The Board is considering two alternative methods of financing this expansion:

1. A rights issue to existing shareholders plus a new issue of shares to employees and trading partners.
2. Medium-term (5 years) debt, interest rate fixed at 7%, secured on the company's fixed assets, mainly land and buildings. The company at present has no long-term debt. It has an overdraft facility that is used for short-term financing needs.

The company pays tax at 30%. Mrs Henry is aware that the method of financing chosen might have an impact on the valuation of the company and also on the company's long-term objectives.

Requirements

Write a report to Mrs Henry that advises on:

(a) the factors that need to be considered by the Board when deciding to raise new equity.
(8 marks)

(b) the effect of each suggested method of financing on the valuation of the company. You only need provide some simple calculations here to support your arguments. You do not have enough information to do a detailed valuation.
(10 marks)

(c) appropriate long-term financial objectives for a company such as PJH Limited.
(7 marks)
(Total = 25 marks)

46 Exam Practice Kit: Management Accounting Financial Strategy

Question 6 – VID

VID Inc. is a US-based company, which was established 15 years ago. It makes and distributes videos, both for the general market and to customer specifications. Its common stock (shares) have been listed on a US stock exchange for the past 8 years. However, there are relatively few stockholders and the stock is not traded in large volumes. The founders of the company no longer participate in its management but own around 10% of the stock in issue.

VID Inc. borrowed US$65 million to purchase new premises three years ago, which have recently been valued at US$85 million. The company is now considering diversifying into mainstream film production which will require raising US$50 million for additional fixed and working capital. This new business will involve joint ventures with UK partners and much of the filming will be done in the UK or Spain. The new investment is not expected to have a significant effect on profits for at least 18 months.

The three methods being considered for raising capital are:

(i) New equity in the UK, subject to US stockholders' approval;
(ii) Long-term fixed rate US$ debt;
(iii) Floating rate sterling-denominated Eurobonds.

Summary financial statistics for the last financial year for VID Inc. are as below.

	US$m
Turnover	175.00
Operating profit	45.00
Post-tax profits	31.36
Non-current assets (book value)	95.00
Net current assets	58.00
Long-term loans	
8% redeemable 2030	65.00
Common stock (in units of US$1)	25.00
Retained earnings	63.00
Share price (US$)	
High for year	28.56
Low for year	18.50
As at today (25 May 2004)	22.58

Current annual fixed interest rates for secured long-term borrowing are as follows:

US$6%   UK£7%   European common currency area Euro 5%

Floating rate sterling Eurobond notes are available at the bank base rate +0.5%. Tax will continue to be payable at 20% per annum.

Requirement

Assume you are a financial adviser to VID Inc. Evaluate the three methods of finance being considered at the present time and advise the directors of VID Inc. Support your advice with any calculations you consider appropriate. Assume, for the purposes of this evaluation, that the P/E ratio of the company will rise to 20 if equity finance is used, or 19 if fixed or floating rate debt is issued. Make only other simplifying assumptions you think necessary and appropriate.

(Total = 25 marks)

Note: Up to 10 marks are available for calculations. A report structure is not required for this question.

Question 7 – Rump

Rump plc is an all-equity financed, listed company which operates in the food processing industry. The Rump family owns 40% of the ordinary shares; the remainder are held by large financial institutions. There are 10 million £1 ordinary shares currently in issue.

The company has just finalised a long-term contract to supply a large chain of restaurants with a variety of food products. The contract requires investment in new machinery costing £24 million. This machinery would become operational on 1 January 2002, and payment would be made on the same date. Sales would commence immediately thereafter.

Company policy is to pay out all profits as dividends and, if Rump plc continues to be all-equity financed, there will be an annual dividend of £9 million in perpetuity commencing 31 December 2002.

There are two alternatives being considered to finance the required investment of £24 million:

1. A 2-for-5 rights issue, in which case the annual dividend would be £9 million. The cum rights price per share would be £6.60.
2. Issuing 7.5% irredeemable debentures at par with interest payable annually in arrears. For this alternative, interest would be paid out of the £9 million otherwise available to pay dividends.

For either alternative, the directors expect the cost of equity to remain at its present annual level of 10%.

Requirements

(a) Calculate the issue and ex-rights share prices of Rump plc assuming a 2-for-5 rights issue is used to finance the new project at 1 January 2002. Ignore taxation.

(6 marks)

(b) Calculate the value per ordinary share in Rump plc at 1 January 2002 if 7.5% irredeemable debentures are issued to finance the new project. Assume that the cost of equity remains at 10% each year. Ignore taxation.

(4 marks)

(c) Write a report to the directors of Rump plc which:

(i) compares and contrasts the rights issue and the debenture issue methods of raising finance – you may refer to the calculations in your answer to requirements (a) and (b) and to any assumptions made; and

(ii) explains and evaluates the appropriateness of the following alternative methods of issuing equity finance in the specific circumstances of Rump plc:

- a placing
- an offer for sale
- a public offer for subscription.

(15 marks)
(Total = 25 marks)

Question 8 – RZ

RZ is a privately owned textile manufacturer based in the UK with sales revenue in the last financial year of £68 million and earnings of £4.5 million. The directors of the company have been evaluating a cost saving project, which will require purchasing new machinery from the USA at a capital cost of $1.5 million. The directors expect the new machinery to have a life of at least 5 years and to provide cost savings (including capital allowances) of £240,000 after tax each year. Cash flows beyond 5 years are ignored by RZ in all its investment decisions. The discount rate that the company applies to investment decisions of this nature is its post-tax real cost of capital of 9% per annum.

RZ at present has no debt in its capital structure. The directors, who are the major shareholders, would be prepared to finance the purchase of the new machinery via a rights issue but believe an all-equity capital structure fails to take advantage of the tax benefits of debt. They therefore propose to finance with one of the following methods:

(i) Undated debt, raised in the UK and secured on the company's assets. The current pre-tax rate of interest required by the market on corporate debt of this risk is 7% per annum. Interest payments would be made at the end of each year.

(ii) A finance lease raised in the USA repayable over 5 years. The terms would be 5 annual payments of US$325,000 payable at the *beginning* of each year. The machinery could be bought by RZ from the finance company at the end of the five year lease contract for a nominal amount of $1. Assume the whole amount of each annual payment is tax deductible.

(iii) An operating lease. No cost details are available at present.

Other information

- The company's marginal tax rate is 30%. Tax is payable in the year in which the liability arises.
- Capital allowances are available at 25% reducing balance.
- If bought outright, the machinery is estimated to have a residual value in real cash flow terms, at the end of five years, of 10% of the original purchase price.
- The spot rate US$ to the £ is 1.58.
- Interest rates in the USA and UK are currently 2.5 and 3.5%, respectively.

Requirements

(a) Discuss the advisability of the investment and the advantages and disadvantages of financing with either (i) undated debt, (ii) a finance lease or (iii) an operating lease compared with new equity raised via a rights issue and comment on whether the choice of method of finance should affect the investment decision. Provide appropriate and relevant calculations and assumptions to support your discussion.

(18 marks)

(b) Discuss the benefits and potential problems of financing assets in the same currency as their purchase.

(7 marks)
(Total marks = 25)

✓ Answers

Question 1 – X rights

$$\text{Ex-rights price} = \frac{(150p \times 1m) + (500{,}000 \text{ shares} \times 75p)}{1{,}500{,}000 \text{ shares}}$$

$$= \frac{1.5m + 0.375m}{1.5m} = £1.25$$

Question 2 – Mr Y

	Takes up his rights	Sells his rights	Does nothing
Before	1,000 shares @ £1.50 = £1,500	1,000 shares @ £1.50 = £1,500	1,000 shares @ £1.50 = £1,500
After	Extra 500 shares 1,500 × £1.25 = £1,875 Cost of rights: 500 shares @ 0.75 = £375 Ex-rights wealth = £1,500	No. of shares after rights issue 1,000 × £1.25 = £1,250 Proceeds from sale of rights: 500 × (1.25 − 0.75) = £250 Ex-rights wealth = £1,500	No. of shares after rights issue = 1,000 shares 1,000 × £1.25 = £1,250
Change in wealth	No change	No change	Loss of £250

As can be seen, the worst thing the shareholder can do is do nothing, as the market value of the existing shares fall.

Question 3 – EPS after project

£m	2003	2004 (Equity)	2004 (Debt)
Profit before interest and tax	5.765	7.565	7.565
Interest	0.240	0.240	0.640
	5.525	7.325	6.925
Taxation @ 30%	1.658	2.198	2.078
Profit after tax	3.867	5.127	4.847
Dividends	1.250	2.250	1.250
Retained earnings	2.617	2.877	3.597

$$\text{EPS} = \frac{\text{Profits avail to shareholders}}{\text{No. of shares}}$$

	2003	2004 (Equity)	2004 (Debt)
	3.867 / 5	5.127 / 7	4.847 / 5
	0.77p	0.73p	0.97p

Gearing = BV debt / BV equity

	2003	2004 (Equity)	2004 (Debt)
	4/6.3 0.63	4/(6.3 + 2.877) = 0.44	(4 + 4)/(6.3 + 3.597) = 0.81

Question 4 – Lease or buy

Investment decision:

	t_0	t_1	t_2	t_3	t_4	t_5
Cost savings		400	400	400	400	
Tax savings			(120)	(120)	(120)	(120)
Invt.	(1,000)					
Scrap					300	
WDA		75	56	42	32	5
CFs	(1,000)	475	336	322	612	(115)
$DF_{10\%}$	1	0.909	0.826	0.751	0.683	0.621
PV	(1,000)	432	278	242	418	(71)

NPV = £205,000 so project is worthwhile

Financing decision:

	t_0	t_1	t_2	t_3	t_4	t_5
Lease payments		(240)	(240)	(240)	(240)	(240)
Tax saving		72	72	72	72	72
On lease payments						
Lost WDA		(75)	(56)	(42)	(32)	(5)
CFs	(240)	(243)	(224)	(210)	(200)	67
$DF_{4\%}$	1	0.962	0.952	0.889	0.885	0.822
PV	(240)	(234)	(213)	(187)	(177)	55

NPV = (996)

Note the after-tax borrowing is 6% × (1 − 0.3) = 4.2%, say 4%.

Therefore, it is cheaper to lease the asset at a cost of £996k, than buy at a cost of £1,000,000. The decision is very marginal.

The NPV will increase from £205,000 to £209,000 if the asset is leased.

Question 5 – PJH

REPORT

To: Mrs Henry
From: Management Accountant
Date: xx of x 2002

Expansion finance, valuations and objectives

This report will consider the factors to be considered when raising new equity, the impact of the method of financing on the valuation of the business and appropriate long-term financial objectives.

1 *Factors to consider*

If the shares are issued to the existing shareholders, the family will have to find 55% of £5 million, which is £2.75 million; this is an average of £275,000 each. The other shareholders only number 25, which mean they would have to contribute an average of £90,000 each. This may be beyond the existing shareholders' means.

However, issuing shares to others will dilute the control of the family, and may mean that decisions are made which are not in their best interests. Ultimately, if the family ends up with a minority stake the company could be sold.

One possibility is to calculate the number of shares the family would have to buy to maintain control.

Suppose the company is worth £35 million (see 'Effect on company value'); this gives a value per share of £35. A rights issue is likely to be at less than current value, say £30.

If the existing shareholders contribute £3 million, this will be 100,000 shares (a 10% rights issue), with the family contributing £1.65 million (an average £165,000 each) and the others £1.35 million (£54,000 each on average). The other £2 million might be raised from new investors at a price of £34.50 (see 'Working'); this would mean issuing a further 57,970 shares.

The family would therefore own $(55,000 \times 1.10)/(1,100,000 + 57,970) = 52\%$ which still gives them day-to-day control of the company. However, the sums required from existing shareholders may be too much, particularly as the above calculations look at averages – in reality some of the family members will have to find more if they have greater shareholdings than the average.

2 *Effect on company value*

We would start with the bid of £25 million from two years ago and add on the NPV of the project, giving £26.2 million. However, this bid was not evaluated and may not have been a realistic value and it takes no account of what has happened over the last two years.

A better approximation might be the present value of future cash flows, assuming earnings approximate to cash and no growth:

$$\text{Value before project} = \frac{(£4.50\text{m} \times 0.70)}{0.09} = £35\text{m}$$

If financed through equity, equity value = 35m + 5m + 1.2m = £41.2m

If financed through debt, equity value = 35m + 1.2m + NPV of tax relief on debt interest and tax relief = £5m × 7% × 30% = £105,000 pa

PV at 7% = 105,000 × 4.100 = £430,500

Therefore equity value = 35m + 1.2m + 430,500 = £36,630,500

Although the equity is worth more under equity financing, bear in mind that £5 million of this is because we have issued more shares!

The second calculation assumes a very efficient market and that debt is effectively risk-free, while both assume that there is no change in the operating risk of the company.

3 *Appropriate long-term financial objectives*

In theory, a company should maximise shareholders' wealth through a combination of dividends and capital value increase. However, other stakeholders set constraints on this objective which will need to be observed if the company is going to thrive in the long term. These include commitments to staff, customers and suppliers. Combining these interests with those of shareholders might give the following objectives:

- dividend payout ratio
- market share and growth in sales
- sales per employee

- amount of repeat business
- employee remuneration as a percentage of costs
- percentage of creditors paid on time.

In addition, the intentions of the family members in the medium term might influence the objectives decided upon.

Working

Existing	1,000,000 shares at £35	£35,000,000
Rights	1,000,000 shares at £30	£3,000,000
	X shares at y	£2,000,000
		£40,000,000

But to ensure no instant gain to the new shareholders, y should be the theoretical price after the issues = £40m/(1.1m + X)

$$= X \times 40/(1,100,000 + X) = 2$$

$$40X = 2,200,000 + 2X$$

$$X = 57,895 \text{ shares}$$

Question 6 – VID

Calculations	Existing	+ Equity	± Debt
Operating profit ($m)	45	45	45
Finance costs ($m)	5.2	5.2	8.2
	39.8m	39.8m	36.8m
Tax ($m)	8	8	7.4
Post-tax profits ($m)	31.8	31.8	29.4
Number of shares (million)	25	27.5	25
EPS ($)	1.27	1.16	1.18
P/E ratio	17.75	20	19
Mkt value equity ($m)	564.5	636	558.6
ROCE (bk values) (%)	29.4	22.2	22.2
ROE (bk value) (%)	36.1	23.0	33.4
Interest cover	8.7	8.7	5.5
Profit margin (%)	18	18	17
Debt/Debt & Equity (book values) (%)	42.5	32.0	56.7%
Debt/Debt & Equity (market values) (%)	13.3	12	19.7

Assumptions

New equity is issued at US$20 or its sterling equivalent.

The current loan is valued as (65 × 0.08)/0.06 = $86.7m, which approximates it as an irredeemable debt.

Generally, the company does not appear to be particularly highly geared (based on market values), although it would be useful to know the average for the industry. The interest cover is also reasonable even if new debt is issued.

The market appears to like the prospects for the investment, given that the P/E ratio is expected to increase. If equity is raised, the total market capitalisation is expected to increase by $72 million, representing the $50 million investment and an additional $22 million for the expected NPV of the project.

The return on capital employed and return on equity both look healthy, but again we need industry averages to be able to comment more. The project will not produce profits for 18 months; the market needs to be aware of this or the disappointment will depress the share price in the short term.

Considering the three financing methods mentioned:

1 *Equity*

- existing shareholders will need to waive their pre-emptive rights
- an equity issue will be more expensive than a debt issue
- equity will have a higher cost than debt, although annual payments do not have to be made unlike debt interest
- the price may have to be lower than $20 to attract investors and this will affect the calculations of the ratios
- gearing will decrease if equity is issued
- EPS will be diluted in the short term to $1.16.

2 *Fixed interest debt*

- easier and cheaper to raise
- gearing increases to roughly 20% by market values
- EPS would still dilute to $1.18 but not as much as with equity.

3 *Floating rate debt*

- interest payments would be affected by market conditions. It is therefore important to take account of the director's expectations of future market rates, given the loan will be in sterling, there will also be a currency exchange rate risk.

Question 7 – Rump

(a) **Rights issue**

$$\text{Offer price} = \frac{\text{Finance needed}}{\text{Number of shares issued}}$$

$$= \frac{£24m}{4m} = £6 \text{ per share}$$

$$\text{Ex-rights price} = \frac{[(5 \times £6.60) + (2 \times £6)]}{7}$$

$$= £6.43$$

(b) **Irredeemable debentures**

Dividends per annum = £9m − (7.5% × £24m) = £7.2m

Dividend per share = £0.72 pa

$$\text{Share price} = \text{PV of dividends} = \frac{0.72}{0.1} = £7.20$$

(c)

REPORT

To: Directors of Rump plc
From: Accountant
Date: xx of 20xx

Raising new finance

The project represents a sizeable increase in the company's operations and the financing of it will have a material impact on the capital structure and the shareholders' wealth.

(i) *Debenture issue or rights issue*

The debentures would introduce significant gearing, and may include restrictive covenants which dictate the repayment timings. In addition there may be restrictions on the operations of the business in order to maintain certain gearing ratios or interest cover. They will probably require security over assets, or compensate for the additional risk of less than full security by applying a higher interest charge.

However, the issue costs associated with the debentures are likely to be lower than those incurred on a rights issue. In addition, the fixed income and asset security will lead to a cheaper cost than the equity which is enhanced by the tax relief available on debt interest.

The calculations in (b) have assumed the cost of equity (and hence the total market value) would stay the same under a debenture issue. However, the risk to the shareholders would increase (as the financial risk of the interest being paid out of profits increases the fluctuation in returns) and so the return required would increase. It therefore may not be as beneficial to shareholders as it appears, as the share value may drop from the price calculated.

Finally, it is possible that not all shareholders will want to take up their rights, which will involve the company selling the rights to other shareholders or the general public if possible. The family would see its shareholding reduced if it could not finance its share of the rights issue.

(ii) *Alternative methods of issuing equity*

A wider issue of equity than a rights issue would have more chance of success but would reduce the holding of current shareholders such as the family, and is likely to have higher issue costs.

A placing is where an issuing house places shares with clients, and is likely to have relatively low costs as it avoids underwriting and much of the advertising. It is likely, however, to concentrate shareholdings which will threaten the family's control. An offer for sale is when an issuing house buys the shares and then offers them to the public, at a fixed price or via a tender, by circulating a prospectus. The costs are likely to be higher as the fees effectively incorporate underwriting of the issue.

A public offer for subscription means that Rump plc itself would issue the prospectus and invite subscription at a fixed price. Costs are likely to be high, as they will have to cover underwriting, publicity and specialist advice.

Question 8 – RZ

(a) **Assessment of investment**

Using equity:

PV of cost savings for 5 years = £240,000 × 3.890 = £933,600
Capital expenditure = $1.5 m/1.58 = (949,367)
(15,767)

While the net present value is negative, it is fairly marginal and the tax benefits which come with other forms of financing may be enough to make it positive.

(i) *Undated debt*

Assume we raise £950,000.

Additional benefit = PV of the tax relief on interest payments
950,000 × 0.07 × 0.30 = £19,950 per annum
Over 5 years this gives 19,950 × 4.100 = £81,795
As a perpetuity it gives 19,950/0.07 = £285,000

Strictly, a risk-free rate should be used to calculate the present value, but the yield on the debt has been used as an approximation.

Advantages

- The benefits of the tax relief on the interest will make the net present value positive (81,795 − 15,767 = £66,000 approximately).
- The financing will not dilute share ownership and is likely to be cheaper and easier to administer than equity.

Disadvantages

- As the debt is undated (in practice this is unusual), the interest will have to be covered indefinitely, even after the benefits from the investment have ceased.

(ii) *Finance Lease*

The easiest way to assess this financing source is to compare the present value of the difference in cashflows from debt finance. This is normally discounted at the post-tax cost of borrowing:

Benefits of leasing over borrow and purchase (in £'000)

	t_0	t_1	t_2	t_3	t_4	t_5
Lease payments	(325)	(325)	(325)	(325)	(325)	
X/R	1.58	1.56	1.55	1.53	1.52	
In £'000	(206)	(208)	(210)	(212)	(214)	
Tax saved		62	62	63	64	64
Purchase saved	949					(95)
Tax benefits lost		(71)	(53)	(40)	(30)	(62)
	743	(217)	(201)	(189)	(180)	(93)
	1	0.952	0.907	0.864	0.823	0.784
	743	(207)	(182)	(163)	(148)	(73)

As the net present value is negative (£30,000), it means that leasing appears to be less beneficial than borrowing using straight debt.

Advantages

- The leasing has a definite five-year life compared with the uncertainty of the undated debt or equity.
- There are quite often lower arrangement costs for leasing than for debt or equity.
- Although our calculation suggests it is more expensive, this is greatly influenced by the resale value estimate and the timing of the cashflows. Further analysis may alter the result.

Disadvantages

- A finance lease will still involve placing an asset and a long-term liability on the balance sheet, and hence will have a similar impact on any ratios as raising finance through debt. This may not be a problem for a (currently) all-equity private company.
- As it entails another four years of payments in US$, it will introduce currency risk.

(iii) *Operating Lease*

With an operating lease, the risks and rewards of ownership remain with the lessor, so that the lessee does not have to include assets, and associated liabilities, on the balance sheet.

Advantages

- There are not likely to be any other costs, such as maintenance or insurance, payable.
- There are likely to be points in the lease at which it can be abandoned.
- There will be no balance sheet impact (although, as above, this may not be an issue for RZ).

Disadvantages

- It may be more expensive as the lessor has to cover all the other costs.
- Operating leases will not be available on all types of machinery.

(b) **Same currency financing**

In this question, RZ could have raised finance in US$ to finance the purchase.

Advantages

- The changes in balance sheet values of the asset and liability would be in the same currency and will offset each other to a large extent.
- There might be cheaper finance available in the US to encourage export sales.

Disadvantages

- The tax implications will be more complex.
- If cashflows are generated in sterling, this will produce currency risk as the interest and capital payments will be made in US$.
- In some cases, exchange controls might be introduced which would cause problems in making the payments.

Stock Market Efficiency 5

✏️ Exam focus

Stock market efficiency underlies all our calculations, as it assesses to what extent the actions undertaken by managers are fed through to the market price. You need to be able to explain the different forms of efficiency, and to identify the form of efficiency which seems to be in operation in a scenario.

🔑 Key points

Principle

An efficient capital market is one where the current market value of a share is a fair price. In other words, it exhibits many of the attributes of a perfect capital market:

- Information easily available (and cheaply)
- Rational investors
- Low transaction costs (not impeding the decision to buy or sell)
- A number of buyers and sellers (to give liquidity)
- No dominant player in the market.

Weak form efficiency

The current share price reflects (at least) the record of past share price movements. So plotting past share price movements (Chartism or technical analysis) will not beat the market consistently.

Semi-strong form efficiency

The current share price reflects all available public information, such as dividend announcements, annual accounts released and items in the media.

Strong form efficiency

The current share price reflects all information that can possibly be acquired, both public and private.

Summary

Form of efficiency	Not efficient	Weak	Semi-strong	Strong
Price reflects				
Previous movements	X	✓	✓	✓
Public information	X	X	✓	✓
Inside information	X	X	X	✓
Can beat market using				
Chartism	✓	X	X	X
Publicly released information	✓	✓	X	X
Inside information	✓	✓	✓	X
General evidence		Good	Reasonable	Not very good

Implications for managers

The more efficient the market, the more the manager can rely on the stock market pricing its equity and debt 'fairly'. So managers should worry less about the presentation of information, or even dividend policy, but concentrate upon investing in positive net present-value projects.

Questions

Question 1 – Investment (Practice Question)

A company has a share price of £2 and has one million shares. On 7th January, the chief executive presents an investment opportunity to the Board. He calculates (and is later proved correct) that the net present value of this project will be £250,000. The Board approve it, but keep the minutes of the meeting confidential.

On 1st March, the company reveals the project to the media, who publish it widely. Investors believe the company's estimates.

Calculate the share prices under weak, semi-strong and strong form efficient market conditions at:

- 7th January
- 1st March

Question 2 – Newspaper (Practice Question)

The following two comments were drawn from separate articles in a highly respected financial newspaper:

> Market efficiency does not mean that share prices can be forecast with accuracy.

> The research department of a large firm of stockbrokers has developed a multiple regression model, based on data collected between 1964 and 1994, which is claimed to give statistically significant results for predicting share prices.

You are required to discuss these comments and explain why they are not contradictory.

(Total = 10 marks)

Question 3 – Founder

Founder has been advised that if he allowed 25% of the shares of F Ltd to be traded on the Alternative Investment Market, the family company would be able to attract additional investors. The company's profits arise from Founder's marketing expertise and financial management.

Each of his two sons currently holds 10% of the equity, his wife owns 25% and Founder himself the remaining 55%.

If they take up other investment opportunities in which they have expressed an interest, Mrs Founder and one son will each sell half of their respective interests for cash. Founder himself and the other son are not willing to sell any of the company's equity they hold. To meet the needs of the market an additional 300,000 shares will be issued. Both the allotment of the shares to be issued and the sale of existing shares will be scheduled to take place on 31 December 2001. The proceeds of the new issue will be used to reduce or to discharge borrowings.

The following table summarises F Ltd's results for 2001 and a budget for 2002 before taking account of the proposed share issue:

	2001 £'000	2002 £'000
Closing balance sheets		
Operating assets	2,767	3,058
Taxes and dividends payable	(344)	(381)
Borrowings	(290)	(118)
	2,133	2,559
Income statements		
Operating profit	764	840
Interest paid	(38)	(33)
Tax provision	(254)	(282)
Dividends declared	(90)	(99)
Retentions	382	426

Advisers believe that the Alternative Investment Market will trade the company's shares at a historical price/earnings ratio of 7, if the current dividend policy is maintained.

Requirements

(a) to calculate the issue price which is implied by the above information

(5 marks)

(b) to prepare a revised budget, assuming that the issue goes ahead as planned, at your calculated price, at a cost of £40,000

(5 marks)

(c) to outline the other factors that a prospective investor would consider when deciding whether to invest in F Ltd

(8 marks)

(d) to outline the changes to F Ltd's financial control and reporting systems that you would expect to follow from the expanded ownership.

(7 marks)
(Total = 25 marks)

Question 4 – COE

COE plc is an all-equity financed, listed company in the pharmaceutical industry which produces a small, specialist range of drugs that treat heart disorders. The drugs are protected by international patent as soon as new research and development has progressed sufficiently.

On 1 March 2002, following many years of testing, a new drug, kryothin, was given government approval in the United Kingdom. It was approved for use in most other countries during April and May 2002. Sales of kryothin will commence on 1 January 2003. The company's accounting year end is 31 December.

Including the earnings generated by sales of kryothin, the company could pay a total annual dividend of £32.2 million in each of the years ending 31 December 2003 to 31 December 2007. Thereafter it is expected that competitors will develop similar drugs and most of the excess profits will disappear, in which case the company could pay a total annual dividend of £19 million from 31 December 2008 onwards. (Assume for simplicity that dividends are declared and paid on 31 December each year.)

In order to manufacture kryothin, it will be necessary to raise £80 million of new capital on 1 January 2003 to finance the purchase of equipment.

The financing options being considered are:

Option (1)   An offer for sale at the market price per share on 1 January 2003.
Option (2)   An issue at par of 7% irredeemable corporate bonds. In this case, the interest would reduce the amount otherwise available to pay dividends.

The directors of COE plc assume that the annual cost of equity will remain at its current level of 10%. The company currently has in issue a share capital of 20 million £1 ordinary shares.

Requirements

(a) Assuming a semi-strong efficient market, explain the nature and timing of the share price reaction to the new drug kryothin at each stage of its development. Calculations are not required.

(9 marks)

(b) Calculate COE plc's price per share at 2 January 2003 under each of the following options for raising the £80 million of new finance:

Option (1) – an offer for sale
Option (2) – an issue at par of 7% irredeemable corporate bonds.

Assume that the directors are correct in assuming that the annual cost of equity will remain at 10%, and that financial markets believe the directors' forecasts of future dividends. Ignore taxation.

(16 marks)
(Total = 25 marks)

✓ Answers

Question 1 – Investment

NPV of £250,000 = an extra 25p per share

Form	Weak	Semi-strong	Strong
7 January	£2.00	£2.00	£2.25
1 March	£2.00	£2.25	£2.25

Question 2 – Newspaper

Market efficiency

Market efficiency looks at how well the share price reflects all the relevant information. Share prices will thus move when new information becomes available, but whether it goes up or down will depend on whether it is good or bad news.

The share price will look like a random walk when plotted, which demonstrates the difficulty in making any reliable prediction. The newspaper quote means that if the market is efficient, then the share price will already reflect all the current relevant information and it will be impossible to predict any future movements, as it will depend on, as yet unknown, information.

Regression model

The multiple regression model will take a number of inputs, relating to areas such as inflation, interest rates, market size and share, and give the predicted share price. The stockbrokers claim that it gave statistically significant results for the thirty years from 1964 to 1994, but this does not necessarily make it any easier to predict future share prices. This is because it will require a prediction of all the inputs in future periods, rather than inputting the values already known.

There is thus no contradiction between the two statements, as neither statement says that future prices can be easily predicted, but that past share prices can be explained in the light of the knowledge of the company and market conditions at the time.

Question 3 – Founder

(a) **Issue price**

If X = original number of shares

$$300{,}000 + (0.05 + 0.125)X = 0.25(300{,}000 + X)$$
$$300{,}000 + 0.175X = 75{,}000 + 0.25X$$
$$225{,}000 = 0.075X$$
$$X = 3{,}000{,}000$$

Issue price $= \dfrac{472{,}000}{3{,}000{,}000} \times 7 = 110\text{p}$

(b) **Revised budget**

Proceeds = 300,000 × £1.10 − £40,000 = £290,000

This will repay the borrowings at the end of 2001 and save interest; if we assume interest at 10% this will be approximately £35,000.

The resulting budget for 2002 is:

Closing balance sheet:

	£'000
Operating assets	3,058
Cash (290 − 118 + 35)	207
Taxes and dividends (381 + 10)	(391)
	2,874

Income statement:

	£'000
Operating profit (840 − 40)	800
Interest (35 − 33)	2
Tax	(282)
Dividends*	(109)
Retention	411

* To maintain dividend per share, total dividend must increase by 10%.

(c) **Other factors**

In deciding whether to invest in F Ltd, a prospective investor would have the last three years' results and an indication of the future prospects on flotation. The historical statements will be endorsed by the auditors, but the investor will need to review carefully the other information and consider it carefully. Other factors might include:

- What are the economic prospects for F, given the likely market conditions?
- How would changes in the economic cycle effect F?
- Who are F's major competitors and how does F maintain its competitive advantage. How much of a threat do new entrants present?
- How likely is F to be able to protect its strengths or to develop new weaknesses?
- How dependent is F on Founder, and are there any succession plans?
- How will the directors' remuneration affect future profits?
- What are the management skills like in the company and how good are the staff relations?

(d) **Financial control and reporting system changes**

Introducing external shareholders means that there is now a split between management and some of the owners, assuming that the family are still involved in the management.

The financial control system was probably focused on cash rather than accounting analysis. The accounting issues are likely to be important for the year-end accounts for Companies House and the Inland Revenue, and the family probably tried to keep profits as low as possible to minimise tax.

This control system will need to change its focus as some shareholders will have no knowledge of the day-to-day operations and will need detailed accounts presented annually, and possibly semi-annually or quarterly. As so much reliance will be placed on these, the management will need to set accurate budgets and monitor progress each month.

Question 4 – COE

(a) **Share price reaction**

A semi-strong efficient market is one in which the share price reflects all publicly available information. As new information is released to the market, the share price will react accordingly. Assuming that the market was aware of the development of kryothin, the market price would try to build in the information, as it became public.

Before it knew about Kryothin, the price would incorporate the general expectation that COE would develop new drugs, some of which might prove successful. When the drug was patented, a general assessment of its viability would suggest that a viable drug has been developed and therefore the share price would rise. This would then fluctuate as the news of its progress through development filtered into the public domain.

When the drug was approved, the share price is likely to have risen, unless the market had already anticipated this decision based on the information it had. As other countries approved it, thus increasing the possible sales, the share price would also rise, again unless the market had already anticipated the news.

On production and the start of sales there is not likely to be a major change in share price, as the expected profits have already been built into the value of the company when the government approvals were given.

(b) **Share price calculation**

(i) *Offer of sale*

Dividends 03–07 = £32.2m pa
08 onwards = £19m pa

PV = (32.2 × 3.791) + (19/0.1 × 0.621) = £240m

New shares will be issued at the new market price so existing shares will be worth: £240m − £80m = £160m

Share value will be £160m/20m = £8

(ii) *Irredeemable bonds*

Interest = 7% × £80m = £5.6m

Dividends 03–07 = (32.2m − 5.6m) = £26.6m pa
08 onwards = (19m − 5.6m) = £13.4m pa

PV = (26.6 × 3.791) + (13.4/0.1 × 0.621) = £184m

Share value will be 184m/20m = £9.20

Cost of Capital

6

📝 Exam focus

The cost of capital is fundamental to project appraisal and valuations, so you need to be able to calculate the various components. However, there are only a limited number of possibilities you will come across in the exam. Remember that the cost of redeemable debt is an approximation, so don't spend a lot of time trying to increase its accuracy. You need to be able to identify when the weighted average cost of capital can be used for project appraisal and when it is unsuitable and why.

🔑 Key points

Cost of equity

Dividend valuation model:

$$k_e = \frac{d_1}{P_0} + g$$

where,
d_1 = dividend in one year's time
P_0 = Today's ex div share price
g = constant annual dividend growth

Remember:

(a) It assumes constant dividend growth
(b) P_0 is ex div
(c) d_1 probably has to be estimated as $d_0 (1 + g)$, where d_0 = today's dividend.

Estimating g

From past dividends:

$20(1 + g)^5 = 28$
$1 + g = 1.4^{0.2}$
$1 + g = 1.0696$
so $g = 6.96\%$

where the dividend paid in 2001 was 20 and the dividend paid in 2006 was 28.

Using Gordon's growth model:

$$g = b \times r$$

where,
b = proportion of profits retained (i.e. not paid out as dividends)
r = return achieved on funds invested

You are less likely to make mistakes if you input both b and r as decimals.

Capital asset pricing model (CAPM)

$$k_e = R_f + [R_m - R_f]\beta$$

where the expected return depends on:
R_f = return required if there was no risk (the 'risk-free rate')
R_m = expected average return on the stock market
β = the risk of investing in the company compared with the whole stock market.

Remember that:

(a) $[R_m - R_f]$ is called the market premium for risk
(b) β is unlikely to be outside the range 0.5–2.0
(c) It assumes that investors in the stock market hold diversified portfolios of shares
(d) It assumes a perfect capital market is in operation.

Cost of debt

Corporate debt is normally traded in the UK in £100 nominal value. However, the market price could be very different and is expressed in different ways:

£120 or 120% or a 20% premium (to par) = a price of £120

$$\text{The yield to an investor} = \frac{\text{Interest paid}}{\text{Market price}}$$

$$\text{The cost of debt to the company, } k_d = \frac{\text{Interest paid}}{\text{Market price}} \times (1 - t)$$

When we have redeemable debt, the interest payments will cease so we do not have a perpetuity of interest and we have to estimate the discount rate used to equate the future interest payments and redemption received by the investor to the current market price.

Weighted average cost of capital (WACC)

The company's cost of capital will be the weighted average of all the costs of long-term finance. Total market values are used to weight the costs together.

$$k_e = \frac{V_E}{V_E + V_D} + k_d(1-t)\frac{V_D}{V_E + V_D}$$

where
V_E and V_D = total market value of equity and debt respectively and
k_d = pre-tax cost of debt

Assumptions and use of the cost of capital

All of the above rely on the market price of any traded investment in the company's equity or debt reflecting the expected risks and returns of holding that investment. This implies a rational, reasonably perfect (or efficient) capital market.

In addition, the cost of capital derived will only be appropriate if the risk in the project is the same as that currently perceived by the investor in the company.

In effect, this means:

- The project must be in the same line of business as the rest of the company (business risk stays the same)
- There must be no change in the gearing level (financial risk stays the same).

Questions

Question 1 – Equity (Practice Question)

Find the cost of equity using the dividend valuation model in the following situations:

(a) Current share price is £2.50. It has just paid its annual dividend of 20p, which has been the same for the last 10 years.

(b) Current share price is £2.50. It will shortly pay its annual dividend of 20p, which has been the same for the last 10 years. The share price is still cum div.

(c) Current share price is £2.30. It has just paid its annual dividend of 20p, and investors expect annual growth in dividends of 5%.

(d) Current market capitalisation (total value of all the equity) is £8 million and it has just paid a total annual dividend of £500,000. Investors expect annual dividend growth of 6%.

Question 2 – Growth (Practice Question)

Estimate g in the following situations:

(a) Previous dividends have been:

4 yrs ago	3 yrs ago	2 yrs ago	Last yr	Now
10p	12p	12p	14p	16p

(b) Previous dividends have been:

6 yrs ago	5 yrs ago	4 yrs ago	3 yrs ago	2 yrs ago	Last yr	Now
3p	4p	16p	17p	19p	21p	23p

Just over 4 years ago, the company floated on the stock market.

(c) Dividend payout ratio averages 70% and the company generates returns of 15% based on book values.

(d) Profits last year in an all-equity company were £100,000, out of which dividends were paid of £60,000. Shareholders' funds at the end of the year were £1.29 million.

Question 3 – CAPM (Practice Question)

The risk-free rate is 3% and the stock market is expected to give 8% on average. Find the cost of equity if the company's beta is:

(a) 1   the same risk as the stock market average
(b) 1.3   more risky than the stock market average
(c) 0.8   less risky than the stock market average
(d) 0   no risk at all

Cost of Capital

Question 4 – Debt (Practice Question)

Find the company's cost of debt in the following situations, if the corporation tax rate is 30%.

(a) A bank loan at 8%.
(b) Irredeemable 5% loan stock, trading at a 10% premium to par.
(c) 7% redeemable loan stock, trading at par and redeemable at a premium of 10% to par in 4 years time.

Question 5 – Loan stock (Practice Question)

A company has 6% loan stock which is redeemable at a premium of 10% in 3 years time. The current market price is 105%. What is the yield to an investor and what is the cost of debt to the company if the corporation tax rate is 30%?

Question 6 – WACC (Practice Question)

A company has the following structure:

	£
8% bank loan	200,000
10% irredeemable loan stock	500,000
Share capital (50p nominal value shares)	100,000
Accumulated reserves	500,000

The share price is currently £5, the irredeemable loan stock is priced at £90, the corporation tax rate is 30% and the company has already calculated its cost of equity to be 12%.

Calculate the company's weighted average cost of capital.

Question 7 – LS

LS is a mature consumer goods company with limited scope for turnover growth in its stable market. The following information is known about the company and its main competitors:

	LS	Competitor A	Competitor B
Equity beta	0.5	0.9	Not available
Actual return on equity per annum (%)	8	9	11 (estimate)
Risk-free return per annum (%)	5	5	5
Market return per annum (%)	10	10	10
Current share price ($)	$2	$3	Not available
Historic turnover growth per annum (%)	3	5	Not available

A recent press announcement from competitor A stated: 'We believe in delivering a return above the norm in our sector of the market and are pleased that we have delivered returns of 1% more than our main competitor. Investors wanting a high return in exciting markets need look no further.'

It is also known that competitor B is looking for financial backing to commence trading and is predicting average annual returns of 11% to equity investors. The company will also be funded with high levels of debt. After five years, the intention is to float the company on the main stock exchange.

The Chief Executive of LS is concerned about these developments and is expecting some shareholders of LS ask some difficult questions. The Chief Executive has made the following three comments to the management team in response to the current situation:

> I have heard that the capital asset pricing model has some limitations, for example it only looks at one part of risk, the risk related to the market. Don't you think we should consider total risk?
>
> Shouldn't we be comparing actual returns on equity with the weighted average cost of capital rather than with the required return calculated by using the capital asset pricing model?
>
> I've heard that our stock market is semi-strong. Is that why our share price is low? If our stock market were strong, would our share price be higher? Can we do anything about our share price if we think it is undervalued?

Requirements

You are a member of the management team. To assist the Chief Executive, set out answers to the following:

(a) Calculate the required return on equity for both LS and competitor A based on CAPM and comment on the results. Compare the actual return with the required return in each case and advise whether LS or competitor A is providing the best performance.

(8 marks)

(b) Assuming the estimated return of 11% accurately reflects the level of systematic risk of competitor B, calculate its beta factor. Discuss the potential risks for a shareholder of investing in competitor B.

(7 marks)

(c) Discuss each of the Chief Executive's three comments.

(10 marks)
(Total = 25 marks)

Question 8 – CAP

CAP plc is a listed company that owns and operates a large number of farms throughout the world. A variety of crops are grown.

Financing structure

The following is an extract from the balance sheet of CAP plc at 30 September 2002.

	£m
Ordinary shares of £1 each	200
Reserves	100
9% irredeemable £1 preference shares	50
8% loan stock 2003	250
	600

The ordinary shares were quoted at £3 per share ex div on 30 September 2002. The beta of CAP plc's equity shares is 0.8, the annual yield on treasury bills is 5%, and financial markets expect an average annual return of 15% on the market index.

The market price per preference share was £0.90 ex div on 30 September 2002.

Loan stock interest is paid annually in arrears and is allowable for tax at a corporation tax rate of 30%. The loan stock was priced at £100.57 ex interest per £100 nominal on 30 September 2002. Loan stock is redeemable on 30 September 2003.

Assume that taxation is payable at the end of the year in which taxable profits arise.

A new project

Difficult trading conditions in European farming have caused CAP plc to decide to convert a number of its farms in Southern Europe into camping sites with effect from the 2003 holiday season. Providing the necessary facilities for campers will require major investment, and this will be financed by a new issue of loan stock. The returns on the new campsite business are likely to have a very low correlation with those of the existing farming business.

Requirements

(a) Using the capital asset pricing model, calculate the required rate of return on equity of CAP plc at 30 September 2002. Ignore any impact from the new campsite project.

Briefly explain the implications of a beta of less than 1, such as that for CAP plc.

(6 marks)

(b) Calculate the weighted average cost of capital of CAP plc at 30 September 2002 (use your calculation in answer to requirement (a) above for the cost of equity). Ignore any impact from the new campsite project.

(12 marks)

(c) Without further calculations, identify and explain the factors that may change CAP plc's equity beta during the year ending 30 September 2003.

(7 marks)
(Total = 25 marks)

Question 9 – WEB

WEB plc operates a low-cost airline and is a listed company. By comparison to its major competitors it is relatively small, but it has expanded significantly in recent years. The shares are held mainly by large financial institutions.

The following are extracts from WEB plc's budgeted balance sheet at 31 May 2002:

	$m
Ordinary shares of $1	100
Reserves	50
9% debentures 2005 (at nominal value)	200
	350

Dividends have grown in the past at 3% a year, resulting in an expected dividend of $1 per share to be declared on 31 May 2002 (Assume for simplicity that the dividend will also be paid on this date.) Due to expansion, dividends are expected to grow at 4% a year from 1 June 2002 for the foreseeable future. The price per share is currently $10.40 ex div and this is not expected to change before 31 May 2002.

The existing debentures are due to be redeemed at par on 31 May 2005. The market value of these debentures at 1 June 2002 is expected to be $100.84 (ex interest) per $100 nominal. Interest is payable annually in arrears on 31 May and is allowable for tax purposes. The corporation tax rate for the foreseeable future is 30%. Assume taxation is payable at the end of the year in which the taxable profits arise.

New finance

The company has now decided to purchase three additional aircraft at a cost of $10 million each. The Board has decided that the new aircraft will be financed in full by an 8% bank loan on 1 June 2002.

Requirements

(a) Calculate the expected weighted average cost of capital of WEB plc at 31 May 2002.

(10 marks)

(b) Without further calculations, explain the impact of the new bank loan on WEB plc's

    (i) cost of equity;
    (ii) cost of debt; and
    (iii) weighted average cost of capital (using the traditional model).

(10 marks)

(c) Explain and distinguish

    (i) debentures; and
    (ii) a bank loan.

In so doing, explain why, in the circumstances of WEB plc, the cost of debt may be different for the two types of security.

(5 marks)
(Total = 25 marks)

Question 10 – Deaton

Deaton plc is a listed company which manufactures quality cut-glass products. The company's sole manufacturing site and 95% of its sales are in the United Kingdom. The company is, however, currently considering entering into a contract to sell a specialist range of glassware to a Japanese retailer. The revenues from the Japanese contract are expected to amount to 25% of all future sales and 15% of future profit. It will require a significant initial investment, but it is expected that the money could be borrowed from the company's bank.

The Deaton family and other directors own the majority of the equity share capital, the remainder being held by employees and small shareholders. The total share capital amounts to 12 million £1 ordinary shares and has been unchanged for many years. Dividends per share paid on 31 May each year have been:

1997	1998	1999	2000
35.64 pence	37.78 pence	40.05 pence	42.45 pence

The dividend on 31 May 2001 will be 45.00 pence per share. The company also has £12.5 million of 8% loan stock to be redeemed on 31 May 2002. Interest is payable annually in arrears on 31 May.

At 31 May 2001, the company's ordinary shares were quoted at £5.50 (cum div) and the loan stock at £98 per £100 nominal (ex interest). The corporation tax rate can be assumed to be 30% for the foreseeable future. Interest is allowable for tax purposes. Ignore any taxation of dividends.

The directors' meeting

The directors of Deaton plc were uncertain whether to proceed with the Japanese contract and in particular they were concerned about the discount rate that should be used for assessing the project.

The marketing director argued: 'We should use the weighted average cost of capital. This is the rate we have used in the past and it reflects the average cost of acquiring funds.'

The production director disagreed: 'If we are going to borrow to finance this project, then we have to pay interest. So long as the cash flows from the project cover the interest payments, we will make a profit on the contract. Common sense dictates that we should therefore simply use the interest rate charged to us by the bank as the discount rate.'

The finance director argued: 'The real issue in deciding the relevant discount rate is the finance that we use. I suggest that instead of paying more and more dividends each year, largely to ourselves as individual shareholders, we should reduce dividends and use the cash saved to decrease the company's debt. If the company can earn a better rate of return than individual shareholders, then the cash should be retained in the company. As it is, the company is in effect borrowing to pay a dividend. Also, this project is high risk and therefore demands a high-risk premium in the discount rate.'

Requirements

(a) Calculate Deaton plc's weighted average cost of capital at 31 May 2001.

(10 marks)

(b) As a member of the treasury team, write a memorandum to the directors of Deaton plc which considers the views expressed by the directors. In so doing, and so far as the information permits, describe the factors to be considered in determining a discount rate for the Japanese project.

(15 marks)
(Total = 25 marks)

74 Exam Practice Kit: Management Accounting Financial Strategy

✓ Answers

Question 1 – Equity

$$k_e = \frac{d_1}{P_0} + g$$

(a) $k_e = \dfrac{20}{250} + 0 = 0.08$ or 8%

(b) $k_e = \dfrac{20}{(250 - 20)} + 0 = 0.087$ or 8.7%

(c) $k_e = \dfrac{20 \times 1.05}{230} + 0.05 = 0.134$ or 13.4%

(d) $k_e = \dfrac{500,000 \times 1.06}{8,000,000} + 0.06 = 0.126$ or 12.6%

Question 2 – Growth

(a) $10(1 + g)^4 = 16$ so $(1 + g) = 1.125$ and $g = 12.5\%$

(b) Ignore years when private, as not representative of the future
$16(1 + g)^4 = 231$ so $g = 1.095$ and $g = 9.5\%$

(c) $b = 0.30$ and $R = 0.15$ $g = 0.30 \times 0.15 = 0.045$ or 4.5%

(d) $b = 1 - 0.60 = 0.40$, $\quad r = \dfrac{\text{Profit}}{\text{Operating Net Assets}} = \dfrac{100,000}{1,290,000 - 40,000} = 0.08$

$g = 0.40 \times 0.08 = 0.032$ or 3.2%

Question 3 – CAPM

(a) $k_e = 3 + (8 - 3)1 \;\; = 8\%$
(b) $k_e = 3 + (8 - 3)1.3 = 9.5\%$
(c) $k_e = 3 + (8 - 3)0.8 = 7\%$
(d) $k_e = 3 + (8 - 3)0 \;\; = 3\%$

Question 4 – Debt

(a) $k_d = 8\% \times 0.70 = 5.6\%$

(b) $k_d = \dfrac{5 \times 0.70}{110} = 3.2\%$

(c) t_0 $\quad\quad$ 100
$\;\;\;\;t_1 - t_4$ $\quad 7 \times 0.70 = (4.90)$
$\;\;\;\;t_4$ $\quad\quad\quad$ (110)

At 5%, PV of future cash flows = (4.9 × 3.546) + (110 × 0.823) = 107.91
At 10%, PV of future cash flows = (4.9 × 3.170) + (110 × 0.683) = 90.66

$$k_d = 5\% + (10\% - 5\%)\frac{(107.91 - 100)}{(107.91 - 90.66)}$$

$$= 5\% + (5\% \times 0.459)$$

$$= 7.3\%$$

Question 5 – Loan stock

Investor's position

t_0	pay market price	(105)
$t_1 - t_3$	receive interest	6
t_3	receive redemption	110

We need to find the discount rate which equates the cash inflows in the future to the current market price. This is the same calculation as an IRR and is subject to the same approximations.

At 5%, PV of future cash flows = (6 × 2.723) + (110 × 0.864) = £111.38
At 10%, PV of future cash flows = (6 × 2.487) + (110 × 0.751) = £97.53

We need the rate which gives a market price of £105.

$$\text{Approximate yield} = 5\% + (10\% - 5\%) \times \frac{(111.38 - 105)}{(111.38 - 97.53)}$$

$$= 5\% + (5\% \times 0.461)$$

$$= 7.3\%$$

Company's position

As interest is tax allowable, but we assume the capital redemption is not, we cannot take the yield and multiply by $(1 - t)$.

The company would pay off the loan at a price of £105 by buying it up now. By not doing so, it continues to have those funds, but at a cost:

t_0	Funds available	105
$t_1 - t_3$	Interest cost (= 6 × 0.70)	(4.20)
t_3	Redemption paid	(110)

Again, we need to estimate the discount rate:

At 5%, PV of future cash flows = (4.20 × 2.723) + (110 × 0.864) = 106.48
At 10%, PV of future cash flows = (4.20 × 2.487) + (110 × 0.751) = 93.06

$$\text{Approximate cost of debt} = 5\% + (10\% - 5\%) \times \frac{(106.48 - 105)}{(106.48 - 93.06)}$$

$$= 5\% + (5\% \times 0.110)$$

$$= 5.5\%$$

Question 6 – WACC

	Cost of capital	Total value
Equity	12%	£1,000,000
Bank loan	$8 \times 0.7 = 5.6\%$	£200,000
Irredeemable loan stock	$\dfrac{10 \times 0.7}{90} = 7.8\%$	£450,000
		£1,650,000

Cost of capital (k) = $\left(12\% \times \dfrac{1{,}000}{1{,}650}\right) + \left(5.6\% \times \dfrac{200}{1{,}650}\right) + \left(7.8\% \times \dfrac{450}{1{,}650}\right) = 10.1\%$ or approximately 10%

Question 7 – LS

(a) **Required return on equity**

LS $5 + (10 - 5)\,0.5 = 7.5\%$
A $5 + (10 - 5)\,0.9 = 9.5\%$

Beta measures the responsiveness of the returns to changes in the market, so A, having a higher beta, is more risky to shareholders and will require a greater return to compensate.

Shareholders require a return of 7.5% from LS, but it is managing to exceed this by giving 8%. On the other hand, they require 9.5% from A but it is only giving 9%. Even though it gives a higher return than LS, it is not high enough for the risk perceived by shareholders. A is therefore an 'inefficient' investment and LS, which is exceeding the return required in compensation for its risk, is providing the better performance.

(b) **Competitor B**

$11 = 5 + (10 - 5)\,\beta$
So $\beta = 1.2$

As B has not yet started trading and has no track record, investors are bound to view it as a more risky investment. In addition, the company intends to raise high levels of debt which will increase the risk to shareholders; this is because interest will be paid before any returns to shareholders and if interest rates rise, could force the company into liquidation. Finally, shareholders will probably only be able to realise their holding in five years' time when the company is floated. All this means that B is a much riskier investment than A (or LS), as reflected in the beta, and hence the return required is higher.

(c) **Chief executive's comments**

(i) *Market risk*

The Capital Asset Pricing Model (CAPM) has a number of assumptions and limitations. Investors are assumed to be fully diversified within the stock market, so that their portfolio reflects the market index. Total risk can be split into market, or systematic risk and specific or unsystematic risk. The unsystematic risk can be diversified away so if our assumption is correct, investors with diversified portfolios will only be interested in the systematic risk. This is measured by beta, which then, via CAPM, gives the return required.

If investors have not diversified their portfolios, there would be some benefit in the company considering total risk and effectively reducing the unsystematic risk by diversifying for these shareholders.

Conversely, investors can diversify outside the stock market (unquoted companies and property, for example) thus reducing their risk further. In this situation, CAPM will overstate the risk and the return required.

(ii) *Weighted average cost of capital (WACC)*

We always need to compare like with like: CAPM gives the required return for equity and should therefore be compared with the actual returns on equity. The WACC estimates the average return required for all sources of capital, including long-term debt, and so should be compared to the average return generated for equity and debt holders. However, the gearing structure will affect the WACC calculation and make it more difficult to compare with other companies which have different gearing levels.

(iii) *Efficiency*

If a market is efficient, then the share price reflects all information that would be relevant to buyers and sellers; this means the price changes rapidly as new information arises. There are three forms described:

1   The weak form states that share prices always reflect past share price movements and trends.
2   The semi-strong form states that share prices always reflect all publicly available information (such as annual reports and media).
3   The strong form states that share prices always reflect all public and private information (including inside information).

Therefore, a semi-strong market does not indicate a share price will be low or high, simply that the share price takes into account all information in the public domain. If the share price is undervalued, it must be that the market is not fully aware of some information about the company and its prospects. This information needs to be identified and released to the public so that it is understood and reflected in the share price.

Question 8 – CAP

(a) Required return on equity = 5 + (15 − 5) 0.8
            = 13%

Beta measures the extent to which CAP's share price has moved with changes in the average market returns. A beta less than 1 means that the share price does not fluctuate as much as the market average (on average it only moves 80% of the change in the market average).

As the fluctuations are lower, it is less volatile, or risky, than the average and will therefore require a lower return than the market average (25%) in compensation.

(b) Cost of preference shares 9/90 10%
Cost of debt (105.6/100.57) − 1 5%
WACC = [(13% × 600) + (10% × 45) + (5% × 251.43)]/896.43 10.6%

(c) **Equity Beta**

Beta is a measure of the risk to a well-diversified stock market investor; changes to both the business risk and the financial risk of CAP will therefore affect beta in the company year.

The new business venture will diversify the company's operations but this will affect the unsystematic risk, not the systematic risk which is measured by beta. The impact on beta will depend on the new business's correlation with the market, not with the current operations. The new beta will then be (ignoring any change in financing) a weighted average of the two betas for the two different operations.

The new debt finance for the camping sites will increase the risk to shareholders, as the interest paid out will make their returns more volatile. This will therefore increase the equity beta.

It is unclear if the current loan stock is to be re-financed next year, or whether this has been allowed for in the new issue. A reduction in the debt finance will reduce the risk to shareholders and hence the beta.

In addition to the above influences, beta changes over time as investors build in expectations of the farming industry. Beta is calculated by looking at historical returns and therefore it can change gradually as new information about the industry and the company emerges; however, this is unpredictable by its very nature.

Question 9 – WEB

(a) **Weighted average cost of capital**

$$K_e = \frac{1 \times 1.04}{10.40} + 0.04 = 14\%$$

K_d given by:

t_0 (100.84)
$t_1 - t_3$ 9 × 0.70 6.30
t_3 100

At 6%, NPV = (6.30 × 2.673) + (100 × 0.840) − 100.84 = 0
So, K_d = 6%
WACC = (14% × 1,040/1,241.68) + (6% × 201.68/1,241.68)
= 12.7%

(b) **Impact of new bank loan**

   (i) *Cost of equity*

   The new bank loan will increase the gearing of the company and therefore make the returns to equity more volatile as interest has to be paid before any payment is made to shareholders. In addition, on liquidation the bank loan will be paid in full before any distribution to shareholders. This means that the risk to shareholders increases and therefore the cost of equity will increase to compensate shareholders for this risk.

   (ii) *Cost of debt*

   Gearing is currently fairly low (measured by market values) but the bank loan will increase this. However, the bank value of assets less current liabilities would appear to be roughly $350 million. This easily covers the $232 million of debt, even with the new $30 million loan and as long as the book values of the fixed assets do not massively exceed their market values, the increase in debt should not affect the risk perceived by the debt-holders. Therefore, we would not expect the cost of debt to change.

   (iii) *Weighted average cost of capital (WACC)*

   As more debt is introduced, it will tend to reduce the WACC as it is a cheaper form of finance than equity. However, the cost of equity is likely to rise, as noted above. As debt is introduced initially, the overall effect, according to the traditional theory, is to decrease until shareholders perceive the risk to be much greater, at which point the cost of equity rises dramatically and pulls the WACC up again. Whether the increase in WEB's debt causes the WACC to increase or decrease depends on whether its current gearing structure is below or above this optional point.

(c) **Debenture or bank loan**

A debenture is a written acknowledgement of a company debt, stating the interest coupon and repayment provisions as well as other conditions. These can be offered to the public if a prospectus is prepared and can be held in trust on behalf of many different investors and traded on a secondary market.

A bank loan is not normally traded and is arranged with a single bank or a syndicate of banks.

The cost of debt may be different between the two for WEB as:

- The current interest rates will affect the terms when issued, so the 9% coupon rate on the debentures will have been influenced by the interest rates ruling at the time.
- The covenants to protect the investor may be different; the one with more protection will be less risky and hence carry a lower cost.
- The debentures are marketable, thus reducing the risk to holders and leading to a lower cost.
- The debentures may have been issued at a premium or a discount and the future cash flows increased or decreased to compensate.
- The cost of debt is not very different between the two. The bank loan is 8% pre tax, whereas the debenture is 6% post tax. Pre tax, the cost of the debenture (or yield) is 8.7%.

Question 10 – Deaton

(a) **WACC**

g given by $35.64(1+g)^4 = 45$
$$1 + g = (45/35.64)^{0.25}$$
$$g = 0.06$$

$$K_e = \frac{45 \times 1.06}{505} + 0.06 = 15.45\%$$

K_d given by $98 = [100 + (8 \times 0.7)]/(1 + K_d)$
$$K_d = 7.76\%$$

WACC $= (15.45 \times 60.6m/72.85m) + (7.76 \times 12.25m/72.85m)$
$ = 14.16\%$

(b) MEMORANDUM

To: Directors of Deaton plc
From: Treasury Member
Date: xx x 200xx

Discount rate and dividends

This memo considers the various views expressed by directors and identifies some of the factors to be considered in deciding on a discount rate for the Japanese project.

Marketing Director
Using the current WACC (14.16%) as the discount rate assumes that the risk in the Japanese project is the same as the existing company. This means that it has the same business risk and is also financed in the same way.

Given that it is overseas, facing different competition and customers, and will also have to manage foreign exchange risk, it seems unlikely that the risk will be the same. The fact that the company has to invest in specialised equipment would also tend to make the project riskier.

However, the project will diversify the company's operations, reducing the risk for undiversified shareholders like the Deaton family and directors. It will also guarantee sales under the contract and possibly offer other opportunities in the Japanese market.

Production Director
Borrowing funds for the project will increase the gearing in the company and hence the risk borne by the shareholders as the owners of the company. This will mean that the return required by shareholders will increase to compensate. The return from the project will need to cover this additional return as well as the cost of the loan finance. As mentioned above, the shareholders' required return may also increase due to the operational risk connected with the new investment.

Finance Director
The dividends paid, finance raised and investments made are directly connected, but the discount rate used in a project may not be the same as the new finance raised as discussed above. Debt is cheaper but will increase the gearing and the cost of equity, whereas equity is more expensive but will reduce gearing which has a beneficial effect.

More generally, enough cash must be left in the company to service the debt, and the company cannot pay out as dividends more than its accumulated profits.

Adjustments to WACC 7

📝 Exam focus

You need to focus on what we want to achieve and how the different theories fit into this. We require a discount rate appropriate to the risk of the project; this may mean adjusting for a change in gearing or a different business risk or both. You should be clear about when to use the existing WACC, when to use M&M to adjust for gearing and when to start with a beta in a different industry from the company.

You also need to be aware of the limitation of these theories and hence the approximate results they give.

🔑 Key points

Financial risk and the cost of capital

Traditional view
The Traditional view was based on observations of the impact of gearing on the market value of a company and its cost of capital. It observed that shareholders viewed some debt as beneficial, as it was cheaper finance and had the effect of magnifying returns to equity.

As a result the weighted average cost of capital, with more cheap debt and no or little increase in the cost of equity, drops before rising as shareholders start to adjust the return required at higher levels of gearing.

However, this was not much good for predicting exactly what would happen to the cost of capital when the gearing changed, as it depended on shareholders' views in a particular company on the appropriate level of debt.

M&M with corporation tax
M&M showed that in a perfect capital market the value of a geared company was higher than that of an identical ungeared company and that the difference was the present value of the tax relief on the debt interest.

i.e. $V_g = V_u + TB$

where:
V_g = total market value of the geared company = $E + D$
V_u = market value of the equity in an identical all-equity company
TB = PV of the tax relief on debt interest.

If the debt is irredeemable and the discount rate used on the tax relief is the pre-tax cost of debt, TB is simply the market value of the debt multiplied by the tax rate. If the value is increasing as gearing increases, the WACC must be decreasing.

$$k = k_{eu}(1 - TL)$$

where:

$$L = \frac{V_D}{V_E + V_D} \quad \text{for the finance used}$$

M&M with corporate taxes implies that the value of the company can be increased by becoming very highly geared. In practice this is unlikely and the theory becomes less useful at higher level of gearing as it did not take account of:

- the company not having any taxable profits left to obtain tax relief on the extra interest (tax exhaustion);
- debt becoming more risky to hold at high gearing levels, thus increasing the cost of debt;
- the additional costs of doing business when supplies and customers see you as at risk of bankruptcy;
- personal tax positions.

In addition, there are practical considerations, such as the assets the company can offer for security, which limit the level of debt which can be issued.

Adjusted present values (APV)

Instead of calculating a new cost of capital for assessing a project, an adjusted present value approach can be used, which separates the investment decision from the financing decision.

This uses the formula:

$$V_g = V_u + PV \text{ of tax relief on debt interest}$$

It evaluates the NPV from the perspective of an ungeared company (giving the increase in V_u) before looking at the benefit to the company of increasing the debt for its funding.

Business risk and the cost of capital

Business risk

Business risk (or operating risk) includes all the risks in a business, apart from financial risk. In other words, it includes the character of the directors, the cost structure of the business and the type of business in which the company operates, as well as other factors.

However, the only one which might be different in a project being considered by a company from that known by investors is the type of business in which it operates. Investors in a brewer of beer, for example, would not have allowed for the risk of book publishing even though the brewer might be considering such a project. The cost of capital derived would, therefore, be inappropriate for the project.

Capital asset pricing model (CAPM)

CAPM states that expected return on an investment is

$$R_f + [R_m - R_f]\beta$$

For a quoted company we would assume the average investor is well diversified. In other words, β only reflects the systematic risk of the investment which cannot be avoided if the portfolio is held in the stock market. The unsystematic risk is diversified away in the portfolio.

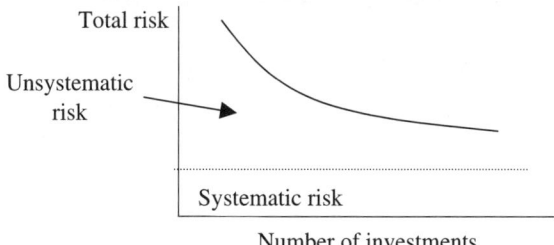

Changing business risk
A brewer, thinking about a project in book publishing, would find the average beta for book publishing by looking at companies already involved in that sector. The cost of equity derived would then be built into the WACC along with the various costs of debt. In practice the brewer should probably make some adjustment to the cost of equity derived, as it reflects the return required by investors from an experienced publisher.

Beta and gearing
One major difference between the brewer and the publishing company, from which it derives the beta, may be in the level of gearing. This will clearly affect the risk to the investor and hence the beta.

We need to strip out the publishing company's gearing and replace it with the brewer's gearing, using:

$$\beta_U = \beta_G \frac{V_E}{V_E + V_D(1-t)} + \beta_D \frac{V_D(1-t)}{V_E + V_D(1-t)}$$

Although this seems complex, β_D is the debt beta and measures the risk of the debt. As debt carries much less risk than equity, its beta is relatively small; many questions do not mention a debt beta, in which case we would assume that it is approximately zero (i.e. the debt is risk-free) and the final term in the above equation disappears.

Terminology
Although there are only two types of beta we use, there are a number of descriptions used. To avoid confusion, here is a list:

Beta including gearing risk	*Beta with no gearing risk*
A company's beta	Asset beta
Equity beta	Ungeared beta
Geared beta	Project beta

Combining betas
A company may comprise several divisions with different risk characteristics. The company's beta will be a weighted average (by total value) of the divisions' betas. In the same way, the beta of a portfolio of shares will be the weighted average, by market value, of the betas of the individual investments.

Arbitrage pricing theory
APT suggests that various independent factors affect the return required, rather than just the systematic risk used by CAPM. However, it is difficult to predict these factors in practice.

84 Exam Practice Kit: Management Accounting Financial Strategy

Questions

Question 1 – Gearing change (Practice Question)

A company has a WACC of 12% and a debt to equity ratio of 1:9 by market value. What will the WACC change to if the company raises more debt and repays equity so that its debt to equity ratio is now 3:7? Corporation tax is 30%.

Question 2 – New values (Practice Question)

A company has market values of £20 million and £80 million for debt and equity respectively. It decides to raise another £20 million of debt (and not pay off any equity or debt). If the corporation tax rate is 30%, what will be the new market values of debt and equity? If the existing cost of capital is 10%, what will it move to? (Assume all debt is irredeemable).

Question 3 – APV (Practice Question)

A company is reviewing a potential investment which will need £150 million now but will produce £30 million a year for the next 8 years. The company is considering financing it by issuing £40 million of 10% debt and using £110 million of its cash reserves. The corporation tax rate is 30% and an identical all-equity company would have a cost of equity of 14%.

Should the company proceed if the debt is

(a) irredeemable?
(b) 8 years in length?

Question 4 – Beta (Practice Question)

The brewer has a beta of 1.1 and estimates the risk-free rate to be 5% and the market premium for risk ($r_m - r_f$) to be 4%. The average beta for publishing appears to be 1.3. What cost of equity should the company use in assessing a publishing opportunity?

Question 5 – Degearing (Practice Question)

The brewer in the previous example has a gearing structure which is 70% equity and 30% debt by market value, while the publisher is geared 60%:40%. The corporation tax rate is 30%. De-gear the publisher's beta (strip out the gearing risk), re-gear to the brewer's gearing level and calculate the cost of equity.

Question 6 – REM

REM is a family-owned business. The family owns 80% of the shares. The remaining 20% is owned by four non-family shareholders. The Board of Directors is considering the purchase of two second-hand (i.e. previously used) freight planes to deliver its goods within its key markets in the USA. The Managing Director, an ex-pilot and one of the non-family shareholders, commissioned an evaluation from the company's accountants and was advised that the company would save money and be more efficient if it performed these delivery operations itself instead of 'outsourcing' them to established courier and postal services. The accountants built into their evaluation an assumption that the company would be able to sell spare capacity on the planes to other companies in the locality.

The Managing Director has decided that the accountants' recommendation will be conducted as a 'trial' for 5 years when its success or otherwise will be evaluated. The net, post-tax operating cash flows of this investment are estimated as:

Year(s)	$m
0	−12.50 (the initial capital investment)
1–4	3.15 each year
5	5.85

Year 5 includes an estimate of the residual value of the planes.

The company normally uses an estimated post-tax weighted average cost of capital of 12% to evaluate investments. However, this investment is different from its usual business operations and the Finance Director suggests using the capital asset pricing model (CAPM) to determine a discount rate. REM, being unlisted, does not have a published beta so the Finance Director has obtained a beta of 1.3 for a courier company that is listed. This company has a debt ratio (debt to equity) of 1:2, compared with REM whose debt ratio is 1:5.

Other information:

- The expected annual post-tax return on the market is 9% and the risk-free rate is 5%.
- Assume both companies' debt is virtually risk-free.
- Both companies pay tax at 30%.

Requirements

(a) Using the CAPM, calculate:

  (i) an asset beta for REM;
  (ii) an equity beta for REM;
  (iii) an appropriate discount rate to be used in the evaluation of this project;
  (iv) the NPV of the project using the discount rate calculated in (iii); and comment briefly on your choice of discount rate in part (iii).

(11 marks)

(b) Evaluate the benefits and limitations of using a proxy company's beta to determine the rate to be used by REM in the circumstances here, and recommend alternative methods of adjusting for risk in the evaluation that could be considered by the company.

(9 marks)

(c) Advise the Managing Director on the benefits of a post-completion audit. A report format is not required in answering this question.

(5 marks)
(Total = 25 marks)

Question 7 – ZX APV

The shares of ZX plc are quoted on a stock market. Two of the directors are also major shareholders in the company. They have been evaluating investment in a project which will require £3.9 million capital expenditure on new machinery. The directors expect the capital investment to provide annual cash flows of £600,000 indefinitely. This figure is net of all tax adjustments.

The company is at present all-equity financed. The discount rate, which it applies to investment decisions of this nature, is 14% net. The directors believe that the current capital structure fails to take advantage of the tax benefits of debt, and propose to finance the new project with undated debt secured on the company's assets. The current annual gross rate of interest required by the market on corporate undated debt of similar risk is 10%. The after-tax costs of issue are expected to be £162,000. The company intends to issue sufficient debt to cover the cost of capital expenditure and the after-tax costs of issue.

The company's marginal tax rate is 30%.

You should use a sensible approach to rounding your answers throughout the question.

Requirement

Calculate the adjusted present value of the investment and the adjusted discount rate, and explain the circumstances in which this adjusted discount rate may be used to evaluate future investments.

(10 marks)

Question 8 – DEB

DEB plc is a listed company that sells fashion clothes over the Internet. Financial markets have criticised the company recently because of the high levels of debt that it has maintained in its balance sheet.

The company's debt consists of $150 million of 8% debentures that are due for repayment by 31 March 2005. Financial markets indicate it would not be possible to issue a new loan under the same conditions. The market value of the debentures is $90 per $100 nominal.

DEB plc's draft balance sheet at 31 March 2002 was as follows:

	$m
Ordinary shares of $1	100
Reserves	20
	120
8% debentures (at nominal value)	150
	270
Fixed assets	200
Net current assets	70
	270

Fixed assets consist of $150 million of capitalised development costs and $50 million of land and buildings. The company's share price has fallen consistently over the past two years as follows:

	Price per share
31 March 2000	$20
31 March 2001	$8
31 March 2002	$4

The company intends to make a 1-for-2 rights issue at an issue price of $2.50 on 30 June 2002. It is assuming that the cum rights price at the issue date will be $4. Immediately thereafter, all the proceeds will be used to redeem debt at its nominal value and thereby reduce its gearing.

Requirements

(a) Calculate the gearing (i.e. debt/equity) of DEB plc at 31 March 2002 using both

  (i) book values; and
  (ii) market values.

(3 marks)

(b) Evaluate the weaknesses and benefits of the two methods used to calculate gearing in requirement (a) above.

(6 marks)

(c) Calculate the gearing of DEB plc in market value terms, immediately after the rights issue and redemption of debt.

(8 marks)

(d) Briefly explain the advantages and disadvantages for DEB plc of redeeming part of its debt using an issue of equity shares.

(8 marks)
(Total = 25 marks)

Question 9 – Imlico

Imlico plc is an all-equity financed listed company. It develops customised software for clients which are mainly large civil engineering companies. Nearly all its shares are held by financial institutions.

Imlico plc's chairman has been dissatisfied with the company's performance for some time. Some directors were also concerned about the way in which the company is perceived by financial markets. In response, the company recently appointed a new Finance Director who advocated using the capital asset pricing model as a means of evaluating risk and interpreting the stock market's reaction to the company.

The following initial information was put forward by the Finance Director for two rival companies operating in the same industry:

Company	Beta
Aztaz plc	0.7
Borran plc	1.4

The Finance Director suggests that the betas of the two companies are used by the stock market to calculate their required rates of return. He also notes, however, that the riskfree rate is 5% each year and the expected return on the market portfolio is 15% each year.

The chairman set out his concerns at a meeting of the Board of Directors: 'I fail to understand these calculations. Aztaz plc operates largely in overseas markets with all the risk which that involves, yet you seem to be arguing that it is a lower risk company than Borran plc, whose income is mainly derived from long-term contracts in our domestic UK building industry. I am very concerned that we can take too much notice of the stock market. Take last year for instance, we had to announce a loss and the share price went up.'

Requirements

(a) Calculate, using the capital asset pricing model, the required rate of return on equity of:

   (i) Aztaz plc;
   (ii) Borran plc.

(6 marks)

(b) Calculate the beta of Imlico plc assuming its required annual rate of return on equity is 17% and the stock market uses the capital asset pricing model to calculate this return.

(3 marks)

(c) As the new Finance Director, write a memorandum to the chairman which explains, in language understandable to a non-financial manager, the following:

   (i) the assumptions and limitations of the capital asset pricing model; and
   (ii) an explanation of why Imlico plc's share price could rise following the announcement of a loss.

In so doing, comment upon the observations and concerns expressed by the chairman. You may refer, where appropriate, to your calculations in (a) and (b) above.

(16 marks)
(Total = 25 marks)

Answers

Question 1 – Gearing change

First find the cost of equity of an identical all-equity company:

$$12 = k_{eu}\left(1 - \frac{1 \times 0.3}{10}\right) \quad \text{so } k_{eu} = 12.37$$

Then re-gear to the new ratio:

$$k = 12.37\left(1 - \frac{3 \times 0.3}{10}\right) \quad \text{so } k = 11.26\%$$

Question 2 – New values

Using $V_g = V_u + TB$

$80 + 20 = V_u + (20 \times 0.30)$

So $V_u = 100 - 6 = £94m$

The identical all-equity company also raises £20m (of equity).

New $V_u = 94 + 20 = £114m$

New $V_g = 114 + (40 \times 0.30)$

$V_g = 126$

Of which $V_D = £40m$

So $V_E = £86m$

$k = k_{eu}(1 - TL)$

$$10 = k_{eu}\left(1 - \frac{2 \times 0.3}{10}\right) \quad \text{so } k_{eu} = 10.64\%$$

$$\text{New } k = 10.64\left(1 - \frac{40 \times 0.3}{126}\right) = 9.63\%$$

Question 3 – APV

First evaluate the project from the all-equity company's perspective:

NPV $= -150 + (30 \times 4.639) = -£10.83m$

(a) Irredeemable debt

Financing impact $= £40 \times 0.30 = +£12m$
Change in V_g = change in V_u + change in TB
APV $= -10.83 + 12$
$= £1.17m$ (so worthwhile)

(b) 8-year debt

Financing impact = PV of tax relief on interest
Interest each year = £40m × 0.10 = £4m
So PV of tax relief = (£4m × 0.30) × 5.335 (10% 8-year annuity)
= £6.40m

Change in V_g = change in V_u + change in TB
APV = −10.83 + 6.40
= −£4.43m (so not worthwhile)

Question 4 – Beta

As the project is in publishing, we should use a beta which reflects the risk of publishing.

$k_e = 5 + (4)1.3 = 10.2\%$

Question 5 – Degearing

Publisher $\beta_U = 1.3 \times \dfrac{60}{60 + (40 \times 0.7)} = 0.886$

Brewer $0.886 = \beta_G \times \dfrac{70}{70 + (30 \times 0.7)}$

$0.886 = \beta_G \times 0.769$ i.e. $\beta_G = 1.152$

$k_e = 5 + (4)1.152 = 9.6\%$

Question 6 – REM

(a) (i) *Asset Beta*

given by: $\dfrac{1.3 \times 2}{(2 + 0.7)} = 0.96$

(ii) *Equity Beta*

$0.96 = \dfrac{\text{Beta} \times 5}{(5 + 0.7)}$

Equity Beta = 1.09

(iii) *Discount rate*

$K_e = r_f + (r_m - r_f)\,\text{Beta}$
$= 5 + (9 - 5)\,0.96$
$= 8.84\%$

This is the discount rate appropriate to the risk of the business of the delivery proposal. It does not take into account the method in which the investment will be financed.

(iv) *Net present value*

Time	t_0	t_1	t_2	t_3	t_4	t_5
Cash flow ($m)	(12.50)	3.15	3.15	3.15	3.15	5.85
Discount factor	1	0.919	0.844	0.776	0.713	0.655
Present value	(12.50)	2.89	2.66	2.44	2.25	3.83

Net present value = $1.57m

(b) **Using a proxy Beta**

Benefits include:

- It gives an idea of the risk of the project as perceived by stock market investors.
- It looks specifically at the risk of the new project.

Limitations include:

- No two companies are identical in their operations, so it will only be an approximation.
- Beta can vary over time, and the estimate only gives a long run average.
- CAPM is a single period model, deals only with systematic risk and is based on historical data.
- CAPM assumes fully diversified investors who are only concerned about systematic risk, while REM being 80% family owned is unlikely to be in that position.

Alternative methods might be:

- Using the company's cost of equity. While this assumes the project is a similar risk to the existing business, shareholders may feel that it is simply an extension of the existing operations.
- Using the company's weighted average cost of capital. However, it is not theoretically correct, as there will be a change in the business risk and probably financial risk. It is also unclear how the WACC has been estimated.
- Using certainty equivalents to reduce the cash flows and then using the risk-free rate to discount them. It is, however, difficult to determine appropriate probabilities.

(c) **Post-completion audits**

A post-completion audit (PCA) allows the company to both monitor and control the progress of the investment, and to improve investment appraisal in the future.

The company needs to set out clearly the objectives of the investment and, where possible, state them in measurable terms. It then allows the company to:

- Assess the extent to which objectives are achieved.
- Allow for reconsideration or abandonment where objectives are not forecast to be met.
- Assess the performance of managers in charge of the implementation.
- Improve estimates in future investment appraisals.

Question 7 – ZX APV

Adjusted present value

$$\text{APV} = (\text{NPV} @ K_u) - (\text{Issue Costs}) + (\text{PV of Tax Relief on Debt Interest})$$
$$= (-3.9 + 0.6/0.14) - (0.162) + (4.062 \times 0.30)$$
$$= 0.386 - 0.162 + 1.219$$
$$= £1.443\text{m}$$

Adjusted discount rate

The ADR is the rate at which APV = 0, i.e. the IRR. To calculate ADR, we calculate the minimum annual income needed to give a zero APV, and calculate the percentage this amount is of the initial investment.

$$\left(-3.9 + \frac{C}{0.14}\right) - 0.162 + 1.219 = 0$$

C = £398,000

$$\text{ADR approximately} = \frac{398}{3,900} = 10.2\%$$

This can be used to assess projects of the same business risk and financed in the same way, and gives the minimum acceptable return as an APV. In other words, such investments should have their APV calculated, using the above 10% as the discount rate, and accept those with positive APVs.

Question 8 – DEB

(a) (i) *Book values*

$$\text{Gearing} = \frac{150}{120} = 125\%$$

(ii) *Market values*

$$\text{Gearing} = \frac{135}{400} = 33.75\%$$

(b) **Weaknesses and benefits**

Measuring gearing using book values has the advantage that it will not fluctuate wildly as the stock market rises and falls, but will be much more closely aligned with the company's historical performance. For this reason, banks and other lenders who have gearing covenants usually base the ratio on book values.

However, measuring gearing using market values allows the equity to reflect the market expectations of future performance through the share price. This is particularly beneficial when much of the equity value is tied up in intangible assets such as staff and reputation in a service company, which are not reflected in the balance sheet.

(c) Ex-rights price $= \frac{[(2 \times 4) + 2.50]}{3} = \$3.50$

Remaining debt = 150m − (2.50 × 50m) = $25m nominal value

New gearing level $= \frac{(25 \times 0.90)}{(150 \times 3.50)} = 4.29\%$

This does not take into account the tax relief on the debt interest that the company, and hence the shareholders, would lose. This is interest of $10 million per annum, so roughly $3 million tax relief per annum for 3 years. This is worth about $7 million in present value terms so has little impact on the total market value or the gearing calculation.

(d) **Advantages and disadvantages**

Advantages

The new equity will reduce the debt levels and so help to address the concerns expressed. This may be important if the company wants to raise more finance, or to refinance the remaining debt, in the future.

Debt covenants may be based on book values for gearing calculations and repayment of much of the debt will prevent any breach of these.

The cost of debt may decrease as the $50 million of land and buildings now covers the remaining debt comfortably and gives the debt-holders some security.

Disadvantages

In market value terms, the gearing was not particularly high and the new equity will have a higher cost than the debt repaid, despite it being lower than the current cost of equity because of the reduced gearing risk. Under the traditional model, it is difficult to predict if the WACC would increase or decrease. Under the theoretical model, the WACC would increase as the gearing reduced.

As the market price is below par, this is currently a cheap source of finance, and paying off over 80% appears excessive.

Question 9 – Imlico

(a) **Return on equity**

(i) Aztac $\quad 5 + (15 - 5)\,0.7 = 12\%$
(ii) Borran $\quad 5 + (15 - 5)\,1.4 = 19\%$

(b) **Beta of Imlico**

$17 = 5 + (15 - 5)\,\beta$
so $\beta = 1.2$

(c) MEMORANDUM

To: Chairman, Imlico plc
From: Finance Director
Date: xx x 20xx

Returns required and share price

1 *Capital asset pricing model (CAPM)*

CAPM has the following assumptions and limitation.

It assumes that shareholders are diversified and hold a portfolio which mirrors the stock market index. This may be true for the institutional shareholders but is not likely to be so for the directors or employees. It may understate the risk involved for these groups.

Shareholders may be able to diversify more widely than just the market index into such areas as property. It may therefore overstate the risk, and hence return required, for them.

The risk-free rate is approximated by an average treasury bill yield.

Beta is calculated from historical data and assumed to be stable over time. However, beta will change gradually over time, which means there is some risk involved in using a cost of equity derived from past information to make a decision regarding the future.

Aztac operates largely in overseas markets and may well have a higher total risk than Borran. However, its operations are likely to have a lower correlation with the UK stock market than Borran's, and hence its systematic risk, as measured by beta, will be lower.

2 *Share price movements*

The semi-strong form of the Efficient Market Hypothesis states that all publicly available information is reflected in the share price. This means that:

The share price responds immediately and fully to new information as it is released.

Analysing information which is already public, including past share price trends, will not benefit an investor.

The Stock market tries to predict future events so that it can profit when the information is confirmed publicly.

In Imlico's case, the stock market had probably already built into the share price an expectation of losses. When the information relating to the actual loss was publicly announced, the share price rose which must mean that it was not as bad as the market had already predicted.

Impact of Financing   8

✏️ Exam focus

This contains little new technical knowledge but combines the financing and ratios parts of the syllabus. You may be required to draft forecast financial statements with and without various forms of finance, so make sure that you understand the impact of new finance on the balance sheet. Don't forget any cash raised! You might then be asked for specific ratios or asked to comment generally, so revise your analysis skills.

Drafting financial statements can be quite time-consuming so watch your time carefully and allow yourself sufficient time to make sensible analytical comments.

🔑 Key points

Remember all the ratios from Chapter 2 as well as the sources of finance from Chapter 4. Read the requirements in the question carefully and watch out for any key ratios that must be checked, such as those specified in bank loan covenants.

Questions

Question 1 – ZX Inc.

ZX is a relatively small US-based company in the agricultural industry. It is highly mechanised and uses modern techniques and equipment. In the past, it has operated a very conservative policy in respect of the management of its working capital. Assume that you are a newly recruited management accountant. The Finance Director, who is responsible for both financial control and treasury functions, has asked you to review this policy. You assemble the following information about the company's forecast end-of-year financial outcomes. The company's year-end is in six months' time.

	US$'000
Receivables	2,500
Inventory	2,000
Cash at bank	500
Current assets	5,000
Fixed assets	1,250
Current liabilities	1,850
Forecast sales for the full year	8,000
Forecast operating profit (18% of sales)	1,440

You wish to evaluate the likely effect on the company if it introduced one of two alternative approaches to working capital management. The Finance Director suggests you adjust the figures in accordance with the following parameters:

	'Moderate' policy	'Aggressive' policy
Receivables and inventory	−20%	−30%
Cash	Reduce to $250,000	Reduce to $100,000
Fixed assets	No change	No change
Current liabilities	+10%	+20%
Forecast sales	+2%	+4%
Forecast profit	No change in percentage profit/sales.	

Requirements

Write a report to the Finance Director that includes the following:

(a) A discussion of the main aspects to consider when determining policy in respect of the investment in, and financing of, working capital, in general and in the circumstances of ZX.

(10 marks)

(b) Calculations of the return on net assets and the current ratio under each of three scenarios shown below:

- the company continues with its present policy;
- the company adopts the 'moderate' policy;
- the company adopts the 'aggressive' policy.

(8 marks)

(c) A recommendation to the company of a proposed course of action. Your recommendation should be based on your evaluation as discussed above and on your opinion of what further action is necessary before a final decision can be taken.

(7 marks)

(Total = 25 marks)

Question 2 – UR

UR is a privately owned machine tool manufacturing company based in the Republic of Ireland. For the past five years, it has operated an aggressive policy in respect of the management of its working capital. The following information concerns the company's forecast end-of-year financial outcomes if it continues with this type of policy.

	Euro'000
Receivables	5,200
Inventory	2,150
Cash at bank	350
Total current assets	7,700
Fixed assets	14,500
Trade payables	4,500
Sales	17,500
Operating costs	14,000
Operating profit	3,500
Earnings	2,625

There are 2.5 million shares in issue.

The company has been experiencing a series of problems because of the type of working capital management policy it has been following and is considering an alternative approach to working capital management.

The percentage figures shown below are changes to the above forecast. These changes are anticipated to occur if a more conservative policy is adopted.

Receivables	−40%
Inventory	+20%
Cash (figures in Euro'000) Increase to Euro	1,000
Fixed assets	No change
Current liabilities	−30%
Forecast sales	−5%
Operating profit and earnings	+5%

Requirement

Evaluate the two working capital management policies described above and recommend a proposed course of action. Include in your evaluation a discussion of the problems that might have arisen as a result of operating aggressive working capital management policies and the key elements to consider and actions to take before making a decision to change. You should calculate appropriate and relevant ratios or performance measures to support your arguments.

[The calculations will earn up to 8 marks]

(25 marks)

Question 3 – ABC services

ABC is a large professional service company listed on a major international stock exchange. ABC has recently appointed a new Finance Director who is concerned about the financing of the company.

Forecast balance sheet at 31 May 2004:

	$m	$m
Fixed assets		555
Current assets	195	
Current liabilities	(50)	
		145
Debentures 7% annual coupon (nominal value) [redeemable 31 May 2008 at par]		(150)
Bank loans		(100)
		(250)
		450
Issued share capital (par value 25 cents)		200
Reserves		250
Shareholder funds		450

On 31 May 2004, market values are $107% ex-interest for debentures and $0.75 ex-dividend for each share. Interest on the bank loan is 5% per annum and the loans are not scheduled to be repaid before 31 May 2007.

The following earnings and closing shareholder funds have been forecast for the next three years:

Year ending	31 May 2005 $m	31 May 2006 $m	31 May 2007 $m
Earnings before interest and tax (EBIT)	58.0	50.0	54.0
Closing shareholder funds at year end	446.8	437.9	431.9

Debenture covenants

There are two covenants relating to the debentures, as follows:

'At no time will the debt ratio of prior charge capital/shareholder funds exceed 60%, based upon book values.'

'The ratio of EBIT/total interest payable shall not fall below 3.5 times.'

Restructuring funding

The Finance Director is concerned that the company is close to breaching debenture covenants and is considering ways of restructuring the company's funding to eliminate this risk.

Two alternatives are being considered:

1 One scheme is to redeem the debentures on 31 May 2004 at market value, funded by a new bank loan. The company's bank has quoted an annual coupon of 5% for a loan maturing on 31 May 2008.
2 An alternative scheme, being recommended by ABC's merchant bank, is a rights issue of 1 for 5 shares to raise $100 million of funds to repay the current bank loan. Assume that tax is recoverable at 30% on interest payments at the time that the interest is paid and that all interest payments are made annually in arrears. Ignore any taxation implications of the redemption premium on the debenture.

Requirements

(a) Calculate gearing and interest cover ratios for the years ending 31 May 2005 to 31 May 2007, and indicate whether ABC is likely to breach either of the two debenture covenants over the next three years. (Ignore any restructuring funding proposals.)

(4 marks)

(b) Calculate the cost of debt for the existing debenture based on the current market value on 31 May 2004 and advise the Finance Director whether or not it is likely to be cheaper to redeem the debenture with a bank loan. Identify what other factors would need to be taken into account when deciding whether to redeem the debenture with a bank loan. (No further calculations are required.)

(10 marks)

(c) Calculate the issue price and ex-rights price of the proposed rights issue. Discuss the advantages of the merchant bank's recommendation to repay the bank loan by raising new equity finance compared with the merits of redeeming the debentures by entering into a new bank loan.

(*Note*: No further gearing or interest cover calculations are required.)

(11 marks)
(Total = 25 marks)

Question 4 – AEF

AEF plc is listed on an international stock exchange. It has an issued share capital of 2 million ordinary shares. Most of the shares are held by large financial institutions. The company currently has an overdraft of $70 million which is carrying an annual interest rate of 10%. The company has no other borrowings. The company's summary profit and loss account for the year ended 30 September 2001 was as follows:

	$'000
Operating profit	22,000
Interest paid	7,000
Profit before taxation	15,000
Taxation	3,000
Profit after taxation	12,000
Ordinary dividend paid	3,000
Retained profit for the year	9,000

Earnings and dividends are expected to grow at a constant rate of 4% each year in perpetuity. Assume, for simplicity, that the dividend is paid on 30 September each year.

100 Exam Practice Kit: Management Accounting Financial Strategy

The company is now considering accepting a major new project which would commence on 30 September 2002. The project is a high-risk investment but the directors expect it to increase the company's annual growth rate of total earnings and total dividends from 4 to 7%. The project would be financed by a 1-for-4 rights issue at an issue price of $10 on 30 September 2002.

The required return by equity shareholders is currently 10% each year, but the directors believe it would rise to 12% each year if the new project is accepted.

One of the directors is concerned about the impact of the project on the overall risk of the company. She is also concerned about the impact of the project on earnings per share. In particular, she is concerned that if earnings per share falls, the share price might be adversely affected.

Requirements

(a) Ignoring the impact of the new project, calculate the following at 30 September 2001:

   (i) the price per share (using the dividend growth model);
   (ii) earnings per share;
   (iii) dividend cover;
   (iv) price earnings ratio;
   (v) gearing (using market value for equity).

   (9 marks)

(b) Write a memorandum to the directors of AEF plc which, as far as the information permits, evaluates the potential impact of the new project at 30 September 2002 (including financing) on:

   (i) the value of the company;
   (ii) the risk profile of the company;
   (iii) the earnings per share of the company.

   Show any relevant calculations to support your arguments.

   (16 marks)

Note: In all relevant calculations, assume that financial markets believe the directors' estimates of future dividends and cost of equity.

(Total = 25 marks)

 **Answers**

Question 1 – ZX Inc.

REPORT

To: Finance Director
From: Management Accountant
Date: x of xx 2001

Working capital management

This report discusses the main aspects of working capital management, calculates the return on assets and current ratio under the different proposals and recommends a course of action.

(a) *Main aspects of working capital management*

Working capital consists of the investment in inventory, receivables and cash; these are partly financed by trade payables and sometimes an overdraft. The amount held in each of these assets and the extent to which the current liabilities cover the current assets give an idea of a company's approach to working capital. A conservative policy would have high inventory levels to ensure that demand can always be met instantly, and high cash levels in order to meet any unforeseen liabilities. A conservative policy would normally mean playing safe and not offering extended credit, while an aggressive policy would try to boost sales by tactics such as giving better credit terms. ZX has included a reduction in credit terms offered, or at least an improvement in collection, as an aggressive policy; this might be described as an aggressive cash management policy as it will collect cash more quickly.

The financing of working capital can also be described as conservative or aggressive. Using only trade payables, by increasing the credit period taken, can be viewed as an aggressive approach, while reducing payables and using long-term finance would be safer and more conservative. Short-term finance is often less expensive (in the case of trade payables almost costless if there is no impact on the trading relationship but is more risky for ZX as the facility can be withdrawn at short notice).

In considering the appropriate policy for ZX, we need to consider the nature of the business and the industry:

- Terms offered by competitors will probably have to be matched by ZX which is a small company. The receivables days are currently 114 and would fall to 89 (moderate) or 77 (aggressive). Whether this will be acceptable to the customers will depend on whether our competitors can supply a comparable product on better terms.
- The type of product will have a major impact on the working capital as a long production process will tie up far more inventory in terms of work-in-progress and may mean that higher finished goods have to be held to meet unexpected demand. ZX has a highly mechanised process and uses modern techniques and equipment which would suggest a shorter production process. If this compares favourably with its competitors, ZX could reduce its inventory levels below those of the industry average without harming its business relationships with customers.
- The efficiency of operations, particularly in terms of credit control and invoicing immediately, will have a direct impact on our working capital in terms of the receivables and cash, but as long as aggressive collection techniques are not employed, there should be little impact on customer relations.

(b) *Ratios under different policies*

The return on net assets and current ratio under the different policies suggested and the current policy are as follows:

Policy	Current	Moderate	Aggressive
Sales	8,000	8,160	8,320
Profit	1,440	1,469	1,498
Receivables	2,500	2,000	1,750
Inventory	2,000	1,600	1,400
Cash	500	250	100
Current assets	5,000	3,850	3,250
Fixed assets	1,250	1,250	1,250
Current liabilities	1,850	2,035	2,220
Net assets	4,400	3,065	2,280
Return on net assets	32.7	47.9	65.7
Current ratio	2.7	1.9	1.5

(c) *Recommendations*

The above ratios would suggest that the aggressive policy is the most attractive as it has the best return on net assets, at double the current return, but only sees the current ratio drop to 1.5, which should still give the company sufficient cover to meet its ongoing liabilities. However, before applying this policy we need to look at the impact this will have on our relationship with our customers and our suppliers. This will depend to a large extent on the terms offered by our competitors as an attempt to reduce our credit period could adversely affect our sales. To this extent, as a small company ZX has less leeway in adjusting its policies than it might appear as it will probably have to follow the industry practices. In addition, cutting inventory levels and reducing the current account cash could incur costs if demand exceeds the inventory held (lost contribution and reputation) or more funds are required (finance costs or bank charges for transferring between accounts). In the light of this, I recommend that we look closely at the industry norms in this area and go for the more cautious approach of the moderate policy. This will allow an increase in the return on net assets, but give sufficient liquidity to compete on an equal basis with the rest of the industry.

Question 2 – UR

Calculations

	Aggressive	Conservative
EPS	2.625/2.5 = E 1.05	2.756/2.5 = E 1.10
ROCE	3,500/17,700 = 19.8%	3,675/18,050 = 20.4%
Current ratio	7,700/4,500 = 1.71	6,700/3,150 = 2.13
Quick ratio	5,500/4,500 = 1.23	4,120/3,150 = 1.31
Inventory days	2,150/14,000 × 365 = 56.1 days	2,580/12,950 × 365 = 72.7 days
Receivables days	5,200/17,500 × 365 = 108.5 days	3,120/16,625 × 365 = 68.5 days
Payable days	4,500/14,000 × 365 = 117.3 days	3,150/12,950 × 365 = 88.8 days
Operating cycle	47.3 days	52.4 days
Op profit margin	3,500/17,500 = 20%	3,675/16,625 = 22.1%

Working capital

Working capital typically consists of inventories, receivables, cash and other short-term assets. Because of uncertainty, companies must hold some inventory and cash based on the forecasts made as well as some surplus. The amount of excess inventory and cash held will be a compromise between the risk of running out, and causing commercial problems, and holding too much, which is a waste of money. An aggressive policy would hold lower safety inventories, a conservative one would hold higher levels. An aggressive policy is therefore more risky.

In a similar way, a conservative policy would not want to take as much risk (of customers not paying) and so is likely to extend less generous payment terms than under an aggressive policy, which would be prepared to take the risk of non-payment in order to increase sales.

Whilst trade payables are not an investment, by taking credit a company can reduce the overall net investment required. An aggressive policy would take as long as possible to pay as long as it did not undermine the commercial relationship with the supplier. This effectively means funding much of the current assets through short-term finance which is inherently more risky than using long-term finance.

Problems of an aggressive policy

UR might have encountered a number of commercial problems in operating its aggressive policies. These might include:

- losing sales or having to stop production because the company ran out of inventory
- overdraft charges due to unexpected cash payments taking the account into overdraft
- legal action from suppliers because of late payment
- increased prices from suppliers or low priority for work
- bad debts and more expensive credit control and debt chasing due to liberal credit policies offered.

Key elements to consider in change

UR needs to look closely at the impact on its relations with customers and sales, and to review carefully the projections made if the change is implemented.

Assuming that the forecasts are reliable, UR should consider the following:

- What are the equivalent credit terms offered by competitors in the industry. Unless UR has a product which is so different that no customer would dream of going to a competitor, any terms which are much worse than the industry average could lead to lost sales.
- The receivable days would fall from 109 to 69 days; this will be beneficial for the company on the face of it but we need to compare it with the terms offered by competitors.
- The operating cycle would reduce slightly from 47 to 52 days which will not make a significant difference to profits. The profit margin also increases slightly from 20 to 22%.
- The current ratio seems relatively high under both policies and actually rises under the proposal. This would suggest that current assets are under-utilised.
- This is particularly true of cash as leaving it in a bank account is not an effective use. Detailed cash-flow projections should be prepared and excess funds invested elsewhere.

Conclusion

Although the proposed change has a beneficial effect on profits, EPS and ROCE, the impact is small. It might be more sensible to review management procedures for each component of working capital. A more rapid invoicing of customers, a tighter and more efficient credit control department or a better inventory control system may do more than this suggested change in policy. External changes in policy will have an impact on the commercial relationships with customers and suppliers, leading to loss of business, while tightening up internal processes will have less impact.

Question 3 – ABC services

(a) **Gearing and interest cover**

	2005	2006	2007
Gearing	250/446.8 = 56%	250/437.9 = 57.1%	250/431.9 = 57.9
Interest cover	58/15.5 = 3.74	50/15.5 = 3.23	54/15.5 = 3.48

The gearing ratio covenant is not broken under these forecasts, but leaves little room for error. The interest cover covenant is forecast to be broken in both 2006 and 2007.

Therefore, there is a high risk that the debenture holders will demand early repayment at some point over the next three years.

The company needs to restructure its financing arrangements as soon as possible.

(b) **Cost of debt**

		3%	PV
t_0	(107)	1	(107)
t_{1-4}	4.90	3.717	18.21
t_9	100	0.8885	88.85
			(0.06)

So, cost of debentures = 3%

The post-tax cost of the new bank loan will be 5% × 0.70 = 3.5%.

The current debenture is therefore cheaper than the proposed replacement bank loan.

Other factors to consider would include:

- whether the debenture could be re-negotiated instead of repaid
- what security might be required by the bank, or other loan covenants
- what other sources of finance might be available
- shareholders' funds are forecast to decrease, showing that dividends will exceed profits; this may concern potential lenders.

(c) **Issue and ex-rights price**

Issue price = $100m/(800/5) = $0.625 each

Ex-Rights price = [(0.75 × 5) + 0.625]/6 = $0.73 per share

The advantages of the rights issue include:

- avoiding redemption premium costs
- giving more ability to raise debt in the future
- not having to consider repayment of the finance

- being able to adjust the cash payments, in terms of dividends, unlike interest
- improving the gearing and interest cover.

The advantage of the bank loan include:

- having a cheaper overall source of finance, due to a lower risk for the investor and tax relief on the interest
- being able to use assets for security to reduce the cost further
- set-up easier and cheaper to arrange than a rights issue
- having a more flexible form of finance which can be repaid easily.

However, the company may not have a free choice between the two. The bank may require covenants similar to those on the debentures which ABC wishes to avoid, thus forcing it to make a rights issue.

Question 4 – AEF

(a) **Ratios**

  (i)   Share price $= (1.50 \times 1.04)/(0.10 - 9.04)$ $= \$26$
  (ii) EPS $= 12m/2m$ $= \$6$
  (iii) Dividend cover $= 12m/3/$ $= 4$
  (iv) P/E ratio $= 26/6$ $= 4.33$
  (v)   Gearing $= 70m/(2m \times 26)$ $= 134.6\%$

(b)

MEMORANDUM

To: Directors, AEF plc
From: Management Accountant
Date: x of xx 2001

Impact of new project

This memorandum will look at the impact of the new project on the value of the company, the risk profile and the earnings per share.

(i) *Company value*

The new project will boost growth in earnings and dividends from 4 to 7%, which will increase the value to shareholders. However, the risk premium increases, putting up the cost of equity from 10 to 12%, and AEF needs to generate more earnings to give the dividends required on the additional shares issued; both of these will have a negative impact on the value.

Overall, the appendix shows that the net effect is an increase in the value of the company by approximately $7.7 million. However, this will only materialise once the market has full information about the project.

(ii) *Risk*

As stated above, the cost of equity for the company will increase from 10 to 12%. This means that the new project must be much higher than the rest of the company in order to bring up the average return required to 12%. Shareholders are therefore likely to require a return considerably in excess of 12% on the new project.

We would expect this required return to have been calculated using the capital asset pricing model which assumes that shareholders are fully diversified and hence only concerned with systematic risk. The risk of the new project is only relevant, under these assumptions, to the extent that it correlates with the market index. As most shares are held by financial institutions, this is likely to be a reasonable assumption for AEF plc.

It is possible that the bank will perceive an increased risk to the servicing and repayment of the overdraft and increase its cost appropriately.

(iii) *Earnings per share (EPS)*

As EPS looks at historical earnings, the earnings generated by the new project will not appear immediately but the number of shares will decrease. The immediate impact will therefore be a reduction in EPS. However, shareholders should consider the future earnings potential when valuing the business rather than historical earnings, so the reduction should not matter as long as the market understands, and believes, the project forecasts.

Appendix

Value

New total value $= [(3m \times 1.04) \times 1.07]/(0.12 - 0.07) = \$66.768m$
Value without project $= [(3m \times 1.04) \times 1.04]/(0.10 - 0.04) = \$54.08m$
Increase $\$12.688m$

Extra finance raised ($\$5m$)
Additional net gain due to project $\$7.688m$

Earnings per share

New EPS at 30 September 2002

$= (\$12m \times 1.04)/2m = \$6.24$ pre-issue
$(\$12m \times 1.04)/2.5m = \$4.99$ post-issue

Part 3

Business Valuations and Acquisitions

Business Valuations 9

📝 Exam focus

The key point to get across in any question is that you understand any calculation is an approximation based on estimates. As a result we would always recommend performing a number of valuations (so do not spend all your time perfecting one calculation!).

It is also important to be able to discuss when the different approaches may be more or less suitable to the situation.

🔑 Key points

Present value of future cash flows

In an ideal world the value of a business should be the present value of the cash flows it generates. However, predicting all of the future cash flows and finding a suitable discount rate is fraught with difficulties and potential buyers will have different estimates both from each other and from the vendor.

The cash flows will also vary with the different plans each has for the business.

The valuation techniques used are all approximations to this, but will often lead to very different results, allowing for a negotiated price.

Price/earnings ratio

Value per share = EPS × P/E ratio.

For a private company this can be a useful technique as the P/E ratio of similar listed companies can be applied to its EPS to arrive at the approximate value it would have if it was quoted. This is often discounted substantially for the lack of liquidity, and hence additional risk, in its shares.

Dividend valuation model

$$P_0 = \frac{d_1}{k_e - g}$$ if we assume constant growth in dividends forever.

In a private business, dividends can be more haphazard as owners are also rewarded through salaries. Adjustments may be needed to alter salaries to market rates before using 'potential' dividends. The cost of equity can be estimated from CAPM using the beta of similar listed companies.

Dividend yield

$$\text{Value} = \frac{\text{Dividend}}{\text{Dividend yield}}$$

An average dividend yield for a similar listed sector can be applied to the target company's dividend.

Asset valuations

The asset values in the balance sheet are historical and are not usually reliable estimates of the current market values. In addition, intangible assets such as inherent goodwill are not recorded.

Where realisable values can be found, it will give the lowest price a vendor will accept, even if he is desperate to sell, as he could break the company up himself and sell off the assets.

Intellectual capital

Intellectual capital forms a major part of the value of many companies. However, it is difficult to measure separately, and is often viewed as the difference between an income based valuation (or current market value) and the book value of the assets. Alternatively, calculate the present value of the excess returns over the industry average.

General comments

(a) The number of potential buyers and the number of potential targets will affect the price.
(b) The asset valuations are likely to be lower than the income-based valuations. For a service business, with few assets, the difference could be very great. In this situation, an asset valuation would be misleading.
(c) Up to 20% premium may be added to a publicly listed share price to gain a controlling interest.
(d) Up to 30% discount may be applied to a private company compared with an equivalent quoted company.

Questions

Question 1 – Target (Practice Question)

Target company recently made a profit of £500,000 and had a pay out ratio of 80% (which is higher than the average for this sector). The average P/E ratio for this sector is 9.

The company's balance sheet shows Shareholder's Funds of £2.25 million for 1 million shares, but the buildings are worth £1 million more than their balance sheet value and stocks would be worth £250,000 less in a break-up of the company.

Dividend growth in the sector is expected to be 4% per annum, the risk-free rate is 6%, the market return 11% and the company's beta estimated as 1.2. The average dividend yield for the sector is 6%.

Find valuations of Target using

(a) P/E ratio
(b) Dividend yield
(c) Dividend valuation model
(d) Balance sheet book values
(e) Net realisable value.

Question 2 – CD

CD Limited is a private company in a computer-related industry. It is based in India and has been trading for 6 years. It is managed by its main shareholders, who are the original founders of the company. Most of the employees are also shareholders, having been given shares as bonuses in 1999. None of the shareholders has attempted to sell shares in the company so the problem of placing a value on them has not arisen.

Turnover last year, the 12 months to 31 December 2002, was 356 million Rupees.

The table below shows earnings and dividends for CD Limited since its creation:

Year	Earnings after tax Million Rupees	Earnings after tax Rupees per share	Dividend declared Rupees per share
1997	25	8.33	0.00
1998	120	40.00	20.00
1999	145	48.33	24.20
2000	185	52.86	26.40
2001	195	55.71	27.80
2002	203	58.00	26.30

Between 1997 and 1999 there were 3 million shares in issue. This was increased to 3.5 million by the issue of bonus shares at the end of 1999. The par value of the shares is 1 Rupee. The company is all-equity financed. The company pays tax at 30%. Dividends declared in one year are paid the following year.

In the current year (2003), earnings are likely to be slightly below 2002 at around 200 million Rupees. The company's directors have decided to pay a maintained dividend for 2003.

They are now evaluating investment opportunities that would require all the company's free cash flow for 2003 plus borrowings of 150 million Rupees of undated debt. If the company does not borrow to invest, growth in earnings and dividends will be zero for the foreseeable future. If the company does borrow and invest, then it expects growth in earnings and dividends of 5% in 2004 (from the 2003 base). The company's expected post-tax cost of equity capital is estimated at 14% per annum, assuming the borrowing takes place. Ignore the effects of inflation.

Requirements

(a) Discuss the relationship between dividend policy, investment policy and financing policy in the context of the scenario and recommend a course of action for the directors of CD Limited.

(10 marks)

(b) Calculate an estimated company value, share price and P/E ratio for CD Limited using Modigliani and Miller's theory of capital structure, assuming the company does borrow and invest.

(6 marks)

(c) Discuss the relevance of the figures you have just calculated in answer to requirement (b) above in placing a value on (i) a small parcel of shares, for example the shareholding of one employee, and (ii) the entire company.

(9 marks)

Note: A report format is NOT required in answering this question.

(Total = 25 marks)

Question 3 – PDQ software

PDQ plc is a software company and Internet provider that was established in the dot-com boom of the late 1990s.

The three founding shareholders, who are still directors and managers of the company, own 30% of PDQ plc. Employees, friends and relatives of the founders own a further 15%. The majority 55% shareholding is owned by a venture capital company that bought a stake in PDQ plc four years ago for £12 million. The venture capital company now wishes to dispose of the holding. The 45% minority shareholders and non-shareholding employees are considering a management buyout.

PDQ plc has sustained losses for the past three years but believes it is now moving into profit. Because of these losses, no liability to tax will arise in 2004 but the company will begin to pay tax at 30% per annum from 2005. It has not declared or paid a dividend since the company was formed. A summary of forecast of key financial information for the current year and for 2004 is as follows:

Income statement for the year end	31 December 2004	31 December 2003
	£m	£m
Sales revenue	15.25	14.52
Direct costs and expenses	12.50	16.97
Profit/(loss) before tax	2.75	(2.45)

Balance sheet at	31 December 2004		31 December 2003	
	£m	£m	£m	£m
Fixed assets (NBV)				
Current assets				
Inventory	1.25		1.25	
Receivables	4.25		3.25	
Cash and marketable securities	0.50		0.00	
		6.00		4.50
Less current liabilities				
Trade payables	2.80		3.20	
Bank overdraft	0.00		0.85	
		2.80		4.05
Total net assets		3.70		0.95
Ordinary share capital		0.25		0.25
(Ordinary shares of £1)				
Total reserves		3.45		0.70
Equity shareholders funds		3.70		0.95

The directors expect growth of 20% each year for the three years 2005–2007 inclusive, falling to 5% each year after that. The average P/E ratio for established listed companies in the industry is currently 28.4 but there is a wide range of between 7.5 and 51.5. The average post-tax cost of equity capital for the industry, according to a recent study, is 15%.

Requirements

Assume today is 31 December 2003.

Advise the founders/employees on the following:

(a) The price they might have to offer the venture capitalist to succeed with a management buyout. You should include in your discussion the various methods of share valuation that might be suitable in the circumstances. Make and state whatever assumptions you feel are necessary and appropriate.

(18 marks)

(b) The advantages and disadvantages of pursuing a management buyout at the present time compared with the possibility of a sale of the venture capitalist's shareholding to another investor.

(7 marks)

Note: A report format is NOT required in answering this question.

(Total = 25 marks)

Question 4 – EQU

EQU plc is a listed company whose shares are mainly owned by large financial institutions. It currently owns and operates a theme park, called 'Dragonland', in the south west of England. It covers five square kilometres and contains various rides, gardens and attractions. Customers pay a single entrance fee. The company's accounting year end is 31 July.

The land is leased and the other fixed assets give poor security, so the company is all-equity financed. The venture has been successful and although it was considered risky initially, it has now stabilised, with a constant stream of customers and steady turnover, profitability and cash flows. The Directors are now considering raising £8 million new finance to be used in full to open a second theme park in Scotland, called 'Phoenixworld'.

The total dividend to be paid by the company on 31 July 2003 will be £1.2 million. The company's shares are already quoted ex div.

The Board meeting

At a Board meeting some concerns were expressed:

The Chairman argued:

> If we want to carry on growing, we need to expand to other sites. I admit that there may be some difficulties in the early years but, basically, Phoenixworld is the same type of business as we have now so the risk should be no different. Therefore the company's cost of equity should not change from its current level, which I think should be about 12% per annum. This seems appropriate for stable earnings such as ours.
>
> If we go ahead with Phoenixworld, I would expect us not to pay any more dividends after 31 July 2003 until 31 July 2006, at which time a total dividend of £2 million would be declared and this should then grow at 4% per annum indefinitely.

The Chief Executive disagreed:

> Of course Phoenixworld would be more risky. This is a new venture with new capital investment and a different customer base. Earnings are therefore bound to be more volatile. This means that the cost of equity will be higher. I think the cost of equity for the company would rise to 15% per annum if Phoenixworld goes ahead. Instead, we should stay at one site and invest £3 million in new rides and facilities to expand and increase profitability and dividends. This will be a lower risk option and will therefore generate a more certain dividend stream. The company's cost of equity should then stay at the current level of 12%. If this option is taken, I would expect dividends to increase at 12% per annum from the current level (at 31 July 2003) up to, and including, the dividend on 31 July 2007. I would expect dividends in all future years thereafter to be constant at this level as we will reach the capacity of our site by that time.

Requirements

(a) Using the dividend valuation model, calculate the total value of the share capital of EQU plc at 1 August 2003 if the Chairman's proposal to open Phoenixworld is accepted. This calculation should be carried out for each of the following assumptions:

  (i) the Chairman's assumption that the company's annual cost of equity stays at 12%;
  (ii) the Chief Executive's assumption that the company's annual cost of equity increases to 15%.

  Comment on the differences in the two calculations.

  (10 marks)

(b) Using the dividend valuation model, calculate the total value of the share capital of EQU plc at 1 August 2003 if the Chief Executive's proposal to expand Dragonland is accepted.

  (4 marks)

(c) Discuss the possible forms of financing the proposed new projects and assess which form of finance is likely to be most appropriate for EQU plc. Describe how each financing method, and each of the projects may affect the company's cost of equity.

(11 marks)

Ignore taxation.

For simplicity, assume that dividends are declared and paid at each accounting year-end.

(Total = 25 marks)

Question 5 – MediCons plc

MediCons plc provides a range of services to the medical and healthcare industry. These services include providing locum (temporary cover for healthcare professionals (mainly doctors and nurses), emergency call-out and consultancy/advisory services to government-funded health organisations. The company also operates a research division that has been successful in recent years in attracting funding from various sources. Some of the employees in this division are considered to be leading experts in their field and are very highly paid.

A consortium of doctors and redundant health service managers started the company in 1989. It is still owned by the same people, but has since grown into an organisation employing over 100 full-time staff throughout the UK. In addition, the company uses specialist staff employed in state run organisations on a part time contract basis. The owners of the company are now interested in either obtaining a stock market quotation, or selling the company if the price adequately reflects what they believe to be the true worth of the business.

Summary financial statistics for MediCons plc and a competitor company, which is listed on the UK Stock Exchange are shown below. The competitor company is broadly similar to MediCons plc but uses a higher proportion of part time staff and has no research capability.

	MediCons plc last year end	Competitor last year end
Date	31.3.2000	31.3.2000
Shares in issue (million)	10	20
Earnings per share (pence)	75	60
Dividend per share (pence)	55	50
Net asset value (£m)	60	75
Debt ratio (outstanding debt as % of total financing)	10	20
Share price (pence)	N/A	980
Beta coefficient	N/A	1.25
Forecasts:		
Growth rate in earnings and dividends (% per annum)	8	7
After-tax cash flow for 2000/2001 (£m)	9.2	N/A

Notes

1. The expected post-tax return on the market for the next 12 months is 12% and the post-tax risk-free rate is 5%. The company pays tax at 30%.
2. The treasurer of the company has provided the forecast growth rate for MediCons plc. The forecast for the competitor is based on published information.
3. The net assets of MediCons plc are the net book values of land, buildings, equipment and vehicles plus net working capital.
4. Sixty per cent of the shares in the competitor company are owned by the directors and their relatives or associates.
5. MediCons uses a 'rule of thumb' discount rate of 15% to evaluate its investments.
6. Assume that growth rates in earnings and dividends are constant per annum.
7. The post-tax cost of debt for MediCons plc and its competitor is 7%.

Requirements

Assume that you are an independent consultant retained by MediCons plc to advise on the valuation of the company and on the relative advantages of a public flotation versus outright sale.

Prepare a report for the directors that provides a range of share prices at which shares in MediCons plc might be issued. Use whatever information is available and relevant and recommend a course of action.

Explain the methods of valuation that you have used and comment on their suitability for providing an appropriate valuation of the company. In the report you should also comment of the difficulties of valuing companies in a service industry and of incorporating a valuation for intellectual capital.

(25 marks)

Note: Approximately one-third of the marks are available for appropriate calculation, and two-thirds for discussion.

Question 6 – BiOs

BiOs Limited (BiOs) is an unquoted company that provides consultancy services to the biotechnology industry. It has been trading for 4 years. It has an excellent reputation for providing innovative and technologically advanced solutions to clients' problems. The company employs 18 consultants plus a number of self employed contract staff and is planning to recruit additional consultants to handle a large new contract. The company 'outsources' most administrative and accounting functions. A problem is recruiting well-qualified experienced consultants and BiOs has had to turn down work in the past because of lack of appropriate staff.

The company's two owners/directors have been approached by the marketing department of an investment bank and asked if they have considered using venture capital financing to expand the business. No detailed proposal has been made but the bank has implied that a venture capital company would require a substantial percentage of the equity in return for a large injection of capital. The venture capitalist would want to exit from the investment in 4–5 years' time.

The company is all-equity financed and neither of the directors is wholly convinced that such a large injection of capital is appropriate for the company at the present time.

Financial information

Revenue in year to 31 December 2003	£3,600,000
Shares in issue (ordinary £1 shares)	100,000
Earnings per share	756p
Dividend per share	0
Net asset value	£395,000[1]

Note:

1 The net assets of BiOs are the net book values of purchased and/or leased buildings, equipment and vehicles plus net working capital. The book valuations are considered to reflect current realisable values.

Forecast

- Sales revenue for the year to 31 December 2004 – £4,250,000. This is heavily dependent on whether or not the company obtains the new contract.
- Operating costs, inclusive of depreciation, are expected to average 50% of revenue in the year to 31 December 2004.
- Tax is expected to be payable at 30%.
- Assume book depreciation equals capital allowances for tax purposes. Also assume, for simplicity, that profit after tax equals cash flow.

Growth in earnings in the years to 31 December 2005 and 2006 is expected to be 30% per annum, falling to 10% per annum after that. This assumes that no new long-term capital is raised. If the firm is to grow at a faster rate then new financing will be needed.

This is a niche market and there are relatively few listed companies doing precisely what BiOs does. However, if the definition of the industry is broadened the following figures are relevant:

P/E ratios

Industry Average	18
Range (individual companies)	12–90

Cost of equity

Industry average	12%
Individual companies	Not available

BiOs does not know what its cost of equity is.

Requirements

(a) Calculate a range of values for the company that could be used in negotiation with a venture capitalist, using whatever information is currently available and relevant. Make and state whatever assumptions you think are necessary. Explain, briefly, the relevance of each method to a company such as BiOs.

(15 marks)

(b) Discuss the advantages and disadvantages of using either venture capital financing to assist with expansion or alternatively a flotation on the stock market in 2–3 years' time. Include in your discussion likely exit routes for the venture capital company.

(10 marks)

(Total marks = 25)

✓ Answers

Question 1 – Target

(a) £500,000 × 9 = £4.5m
(b) (500,000 × 0.80)/0.06 = £6.667m
(c) $k_e = 6 + (11 - 6) 1.2 = 12\%$

$$\frac{400,000 \times 1.04}{0.12 - 0.04} = £5.2m$$

(d) = £2.25m
(e) 2.25m + 1m − 0.25m = £3m

Question 2 – CD

(a) **Dividend, investment and financing policies**

These three policies are fundamental to a company's operation. To increase shareholder wealth, the directors must invest in positive net present value projects, so as to safeguard a stream of income in the future. At the same time, they need to finance the investments, either through raising external finance or using internal resources. The second possibility will then impact on the dividend paid, which could disappoint shareholders who were expecting cash in the near future.

In an efficient market, shareholders would understand that dividends might be reduced or cancelled in the short term in order to invest in projects that will boost the present value of the cash that will eventually be paid out. They would therefore be indifferent to the dividend policy in any one particular year. In practice, companies usually feel that the markets do not like a wildly fluctuating dividend and set policies that allow them to retain sufficient cash to undertake small projects that arise without disturbing dividends. Large projects are often funded with additional external finance.

In the current situation, CD is a private company with its main shareholders still being the founders and managers. The dividend payout ratio has been around 50% (reduced slightly last year to 45%) and it therefore seems quite high for a company in the early years of its life. The main shareholders would also be well aware of the investment opportunity being taken if the dividend was reduced this year.

CD is currently all-equity financed and introducing debt finance is likely to lower the overall cost of capital. The gearing level will rise to roughly 21% (see working below) for Debt: Debt + Equity, which is not excessive and debt is cheaper than equity due to the lower risk to the investor. However, the investment is large and CD may be at risk if the project does not perform according to expectations. It might be sensible to cut the dividend further to reduce the reliance on debt finance.

We would recommend that the directors call a meeting of the shareholders and present the investment details. If the shareholders agree that it is beneficial, it is likely they will agree to a reduced, or cancelled, dividend for 2003 to reduce the external debt finance from its projected R150 million.

Workings

		Rm
Earnings – dividends – bonus shares (1997–2002) =		458.2
200 – (3.5 × 26.3) (2003) =		108.0
	Retained profits	566.2
	Share capital	3.5
	Shareholders' funds	569.7

Gearing = 150/(150 + 569.7) = 21%

(b) **Valuations**

$$\text{Value if ungeared} = \frac{D_1}{k_e} = \frac{(200 \times 1.05)}{0.14} = \text{R1,500m}$$

$$V_g = V_u + D_t$$
$$= 1,500 + (150 \times 0.30)$$
$$= 1,545$$

Value of equity = 1,545 – 150 = R1,395m

$$\text{per share, value} = \frac{1,395}{3.5} = \text{R399}$$

$$\text{P/E ratio} = \frac{399}{(200/3.5)} = 7$$

(c) **Relevance for valuations**

Modigliani and Miller's theory has a number of assumptions that do not necessarily hold, in particular:

- full information in the marketplace about the company's operations
- no transaction costs or irrational shareholder behaviour
- all investors have the same view
- no further growth is expected.

We can see the difference the final assumption makes if we assume CD continues to grow its earnings at 5% per annum. This would make $V_u = (200 \times 1.05)/(0.14 - 0.05) = 2,333$. This increases the value of the equity in CD by R833 million to R2,228 million, the share value to R637 and the P/E ratio to 11.1.

However, the model depends on a large number of investors scrutinising the information about the company and being able to buy or sell the shares in a liquid market accordingly. CD, being a private company, is not in this situation so there would have to be a very careful assessment of the investment plans before an accurate valuation could be deduced for the whole company.

A small parcel of shares would not necessarily be worth the same as a large block of shares, as there is significant value attached to control or influence in a company. This can be seen in listed companies when control costs are far more per share than a small parcel, and it is even truer in private companies, in which a small shareholding carries no power at all. The value per share calculated was looking at the entire company and is unlikely to be the value agreed per share for a small parcel.

Question 3 – PDQ software

(a) **Offer price**

We wish to value 55% of the company; we should value the entire company and adjust this to 55%.

1. *Asset value*

    The current net asset value is £0.95 million but is forecast to rise to £3.7 million. However, a buyer or seller would normally value a business as a stream of cash flows rather than a collection of assets. The asset approach does not allow for intangible assets, particularly the reputation and goodwill which will form most of the value for a service company like PDQ plc.

2. *Earnings multiple*

    A P/E ratio gives the multiple connecting the share value and the earnings per share; in a listed company both are published and the P/E ratio calculated. We would therefore apply the P/E ratio from a similar listed company to our earnings (no tax is payable on 2004 profits) to get an approximate value for the company (if we were listed).

At average P/E ratio	28.4 × £2.75m	£78.1m
At low P/E ratio	7.5 × £2.75m	£20.6m
At high P/E ratio	51.5 × £2.75m	£141.6m

    The P/E ratio implicitly assesses the growth prospects and the risk of the company, and is likely that our company would be viewed as more risky and hence less valuable than the market average. The growth prospects also seem high, given a cost of capital of 15% and a 100% payout ratio:

    $$P = \frac{D_1}{(k_e - g)}$$

    $$P/E = \frac{1}{(k_e - g)}$$

    $$28.4 = \frac{1}{(0.15 - g)}$$

    This gives $g = 11.5\%$ which may be higher than we could achieve in the long term but may be possible in the short term.

    If we look ahead to 2005, it might give investors a better idea of long-term prospects as the tax losses will have been used up. Earnings after tax might be approximately = £2.75m × 1.20 (growth) × 0.70 (tax) = £2.31m

    Value as listed approximately = £2.31m × 28.4 = £66m

    Reducing this for the lack of liquidity in the shares by 25% might give a value of £50 million.

3 *Present value of cash flows*

Using the post-tax earnings as an approximation to cash, and applying the expected growth of 20% for three years followed by 5% per annum, we can discount at the 15% cost of equity.

$$\frac{2.75}{1.15} + \frac{(2.75 \times 1.20 \times 0.7)}{1.15^2} + \frac{(2.75 \times 1.20^2 \times 0.7)}{1.15^3}$$
$$+ \frac{[(2.75 \times 1.20^3 \times 0.7)/(0.15 - 0.05)]}{1.15^3}$$
$$= 2.39 + 1.75 + 1.82 + 21.87 = £27.8m$$

4 *Summary and conclusion*

As the company has not paid dividends, we cannot use a dividend valuation approach so the calculations can be summarised as:

	Total company	Venture capitalist (55% share)
Asset value (£m)	1	0.6
Earnings multiple (£m)	50	27.5
Present value of cash (£m)	28	15.4

There is a wide range of values and a number of other factors will determine the price paid. These include:

- the minimum the venture capitalist requires
- the other options available to the venture capitalist and how desperate they are to realise their investment
- the other options available to the buyout team and how anxious they are to secure the shares
- the method of financing used for the buyout.

(b) **Management buyout (MBO)**

The MBO has advantages and disadvantages over a sale to another investor for both the venture capitalist and the MBO team.

From the venture capitalists perspective, a quick sale to a ready buyer such as the MBO team is preferable to finding another investor who will want to undertake lengthy investigations. They may be prepared to accept a lower price, although they are likely to assume that you value the stake more highly than a third-party investor and try to negotiate a higher price.

From the MBO teams viewpoint, the MBO team would not bring any new skills or knowledge to the company (which a new outside investor might). However, the new investor might want a greater role in the management of the business. The main advantage is in maintaining control of the company within the existing shareholders and employees, but as discussed in (a) this will be costly and the financing and its associated risk will need to be considered carefully.

Question 4 – EQU

(a) **Total value if Phoenix World opened**

  (i) *Constant cost of equity*

  $$\text{Value} = \frac{[2/(0.12 - 0.04)]}{1.12^2} = £19.93\text{m}$$

  (ii) *Increased cost of equity*

  $$\text{Value} = \frac{[2/(0.15 - 0.04)]}{1.15^2} = £13.75\text{m}$$

  The difference in value is entirely due to the change in estimate for the cost of equity. This is because at 15% the shareholders require a greater return for the risk perceived in the company and the cash flows predicted do not exceed this return required by as much.

  The new project itself will have a much higher risk profile under the Chief Executive's assumptions as it has raised the average return required across the company's entire operations to 15%.

(b) **Dragonland expansion**

  $$\begin{aligned}
  \text{Value} &= \frac{(1.2\text{m} \times 1.12)}{1.12} &&= 1.2\text{m} \\
  &+ \frac{(1.2\text{m} \times 1.12^2)}{1.12^2} &&= 1.2\text{m} \\
  &+ \frac{(1.2\text{m} \times 1.12^3)}{1.12^3} &&= 1.2\text{m} \\
  &+ \frac{[(1.2\text{m} \times 1.12^4)/0.12]}{1.12^3} &&= 11.2\text{m} \\
  & && \overline{£14.8\text{m}}
  \end{aligned}$$

(c) **Possible financing and impact on cost of equity**

  The main forms of finance fall into four catergories: issue of shares, bank loans, corporate bond or debenture, or leasing.

  1 *Issue of shares*

  Shares can be issued via a rights issue, an offer for sale and or public offer, or a placing. However, the £3 million required is too small for an offer for sale or a public offer, which would have higher issue costs than the other two methods anyway. Even a rights issue or a placing is likely to have higher issue costs than debt, and the relative control of shareholders would change unless everyone took up their rights.

  If finance was raised from equity, the company would still be all-equity financed, so there is no change in the financial risk to shareholders. There would be no impact on the cost of equity beyond that identified by the Chief Executive if the company undertook the Dragonland project.

2 *Bank loans*

A bank loan is with a single bank or a syndicate, and is likely to have much lower set-up costs. The bank will, however, require a charge over the assets for security, which may be a problem given that the assets in the existing site were deemed to be inappropriate, and the company will have to arrange repayment of both capital and interest over an agreed time frame.

The bank loan would introduce gearing to the company and some financial risk for shareholders. The interest paid will make the earnings and potential dividends more volatile, while the possibility of default leading to liquidation introduces additional risk. The cost of equity will therefore rise above any increase due to the change in business.

3 *Corporate bonds or debenture*

The issue of corporate bonds to the public, or a debenture with a prospectus, will contain restrictive covenants, which may limit the ability to borrow more. The issue costs are likely to be higher than for a bank loan but less than those for equity, and as with the bank loan the capital and interest will have to be paid over a pre-determined schedule. These will also increase the gearing level of the company and hence the financial risk to shareholders, leading to an increase in the cost of equity over and above any increase due to the nature of the business.

4 *Leasing*

Leasing allows the company to effectively obtain 100% of the finance for the leased asset and has low initial set-up costs. However, the implicit interest rate charged can be high to compensate for this.

If the lease is long term it is likely to be regarded as long-term debt which will increase the financial risk perceived by shareholders. As with the other forms of debt, this would therefore increase the cost of equity.

5 *Conclusion*

Given the high issue costs of new equity, and the absence of any gearing, it would seem appropriate to raise debt-finance, probably in the form of bank loans. Although this will increase the cost of equity, it will be partly offset by the cheaper cost of debt, due to the lower risk to the lender and the tax relief on debt interest.

Question 5 – MediCons

REPORT

To: Directors of MediCons plc
From: Independent Consultant
Date: xx of x 20xx

Valuation of the company

This report looks at possible valuations of the company and discusses their suitability, as well as looking at some of the difficulties in valuing a business accurately.

1 *Valuation*

In the appendix, I have outlined three valuations which give the following results:

	Per share	Total value
Net assets	£6.00	£60m
Earnings multiple	£12.75	£127.5m
Dividend stream	£11.88	£118.8m

A company is usually bought as a source of future cash streams, rather than to access and sell the assets, so the asset value, which simply looks at the book value of tangible net assets, is not particularly relevant unless it is the intention to liquidate the company. This is clearly not the case here, and is likely to severely underestimate the value of a service company which might have few tangible assets, but a high-income stream generated by intangible assets. Foremost amongst these are the skills of its staff (or intellectual capital) which generates the company's reputation, but it is very difficult to put any kind of objective value on such an intangible asset (except by comparing the difference between an asset valuation and income-based valuations). In the case of MediCon, the income valuations appear to be about double the net asset valuation.

The earnings multiple approach assumes that last years' earnings were fairly typical and that the market will view MediCon in a similar light to its competitor. Subject to these limitations, it gives a quick and easy approximation for the value of the company if floated on the stock exchange. A single buyer of the company may not be prepared to pay as much due to the lack of a liquid market in the shares; conversely another company may be prepared to pay more if it can see synergistic gains to be made on acquisition.

The dividend valuation model assumes constant growth in dividends (at 8%) forever and it's more appropriate for minority shareholdings who would be unable to alter the dividend policy. However, it is useful to see that it is in a similar range to the earnings multiple approach.

2 *Other methods*

Other methods exist for estimating a value, but they will not give any more accuracy; rather they lend comfort to the current range of values and give assurance that we are in the right area. One such is to try and estimate the cash flow for the period over which it is expected to grow often 5–10 years, and discount to a present value.

3 *Flotation or sale*

To make a sale requires a potential buyer to be identified or to come forward. If none has emerged so far, advisers may be able to make enquiries, but as it is likely that a buyer would be a company in the same or similar industry, most of the possible candidates are probably already well aware of MediCon's plans. Therefore, if no offer has been forthcoming, a flotation seems the more likely option.

A flotation will incur higher costs than an outright sale and the market would be concerned if existing shareholders realised all their investment. It will therefore be necessary to issue new shares for cash, whilst an outright sale would buy all the existing shares, paying cash or new shares in the new parent company.

4   *Conclusion*

A current valuation would appear to be around £120 million to £125 million or £12 to £12.50 per share. A public flotation would enable you to keep control of the company as you will have to maintain your shareholding, while any declared interested parties in an outright sale may be prepared to buy your shares at a higher price, in cash, for the synergy they anticipate.

Appendix

(i) Net asset value $= \dfrac{£60m}{10m} = £6.00$ per share

(£60m for the entire company)

(ii) *Earnings multiple*

Competitor's P/E ratio $= \dfrac{980}{60} = 16.3$

As MediCon's forecast growth in earnings and dividends are greater, approximate MediCon's P/E ratio as 17.

Value = £0.75 × 17 = £12.75 per share (£127.5m for the entire company)

(iii) *Dividend valuation model*

Ungearing competitor's beta:

$$\beta_u = \dfrac{1.25 \times 80}{[80 + (20 \times 0.7)]} = 1.064$$

Regear at MediCon's Gearing level:

$1.064 = \beta \times 90/[90 + (10 \times 0.7)]$

so $\beta = 1.15$

and $K_e = 5 + (12 - 5)\,1.15 = 13\%$

Value $= \dfrac{(0.55 \times 1.08)}{(0.13 - 0.08)} = £11.88$ (£118.8m for the entire company)

Question 6 – BiOs

(a) **Valuation of company**

The true value of a business will be the cash flows it produces, discounted to their present value. However, identifying the cashflows is difficult and a number of different estimates can be made.

Asset valuation

An asset valuation assumes that the company is broken up and the assets and liabilities realised. We are told that the market values of these are approximately £395,000.

As the owners, or those they are contemplating sharing the company with, have no intention of closing the company down, this valuation is less relevant. It is likely to be substantially less than its value as a going concern as it takes no account of assets not included in the balance sheet, or capable of being sold separately, such as goodwill and reputation. For a professional services company such as BiOs this is likely to form a substantial part of the value of the company.

PE multiple valuation

The PE multiple approach compares the price of similar companies to their earnings and then applies a similar multiple, with suitable adjustments, to BiOs. The main problems come in finding companies that are similar, as no two companies are identical, and in making suitable adjustments to take account, for example, of the fact that BiOs is unlisted.

Using different PE ratios will clearly give different values:

Industry average $18 \times 7.56 \times 100{,}000 = £13.6$ m
Low $12 \times 7.56 \times 100{,}000 = £9.1$ m
High $20 \times 7.56 \times 100{,}000 = £15.1$ m

As these are listed companies, shareholders are likely to value them more highly than BiOs as the liquid market in their shares makes them less risky. This would suggest a value of perhaps £10 m, though the prospect of listing on the stock market in the medium term may reduce the discount applied.

Cashflow valuation

A cashflow valuation attempts to estimate cashflows accurately before discounting them, but clearly has to abandon this at some point and make some assumption about the longer term. This is often to assume a constant perpetuity of cashflows at the same level as the last year of the detailed analysis. Here, we are told that growth will be 30% for the first two years after 2004 and then 10% thereafter.

The cashflows, are, therefore:

2004: £4.25 m × 0.50 × 0.70 = £1.488 m
2005: £1.488 m × 1.30 = £1.934 m
2006: £1.934 m × 1.30 = £2.514 m rising at 10% thereafter

As BiOs does not know what its cost of equity is, we will have to use the industry average of 12%, although BiOs' cost is likely to be higher than that of listed companies.

$$PV = 1.488/1.12 + 1.934/1.12^2 + (2.514/(0.12 - 0.10))/1.12^2 = £103.1 \text{ m}$$

This is much higher than the other valuations, but is largely due to the value of the tail. The value of the first three years is £4.7 m and assuming a constant level of cashflows after 2006 gives a total value of £19.6 m.

It is, therefore, very sensitive to the assumption about the long-term growth rate. Without justification for the 10%, it might be more realistic to assume no long-term growth. If we also increase the cost of equity for the increased risk in a private company shareholding to 15%, this would reduce the value to:

$$1.488/1.15 + 1.934/1.15^2 + (2.514/0.15)/1.15^2 = £15.4 \text{ m}$$

Summary

In summary, a wide range of values can be produced, depending on the assumptions built in:

Assets	£395,000
PE multiple range	£9.1–£15.1 m
PE average	£13.6 m
PE likely BiOs	£10 m
Detailed cashflow projections	
Growth estimates given	£103.1 m
First three years only	£4.7 m
Constant tail and 15% discount rate	£15.4 m

We would, therefore, need to do substantial work on the assumptions built into these valuations. However, at this stage a tentative estimate, ignoring the asset valuation, might be in the range £10–£16 m.

(b) **Venture capital or flotation**

The main factors to consider in anticipating flotation in two to three years' time are

- The value of the company would appear to be very low for a main listing, and even on the small side for listing on the AIM.
- It may take some time to achieve as the exchange will control the number of new companies listing through a queuing system.
- The finance will be raised and ownership sold into the indefinite future. Venture capital is likely to be temporary and therefore consideration needs to be given to the likely exit route for the investors.
- The investors in a stock market company are likely to be far less involved in the company than venture capitalists, who may well want to participate in board decisions.

Overall, it is important the owners decide on their longer-term objectives as it will be a major influence on the choice of longer-term expansion finance.

Mergers and Acquisitions   10

✏️ Exam focus

The exam will want you to show that you understand the motivation for mergers or acquisitions in practice. Ensure that you can comment on the pros and cons of the various possible considerations and are able to advise directors and shareholders on hostile bids and management buyouts.

🔑 Key points

Synergy

Synergy represents a benefit to the organisation and its shareholders which comes about because two businesses are now operating together. Ultimately, this means some reduction in costs or increase in revenues.

Synergy could be a one-off cost saving such as:

- Selling one of the head office sites
- Selling other duplicated assets.

It could also be a cost saving or revenue boost which is felt every year, such as:

- Cross-selling to the other business's customers
- Production economies of scale
- Storage, distribution and marketing rationalisation
- Elimination of overlapping jobs
- Sharing of assets
- Elimination of a competitor
- Possibly cheaper financing costs.

More generally, any transfer of skills or sharing of resources (from warehouses to customer lists and goodwill) is likely to lead to synergy.

In income-based valuations,

- One-off synergy should be added to the total value as a 'bonus' on top of the income stream which can be produced by the business.
- Ongoing synergy should be included in the annual income before valuing the income stream.

Synergy makes no difference to asset-based valuations. This is because cost savings or revenue boosts are irrelevant, and surplus assets are already included in the list of all the assets being valued.

Studies tend to suggest that a predator often overestimates synergy and underestimates the costs of reorganising the merged entity. In the excitement of a contested bid, this can lead to them offering too much for the target's shares and hence reducing the wealth of their own shareholders.

Consideration for purchase

The main ways to pay for the purchase are in cash, shares or loan stock:

	Advantages for purchaser	*Advantages for vendor*
Cash	no sharing of control	certainty of consideration
Shares	no liquidity problems	no Capital Gains Tax on sale share in future profits
Loan stock	less of an immediate liquidity problem but no sharing of control	a guaranteed income stream without suffering immediate Capital Gains Tax

Hostile bids and defence strategies

A friendly bid is when the management of the target company view it favourably and recommend it to their shareholders.

A hostile bid is when the management of the target company are against it. The potential purchaser (or predator) therefore approaches the shareholders directly. In a hostile bid, the predator is unlikely to have as much detailed operational information on which to base the bid.

In a hostile bid, there are a number of defence strategies the management of the target can use to stop the predator taking over the company.

To discourage any interest, the management might use:

(a) a clear strategic plan to demonstrate the benefits of the current management team
(b) poison pills, to make the company unattractive if taken over
(c) strategic shareholdings, where the managers or associates control a number of shares.

If the predator expresses interest, the management might:

(d) dispose of the assets attracting their attention (Crown Jewels)
(e) persuade a more friendly predator to bid for them (White Knight)
(f) launch a management buyout themselves
(g) try to take over the predator (Pac Man)
(h) try to have it referred to the Competition Commission.

If a full bid is launched, the management of the target company will circulate a defence document to shareholders, explaining why they should stay with the present management.

City code and company law

The general principle is that all shareholders must be treated equally. In addition, there are percentage shareholdings which trigger certain actions:

- 3%+   must disclose to target company
- 30%   must make a conditional offer to all shareholders
- 90%   can usually force other shareholders to sell (at a price offered to others).

Management buyout (MBO)

An MBO is where the managers of a business, possibly only part of a company, buy it from the shareholders. In the past this has often meant taking on very high levels of debt (a highly leveraged buyout) but the growth of venture capital has reduced the amount of long-term interest-bearing loans needed. Venture capitalists will look for high capital growth and will often have identified an exit route before investing.

Questions

Question 1 – Company A (Practice Question)

Company A has earnings of £1 million and a P/E ratio of 7.5. It is considering a bid for company B, which has earnings of £0.5 million and a P/E ratio of 6. It estimates that the P/E ratio after acquisition will change to 7.

What is the maximum A can realistically offer B if

(a) there is no expected synergy?
(b) A expects annual post-tax synergy of £0.25 million?

Question 2 – PR

PR plc is listed on the London Stock Exchange. The directors have made a bid for its main UK competitor, ST plc. ST plc's directors have rejected the bid. If the bid eventually succeeds, the new company will become the largest in its industry in Europe. However, it will still be smaller than some of its US competitors. The directors of PR plc are aware that the company must continue to expand if it is to remain competitive in a global market and avoid being taken over by a larger US company.

Relevant information is as follows:

	PR plc	ST plc
Share price as at today (21 May 2002) (pence)	671	565
Shares in issue (million)	820	513
P/E ratios as at today	14	16
Debt outstanding (market value) (£ billion)	2.2	1.8

Other information:

The average P/E for the industry is currently estimated as 13.

- The average debt ratio for the industry (long-term debt as proportion of total funding) is 30% based on market values.
- 40% of PR plc's debt is repayable in 2005; 30% of ST plc's in 2006.
- PR plc's cost of equity is 13% net of tax.
- PR plc has cash available of £460 million following the recent disposal of some subsidiary companies. ST plc's cash balances at the last balance sheet date (31 December 2001) were £120 million.

Terms of the bid

PR plc's directors made an opening bid one week ago of 10 PR plc shares for 13 ST plc shares. They are aware that they might have to raise the bid in order to succeed and also may need to offer a cash alternative. Their advisers have told them that, typically, 50% of shareholders might be expected to accept the share exchange and 50%, the cash alternative.

Requirements

Assume you work for PR plc's financial advisers. You have been asked to write a report advising the directors of PR plc. Your report should cover the following issues:

(a) A discussion of the implications that the current share prices of the two companies have for the bid. Recommend terms of a revised share exchange.

(8 marks)

(b) The advantages and disadvantages of offering a cash alternative and how the cash alternative might be financed, based on your revised bid terms recommended in answer to (a) above. Your discussion should include an evaluation of the impact of the proposed finance on the merged group's financial standing. Assume a rights issue is not appropriate at the present time.

(17 marks)
(Total = 25 marks)

Question 3 – AB plc

AB plc is a firm of recruitment and selection consultants. It has been trading for 10 years and obtained a stock market listing 4 years ago. It has pursued a policy of aggressive growth and specialises in providing services to companies in high-technology and high-growth sectors. It is all-equity financed by ordinary share capital of £50 million in shares of £0.20 nominal (or par) value. The company's results to the end of June 2002 have just been announced. Profits before tax were £126.6 million. The Chairman's statement included a forecast that earnings might be expected to rise by 4%, which is a lower annual rate than in recent years. This is blamed on economic factors that have had a particularly adverse effect on high-technology companies.

YZ plc is in the same business but has been established much longer. It serves more traditional business sectors and its earnings record has been erratic. Press comment has frequently blamed this on poor management and the company's shares have been out of favour with the stock market for some time. Its current earnings growth forecast is also 4% for the foreseeable future. YZ plc has an issued ordinary share capital of £180 million in £1 shares. Pre-tax profits for the year to 30 June 2002 were £112.5 million.

AB plc has recently approached the shareholders of YZ plc with a bid of 5 new shares in AB plc for every 6 YZ plc shares. There is a cash alternative of 345 pence per share. Following the announcement of the bid, the market price of AB plc shares fell 10% while the price of YZ plc shares rose 14%. The P/E ratio and dividend yield for AB plc, YZ plc and two other listed companies in the same industry immediately prior to the bid announcement are shown below. All share prices are in pence.

		2002		
High	Low	Company	P/E	Dividend yield %
425	325	AB plc	11	2.4
350	285	YZ plc	7	3.1
187	122	CD plc	9	5.2
230	159	WX plc	16	2.4

Both AB plc and YZ plc pay tax at 30%.

AB plc's post-tax cost of equity capital is estimated at 13% per annum and YZ plc's at 11% per annum.

Assume you are a shareholder in YZ plc. You have a large, but not controlling, shareholding and are a qualified management accountant. You bought the shares some years ago and have been very disappointed with their performance. Two years ago you formed a 'protest group' with fellow shareholders with the principal aim of replacing members of the Board. You call a meeting of this group to discuss the bid.

Requirement

In preparation for your meeting, write a briefing note for your group to discuss. Your note should:

(a) Evaluate whether the proposed share-for-share offer is likely to be beneficial to shareholders in both AB plc and YZ plc. You should use the information and merger terms available, plus appropriate assumptions, to forecast post-merger values. As a benchmark, you should then value the two companies using the constant growth form of the dividend valuation model.

(13 marks)

(b) Discuss the factors to consider when deciding whether to accept or reject the bid and the relative benefits/disadvantages of accepting shares or cash.

(8 marks)

(c) Advise your shareholder group on what its members should do with their investment in YZ plc, based on your calculations/considerations.

(4 marks)
(Total = 25 marks)

Question 4 – TDC

TDC Inc. is a transport and distribution company listed on the New York Stock Exchange. On 14 November 2003, the directors made a bid for a competitor, UED plc, that is based in the UK. UED plc's directors are considering the bid, but have indicated the terms are inadequate and would have to be improved if they were to feel able to recommend it to their shareholders.

The merger would create the fourth largest company in the industry worldwide, but it would still be substantially smaller than the three largest companies. TDC Inc. has suffered from slow growth over the past few years and has long been rumoured by market professionals to be a likely target of a hostile bid from one of the three larger companies, or even a reverse takeover by a smaller company. The bid for UED plc is therefore being seen by the market as defensive.

	TDC Inc.	UED plc
Market data		
Common stock/share price as at today (18 November 2003)	US$11.36	425 pence
Common stock/share price on 18 October 2003	US$12.45	305 pence
Common stock/shares in issue	120m	145m
P/E ratio as at today	11	13.5

Accounting data	US$m	£m
Forecast profit after tax for the current financial year	98.5	45.5
Net asset values at last balance sheet date (30 June 2003)	825.2	230.5
Including cash balances of	125.5	65.2
Debt outstanding (market value)	250	75
[Repayable	2007	2008]

Other information:

The average P/E for the industry is currently estimated as 10 in the UK and 13 in the USA.

The average debt ratio for the industry internationally (long-term debt as proportion of total funding) is 15% based on market values.

TDC Inc's cost of equity is 12% net of tax.

The US$/£ exchange rate today is 1.53.

Terms of the bid

TDC Inc's directors have made an opening bid of 1 TDC Inc. common stock for 2 UED plc shares. No cash alternative has been offered so far.

Requirement

Assume you are the Financial Manager with TDC Inc. Write an internal memorandum for the Board that:

(a) discusses how the recent price movements of the two companies' shares might impact on the bid negotiations;

(6 marks)

(b) recommends revised bid terms that might be acceptable to the directors and shareholders of UED plc and also to your own Board. Your recommendation should be fully evaluated;

(12 marks)

(c) evaluates the strategic implications of making a hostile bid compared with an aggressive investment programme of organic growth.

(7 marks)
(Total = 25 marks)

Question 5 – RD

RD plc has made a takeover bid for LO plc. RD plc's share price has been performing well in recent months as the market believes its Managing Director, Mr Jones, has the ability to improve dramatically the company's earnings. The acquisition of LO plc, an erratic performer in recent years, seems to be a sensible move in commercial terms. However, the market does not react to the terms of the bid as Mr Jones expected and he finds RD plc's share price falling.

A summary of the financial data before the bid is as follows:

	RD plc	LO plc
Number of shares in issue (million)	5	15
Earnings available to ordinary shareholders (£m)	2.5	7.5
P/E ratio	12.5	7.5

Mr Jones estimated financial data post-acquisition

Estimated market capitalisation	£125m
Estimated share price	£8.33
Estimated EPS	£0.67
Estimated equivalent value of one old LO plc sh	£5.55

The offer is 10 RD plc shares for 15 LO plc shares. At the time of the bid announcement, no information is released other than the bid terms and the comment by Mr Jones that he hopes to 'turn LO round'. The expected rate of return on RD plc's equity capital is 15% per annum constant.

(a) *Requirements*

    (i) to suggest how Mr Jones might have calculated post-acquisition values

    (ii) to write a short report suggesting a probably post-acquisition share price and advising shareholders in both RD plc and LO plc on whether the bid should proceed

(15 marks)

(b) It is later announced that the proposed merger is expected to result in immediate administrative savings of £5 million. Sales of redundant assets by the end of the first year are expected to realise £10 million. Net income is expected to increase by £7.5 million per annum for the foreseeable future as a result of a more aggressive marketing policy for LO plc's business.

Note: You should assume all figures are net of tax.

You are required to explain how this new information would affect your estimate of a probable post-acquisition share price, and comment on how it might affect LO plc's bargaining position.

(10 marks)
(Total = 25 marks)

Question 6 – PCO plc

PCO plc operates in oil and related industries. Its shares are quoted on the London International Stock Exchange. In its retailing operations the company has concentrated on providing high quality service and facilities at its service stations rather than competing solely on the price of petrol. Approximately 75% of its Revenue and 60% of its profits are from petrol, the remainder coming from other services (car wash and retail sales from its convenience stores which are available at each service station).

The company has been highly profitable in the past as a result of astute buying of petroleum products on the open market. The company does not enter into supplier agreements with

Mergers and Acquisitions

the major oil companies except on very short-term deals. However, profit margins are now under increasing pressure as a result of intensifying competition and the cost of complying with environmental legislation.

The managing director of the company is assessing a possible acquisition that would help the company increase the percentage of its non-petroleum revenue and profits. OT plc specialises in oil distribution from the depots owned by the major oil companies to their retail outlets. Its shares have been quoted on the UK Alternative Investment Market for the past 2 years. It operates a fleet of oil tankers, some owned and some leased. PCO plc has used its services in the past and knows it has an up to date and well-managed fleet. However, a bid for OT plc would almost certainly be hostile and, as the directors and their families own 40% of the shares, a successful bid is far from assured.

Extracts from PCO plc's Balance Sheet at 31 December 2003

Assets Employed	£m
Cash and marketable securities	105.00
Accounts receivable and inventories	95.00
Less current liabilities	(75.00)
Working capital	125.00
Property, plant and equipment	160.00
Less long term liabilities:	
Secured loan stock 7% repayable 2009	(80.00)
	205.00

Shareholders' equity	
Stated capital	
(Authorised £50 million)	
Issued	40.00
Accumulated profits	165.00
Net Assets Employed	205.00

PCO plc's financial advisors have produced estimates of the expected NPV and the first full year post-acquisition earnings of PCO plc and OT plc:

PCO plc plus OT plc   *Estimated post-acquisition earnings in first full year following acquisitions:* £70 million   *Estimated NPV of combined organisation:* £720 million

Summary financial statistics

	PCO plc	OT plc
Last year end	31 December 2003	31 December 2003
Shares in issue (millions)	40	24
Earnings per share (pence)	106	92
Dividend per share (pence)	32	21
Share price (pence)	967	1020
Book value of fixed assets and current assets less current liabilities (£ million)	285	145
Debt ratio (outstanding debt as % of total market value)	17.0	14.0
Forecast growth rate % (constant, annualised)	5	9
Beta coefficient	0.9	1.2

Requirements

(a) Calculate, for PCO plc and OT plc *before* the acquisition:

   (i) The current market value and P/E ratio.
   (ii) The cost of equity using the CAPM, assuming the return on the market is 8% and the return on the risk free asset is 4%.
   (iii) The prospective share price and market value using the dividend valuation model.

   (6 marks)

(b) Discuss and advise on the following issues:

   (i) The price to be offered to the target company's shareholders. You should recommend a range of terms within which PCO plc should be prepared to negotiate.
   (ii) The most appropriate form of funding the bid and the financial effects (assume cash or share exchange are the options).
   (iii) The business implications (effect on existing operation, growth prospects, risk and so on).

   (19 marks)

Marks are split roughly equally between sections of part (b) of the question

(Total marks = 25)

✓ Answers

Question 1 – Company A

(a) Value combined = (1m + 0.5m) × 7 = 10.5m
    Value of A alone = 1m × 7.5 = 7.5m
    Maximum bid = £3m

(b) Value combined = (1m + 0.5m + 0.25m) × 7 = 12.25m
    Value of A alone = 7.5m
    Maximum bid = £4.75m

This therefore gives A some leeway in its bid (£1.75m).

Question 2 – PR

REPORT

To: Directors of PR plc
From: Adviser
Date: xx of x 2002

Bid for ST plc

This report will discuss the implications for the bid of the current share prices, and the advantages and disadvantages of a cash bid and how it could be financed.

(a) *Current share prices*

The bid terms are 10 PR shares for 13 ST shares. At today's prices, the PR shares would be worth £67.10 and the ST shares £73.45. It is therefore unlikely that the bid will be accepted at today's prices, and it would have to be increased to roughly 17 PR shares for 20 ST shares.

However, the share prices are based on the market expectations of the gain to the respective shareholders, and in particular a bid at this level may not represent good value to the existing shareholders of PR. The benefits of the acquisition need to be assessed carefully to decide what it is worth paying.

The earnings of ST are approximately £181m (£5.65/16 × 513m), which gives an approximate value at your cost of equity (13%) of £1.4 billion (valued as a perpetuity). Given that the current market capitalisation of ST is £2.95 billion, the market has already built in a substantial premium to allow for any operating synergy. Only if the cost savings and revenue increases are likely to exceed £1.5 billion in present value terms (or £200 million per annum in post-tax earnings), should the directors consider increasing their bid.

(b) *Cash alternative*

The main advantage of a cash offer is that the benefits of the merger in the future operations all accrue to those that remain as shareholders in PR plc. The disadvantage is that the cash has to be found to fund the payments required.

If the bid of 17 PR shares for 20 ST shares is accepted, each ST share is being valued at 17 × £6.71/20 = £5.70. We are assuming that 50% × 513m × 50% = £1,462m. The two companies have total cash of £580 million, leaving £882 million to be raised.

This is best financed through long-term debt finance, although we need to examine the impact on the group's capital structure. If we do not allow for any synergy over and above that reflected in ST's share price, and assume that the market takes no account of the change in the capital structure, the equity after merger = £5.5 billion + £2.9 billion = £8.4 billion, and the debt will be £4.9 billion approximately (including the £882 million raised). This gives gearing of 37%, which is higher than the industry average but not excessive.

However, this ignores any extra synergy not anticipated by the market (which would increase equity and reduce gearing) and the impact of increased gearing from PR's perspective, which might increase the cost of equity from 13% and reduce the equity value, hence increasing the ratio.

In addition, £1.4 billion of debt is repayable within four years, which will decrease the gearing to 30% (using the same equity value). Much will therefore depend on the earning potential of the merged entity and how much can be generated to pay off this debt without having to refinance.

Question 3 – AB plc

(a) **Share-for share offer**

	AB	YZ	Combined
Profit after tax (£m)	88.62	78.75	167.37
EPS (p)	35.45	43.75	41.84
P/E ratio	11	7	
Share price (pre bid)	£3.90	£3.06	£3.82
MV of company (£m)	974.8	551.3	1,526.1
No. of shares (million)	250	180	400

This assumes that there is no operating synergy and so no increase in the combined earnings; it is unlikely a bid would be launched if substantial synergy was not envisaged.

On these assumptions, even though the EPS increases for a shareholder in AB, the share value decreases from £3.90 to £3.82. A shareholder in YZ who held 6 shares had a value of £18.36 but will now have 5 shares in the combined entity worth £19.10. There is therefore a transfer of wealth from the existing AB shareholders to the YZ shareholders. This would partly explain the 10% fall in the AB share price and the 14% increase in YZ's. However, AB clearly feel there are substantial savings to be made as they are offering cash of £3.45 per YZ share.

This gives a combined market value of £167.37m × 11 = £1,841m or £4.60 per share. Original AB shareholders gain 70p per share and original YZ shareholders [(5 × 4.60) − (6 × 3.06)]/6 = 77p per original share.

The dividend valuation model estimates the share value for each company as:

$$AB = \frac{(0.3545 \times 1.04)}{(0.13 - 0.04)} = £4.10 \text{ per share}$$

$$YZ = \frac{(0.4375 \times 1.04)}{(0.11 - 0.04)} = £6.50 \text{ per share}$$

This would suggest that AB is slightly undervalued, but that YZ is hugely undervalued in the marketplace. It is possible that the market does not believe YZ's growth estimates, given its poor performance to date.

(b) **Factors to consider**

In considering whether to accept or reject the bid, and whether to take shares or cash, we need to consider the following:

The market does not appear to believe the growth rate predicted by YZ.
In the short term, target companies tend to gain most.
YZ share price is near its lowest level for the year, suggesting that AB are buying when our price is depressed.
If we reject the bid, will AB improve the terms?
Cash may give rise to a tax charge.
We do not know what AB's future dividend policy will be.

(c) **Recommendations**

It is difficult to make a definite recommendation, as it will depend on shareholders' views of the future. We could sell for cash, at a higher price than our shares are currently worth. Alternatively, we could accept shares if we feel the AB management will revitalise the company.

A final possibility would be to reject the bid and continue to push for the Board of YZ to be replaced. Some of the valuations considered suggest that we are very undervalued by the market.

Question 4 – TDC

MEMORANDUM

To: Directors of TDC Inc.
From: Financial Manager
Date: xx of x 2003

Bid for UED plc

This memo will discuss the impact of the recent price movements, recommend revised terms and evaluate the strategic implications of a hostile bid as against organic growth.

(a) *Impact of recent price movements*

In the last month our share price has fallen 9% from $12.45 to $11.36 while UED's has risen by 40% from £3.05 to £4.25. Even though the bid was only made four days ago, it appears the stock market had already anticipated it.

The market would appear to think that our management can get better growth in the earnings than UED and have allowed for this benefit in the price. Additionally, it is likely that they are aware bidders usually pay more than the target company appears to be worth in order to gain control.

Our share price has fallen, which suggests that the market feels we are likely to offer more than it will be worth to us, thus decreasing shareholders' wealth.

We will need to offer a cash alternative at some stage, which is likely to mean raising more finance, probably debt; cash stands at $125 million, which is probably not enough to cover those that want the cash alternative, and UED's cash may be spent by the time we acquire it.

(b) *Recommended revised terms*

The current bid terms are 1 TDC share for 2 UED share; based on today's prices, the TDC share is worth $11.36 while 2 UED shares are worth $13 at today's exchange rate. The bid needs to be increased to be successful; without allowing for any other changes in share prices (which is unlikely) it would need to increase to 4 TDC shares (worth $45.44) for 7 UED shares (worth $45.50).

Using our own cost of equity and assuming 100% payout ratio, we can calculate the growth which the market has already assumed in the current price:

$$6.50 = \frac{[6.50/13.5 \times (1 + g)]}{(0.12 - g)}$$

which gives $g = 4.3\%$ per annum

Therefore, we should only raise our bid to that recommended above if we feel that we can achieve in excess of this growth rate. At these terms, all of the benefits of the 4.3% growth will accrue to the existing shareholders of UED.

A cash alternative will also need to be offered, as many UK shareholders may not want American shares. This may require raising additional debt finance; if all the shareholders required the cash alternative we would need to raise an additional $[(6.50 \times 145m) - 225m]$ or 717m.

Thus for the combined group, market values might be:

```
Equity = 1,363 + 943 = 2,306
Debt   = 717 + 365   = 1,082
                       $3,388m
```

The gearing in this worst-case scenario would rise to 32%, which is more than double the industry average, which may mean that shareholders will feel interest cover will be at risk.

These calculations are approximations based on a number of assumptions, and using the current market valuations and exchange rate. The asset value per share is $6.88 for TDC and $2.43 for UED; given that they are in the same industry it would seem that UED's assets are either undervalued or much older than TDC's and probably need replacing. This may affect the amount we are prepared to offer for the company.

(c) *Strategic implications of a hostile bid*

The advantages of making a hostile bid as opposed to organic growth include:

- It reduces the competition, and allows a large increase in market share quickly.
- Allows some diversification of risk, unless the companies are identical.
- Will achieve the company's strategic aims more quickly than organic growth.

However, disadvantages include:

- Evidence suggests that hostile bid purchases tend to overpay for the business.
- It is expensive to integrate two businesses and it is particularly difficult after a hostile bid when the people who work in the two organisations are probably against the change.

Question 5 – RD

(a) **Post acquisition values**

(i) *Mr Jones' estimate*

Mr Jones has used RD's P/E ratio to deduce a value from the combined earnings:

$12.5 \times £10m = £125m$
Share price $= £125m/15m = £8.33$ per share
EPS $= £10m/15m = £0.67$

Value of one old LO share $= £8.33 \times 10/15 = £5.55$

(ii)

REPORT

To: Shareholders
From: Management Accountant
Date: xx of x 20xx

Acquisition of LO plc by RD plc

Assuming that no synergy arises, the value of the combined group will be the sum of the values of the parts.

Value $= (12.5 \times £2.5m) + (7.5 \times £7.5m) = £87.5m$

The share price will then be, assuming the terms of 10 RD shares for every 15 LO is taken up, $£87.5m/15m = £5.83$.

Before the acquisition, RD's share price was $£0.50 \times 12.5 = £6.25$, so each RD shareholder will lose 42p per share, a total of £2.1 million from this group being transferred in value to the old shareholders of LO. Without any synergy, it would seem likely that RD's shareholders will not proceed on these terms, while LO's shareholders will gain and will want it to go ahead. As the bidder has already made a bid, it is unlikely that it can be retracted, and RD's shareholders must hope that the 'turnaround' of LO will generate substantial savings.

(b) **New information**

Value without synergy = £87.5m
Admin. savings = £5m
Assets sale = 10/1.15 = £8.7m
Income increase = 7.5/0.15 = £50m
Market capitalisation = £151.2m

Share price = £151.2m/15m = £10.08 per share.

Existing shareholders in RD thus gain £3.83 per share or a total of £19.15 million. As the total synergy has a value of £63.7 million, the main part of the gain (£44.55 million) is still going to the current LO shareholders. It appears that LO's performance has been erratic in the past and LO's shareholders may not have many other options available to them. RD should therefore try to restructure the deal so that the majority of the synergistic gains accrues to the RD shareholders.

If the synergy could be achieved by LO combining with a number of companies, it would raise its value as they could approach other possible purchasers. This would have the effect of increasing their share of the savings achieved.

Question 6 – PCO plc

(a) **Values before the acquisition**

	PCO	OT
Current Market Value	9.67 × 40 = £386.8 m	10.20 × 24 = £244.8 m
PE Ratio	967/106 = 9.1	1020/92 = 11.1
Dividend Valuation		
Cost of Equity	4 + (4 × 0.9) = 7.6%	4 + (4 × 1.2) = 8.8%
Share Price	(32 × 1.05)/(0.076 − 0.05) = 1292p	
Prospective Market Value	12.92 × 40 = £516.8 m	

Note that the value for OT cannot be calculated in the dividend valuation model as the prospective growth rate exceeds the cost of equity.

(b) (i) *Price to be offered*

- As a going concern which has its shares traded on a public exchange, the asset valuation of £145 m is likely to be some way below any income valuation.
- The total increase in value as a group has been estimated as 720 m − 387 m − 245 m = £88 m.
- PCO should not offer more than 245 + 88 = £333 m but will have to offer more than the current value of £245 m.
- The value of the synergy will need to be split between the two groups of shareholders. A possible offer would be to split it in proportion to the original market values. This would mean offering 245 + (88 × 245/631) = £279 m.

This would give an offer price of £11.62 per share.

(ii) *Form of funding*

Cash

- PCO does not have sufficient cash to fund the acquisition and would have to raise debt finance. Allowing for the £105 m in cash, it would have to raise £174 m (assuming a price of £279 m).
- If PCO has to repay OTs £40 m debt, the finance raised will have to increase by this amount. If they do not have to repay it, then it will still be in the consolidated balance sheet. In either case, debt will rise to 80 + 174 + 40 = £294 m which exceeds shareholders' funds in the balance sheet.

Shares

- A share for share exchange would need to be calculated to ensure that each original group gains by the agreed amount.
- If we wish £279 m to be the value of the bid, this gives a gain of £34 m to OT shareholders and £54 m to PCO shareholders.

  If X = number of new shares issued, then:
  $720 \times 40/(40 + X) = 387 + 54$ giving X = 25.306 m shares
  This gives an exchange of 1.0544 PCO shares for every OT share.

- Unfortunately, such an offer may well be rejected as on current share prices, it would mean losing on the exchange for the OT shareholders:
  24 m × £10.20 = £244.8 m becomes 25.306 m × £9.67 = £244.7 m
- The management will, therefore, have to make very clear the benefits of the acquisition for shareholders, and specify the value of £88 m.
- As soon as this becomes widely known, the share prices of each company will, in theory, move towards the post-merger values of £441 m and £279 m, which give share prices of £11.025 and £11.625. This equates to a correct exchange of 1.0544 PCO shares for every OT share, and the gain of £88 m has been apportioned by market forces before the acquisition takes place.
- In practice, the share prices would be different, due to the risk of the deal not going through, as well as because of market speculation and the imperfect information held by the market.
- Issuing another 25 m or so new shares would need approval to increase the authorised share capital as it only has leeway of another 20 m. This might be one way to encourage the share price to rise if investors anticipated a bid, thus making any eventual offer appear more attractive.

(iii) *Business implications*

- It is likely to be a hostile bid, which will involve extensive costs for advisors.
- Market activity and speculation may drive the share price of OT so high that a bid offer becomes unattractive or PCO increases its bid so that virtually all the gains pass to the OT shareholders.
- Given the nature of the businesses, there may be some reduction in petrol delivery costs but it is difficult to see this being worth £88 m and the disadvantage is that PCO will lose a degree of flexibility in its suppliers.
- A rights issue of equity rather than debt might be more appropriate if a cash purchase is intended. Alternatively, a choice of cash or shares could be given to help keep the gearing down.
- Other possible acquisition targets should be considered and analysed before settling on OT as there may be more synergy available through other combinations.

Part 4

Investment Decisions and Project Control

Investment Appraisal

📝 Exam focus

This is a large area but one with plenty of easy marks available. Make sure you can apply the basic appraisal methods and identify relevant costs for a net present value. Tax, inflation and working capital will often appear in NPV questions, while asset replacement and capital rationing are likely to be stand-alone topics.

🔑 Key points

Appraisal methods

Payback period
The payback period is the time taken to recoup the initial investment (in cash terms).

Advantages

Use cash
Emphasises liquidity
Simple

Disadvantages

No account of time value of money
Ignores cash flows after payback period

Accounting rate of return (ARR)

$$\text{ARR} = \frac{\text{Average annual profit}}{\text{Investment}}$$

Although normally calculated on initial investment, longer projects may be assessed based on average investment. This is the net book value halfway through the project's life.

Advantages

Similar approach to ROCE
Uses accounting figures

Disadvantages

No account of time value of money
Needs a target percentage
Percentages are relative and misleading in comparisons

Net present value

NPV = present value of cash inflows − present value of cash outflows

Advantages

Takes account of time value of money
Theoretical link to shareholders wealth
Looks at cash and considers whole project
Builds risk into discount rate

Disadvantages

Estimates of discount rate
Not easily understood
Does not build in all risks

Internal rate of return

This is the return the project gives, on a discounted cash-flow basis. It can be calculated by finding the discount rate which would completely absorb the returns from the project and give an NPV of zero.

This can be estimated using two discount rates and their NPVs, using the formulae

$$IRR = r_1 + (r_2 - r_1)\frac{(NPV_1)}{NPV_1 - NPV_2}$$

Advantages

Takes account of time value of money

Does not rely on exact estimate of cost of capital

Disadvantages

Can have multiple IRR (up to as many as changes in sign of cash flow)
Percentage is relative
No direct connection to shareholders wealth
Not designed for comparing projects

Conflict between NPV and IRR

When choosing between two mutually exclusive projects, you may get conflicting results with NPV and IRR. Where this is the case choose the project with the higher NPV.

Alternatively, a modified IRR can be used, which compounds all future cash flows to the final year at the cost of capital. It then calculates the IRR based on the initial investment and the single final value representing all other cash flows.

Relevant costs in a net present value

In making investment decisions, relevant costs are crucial. We need to identify *future, incremental cash flows* so that we can assess the impact on the business of undertaking the project compared with not doing so:

Future   ignore 'sunk' costs (i.e. costs already incurred) as they will not change no matter what decision is taken.

Incremental   only include the extra cash flows incurred or earned by undertaking the project (including all the knock-on results).

Cash   only include additional cash flows for the company as a whole, so exclude depreciation (include the full cash expense) and absorbed overheads.

Investment Appraisal

Inflation

If the cash flows are not yet inflated by their specific inflation rates, then we need to calculate the actual cash payment or receipt that will take place.

The cost of capital must also include an allowance for general inflation (the money cost of capital):

$$(1 + m) = (1 + i_g) \times (1 + r)$$

where

m = money cost of capital
i_g = general inflation rate (e.g. RPI)
r = 'real' cost of capital (i.e. excludes inflation)

An alternative approach is not to include inflation but to then exclude the general inflation expected from the cost of capital (i.e. deduce r above, given m and i_g).

Taxation

There are two effects caused by tax for our purposes – tax on operating cash flows and capital allowances.

Assume tax on operating cash flows arises with a 1-year delay unless told otherwise.

Assume capital allowances are taken as soon as possible, that is assume the asset is purchased on the last day of the year, unless told otherwise. Therefore, the capital allowance is obtained immediately and the tax saved 1 year later.

Working capital

Remember that the cash flows to include are the amounts needed to take the working capital up (or down) to the level required for the forthcoming year. Working capital does not attract any tax relief so should be calculated after the tax impacts.

Asset replacement

- Identify all the cash flows associated with purchasing the asset, the initial cost, maintenance charges and scrap value.
- Calculate the present value of the cash flows.
- Calculate the Annual Equivalent Cost of holding the asset over its entire life:

$$AEC = \frac{NPV}{CDF}$$

  where CDF = cumulative discount factor
- Repeat this for each possible length of asset life. The optimum replacement cycle will be that which has the lowest annual equivalent cost.

Capital rationing

Single period capital rationing occurs when there is inadequate funding to finance all of the initial investment needed to undertake all positive net present value projects, but finance is freely available in subsequent years.

Projects can either be divisible, that is the whole or any fraction of the project can be undertaken, or indivisible, that is only the whole project can be undertaken.

A summary of possible situations and approaches is as follows:

Divisible projects   Maximise NPV per £ invested (using profitability index).
Indivisible projects   Consider, by trial and error, the NPV of the different possible combinations.

Questions

Question 1 – Machine (Practice Question)

A company has the chance to invest £100,000 in a machine which will produce the following net cash flows and be sold after 5 years for £10,000:

Year	Net cash flow
1	30,000
2	40,000
3	60,000
4	30,000
5	40,000

Find the payback period, the ARR based on initial and average investment, and the NPV if it has a cost of capital of 10%.

Question 2 – IRR (Practice Question)

Using the information in Question 1, the NPV was £57,000 at a discount rate of 10% and would be £9,000 at a discount rate of 25%. Estimate the Internal Rate of Return.

Question 3 – Labour (Practice Question)

A company is looking at a new contract for which the labour required is:

- Skilled labour 400 hours @ £8 per hour
- Unskilled labour 600 hours @ £5 per hour.

There is currently a shortage of skilled labour in the company and if the contract is accepted it will remove skilled staff from other work on which they generate a net contribution of £7 per hour.

There is currently a large amount of idle time amongst unskilled labour, but the company has refused to lay any staff off. Calculate the relevant cost of labour.

Question 4 – RBS (Practice Question)

A company has just received a last minute order to manufacture a complex component, the RBS 2. RBS 2 is made up of two materials, X and Y. 2,500 kg of material X is required and 1,200 kg of material Y. 5,000 kg of Material X is currently in stock. X originally costs £5 per kg 5 years ago. Its current purchase price is £9 per kg, and if sold today it has an NRV of £4 per kg. 1,200 kg of Material Y is required. Y is used frequently. 1,000 kg of Y is in stock which costs £10 per kg. The supplier has just increased the cost to £12 per kg and it has an NRV of £9 per kg.

RBS 2 will require 100 hours of skilled labour and 40 hours of unskilled labour. The skilled labourers are paid £24,000 per annum and currently have spare capacity. The unskilled labour is at full capacity and currently working on another project. Unskilled labour is paid £5 per hour. The other project is making the RBS 1.

The standard cost card of RBS 1 is as follows:

Price	200
Material cost	60
Labour cost	100
Contribution	40

The manager in charge of RBS 1 will also oversee production of RBS 2. He is currently paid £25,000 and expects to spend 1 week of his time in total on RBS 2.

What is the minimum price the company would accept for manufacturing the RBS 2?

Question 5 – Money (Practice Question)

An investment of £10,000 is to be made and cash inflows of £5,000 per annum for 3 years expected, inflating at 5%. The money cost of capital is 10%.

Calculate the NPV using the money method.

Question 6 – Taxation (Practice Question)

A company buys an asset for £10,000 on the last day of the previous accounting period (31 December 2003). It undertakes a 2-year project generating cash flows of £5,000 in year 1 and 2. The asset is scrapped at the end of year 2 for £4,000.

Corporation tax = 30% with 1-year delay, writing down allowances = 25%.

Discount rate of 10%.

Calculate the NPV.

Question 7 – Cycle (Practice Question)

A company buys a machine costing £50,000. It can replace the machine after 1 or 2 years. The running costs in year 1 and 2 are £10,000 and £12,000 respectively. If the machine is scrapped after one year £35,000 will be received, however if the machine is used for another year the scrap proceeds will only be £25,000. Calculate the optimum replacement cycle if the discount rate used is 10%.

Question 8 – Rationing (Practice Question)

A company has the option of 5 projects, which are all divisible. Capital is rationed to £100,000 at T₀ only. Surplus funds generate 5%.

	A	B	C	D	E
NPV	200	100	(10)	160	54
Initial investment	(100)	(20)	(5)	(40)	(30)

Which projects should the company undertake?

Question 9 – Indivisible (Practice Question)

Using the information in Question 8, advise the company what to do if all the projects are indivisible.

Question 10 – ZX Rationing

The company is considering three other investment opportunities. The initial capital investment required, the NPVs and duration of these three projects are as follows:

	Initial investment £m	NPV £m	Duration Years
Project 1	3.85	0.85	3
Project 2	4.25	0.90	4
Project 3	2.95	0.68	2

However, resource constraints mean that the company cannot invest in all three projects. It wishes to restrict investment to £7.5 million.

Notes

- The projects are not divisible.
- The company has used its cost of capital of 14% to evaluate all three investments.
- Any surplus cash could be invested in the money market at 6%.
- Assume all rates in this part of the question are net of tax.

Requirement

Discuss and recommend, with reasons, which project(s) should be undertaken.

(15 marks)

Question 11 – TFC

The Translavian Ferry Company (TFC) operates four ferries. It wishes to acquire a further new ferry due to high demand for its services from passengers.

At a Board meeting, proposals were put forward for three different methods of financing the new ferry. It was made clear at the meeting that the company is unable to raise any further equity finance.

The ferry being acquired is identical under all three methods of financing. The price of the ferry will be $10 million at 1 January 2004 and it will have a 10-year life. After this time, the terms of the operating licence given by the Translavian government require that the ferry should be scrapped for health and safety reasons. The net proceeds are expected to be zero. The company's accounting year end is 31 December. The company uses an annual net of tax discount rate of 7% to evaluate financing projects.

Method 1 – Long-term lease
The ferry can be leased with equal annual rentals of $2.8 million payable in arrears. The lease term would be 5 years, but this can be extended indefinitely, at the option of the company, at a nominal rent. The lease cannot be cancelled within the minimum lease term

of 5 years. TFC would incur all the maintenance costs of $200,000 per year, payable at the end of each year of the life of the asset.

Method 2 – Short-term lease

The ferry can be leased using a series of separate annual contracts. The annual expected lease rental would be $1.7 million payable annually in advance, with the first payment being on 1 January 2004. Maintenance costs would be paid in full by the lessor. There is no obligation on either party to sign a new annual contract on the termination of the previous lease contract.

Method 3 – Loan

TFC's bank is willing to make a 4-year loan of $10 million so that the ferry can be purchased. Annual repayments would be $3.154 million including both capital and interest. These payments are to be made at the end of each of the four years. The loan would be secured by fixed and floating charges over the company's assets.

Taxation

Taxation payments are made one year after the relevant transaction occurs. The tax rate is 30%. All lease payments, interest payments and maintenance charges are allowable in full for tax. Similarly, the purchase price of the ferry is allowable in full as a tax deduction in the year in which the expenditure is incurred. The company has sufficient profits from the existing ferries to ensure that tax allowances can be offset immediately.

The Marketing Director's view

After the meeting, the Marketing Director expressed concerns about the Board's decision to consider only the three funding methods proposed. He argued that: 'All three methods involve financing charges. Yet we can obtain just about enough cash to fund the new ferry from our own resources, even though we may need to sell some of our short-term investments. Why should we pay interest and other finance charges to outsiders when we can fund the new ferry for free ourselves?'

Requirements

(a) Calculate the pre-tax rate of interest implicit in the 4-year loan under financing Method 3 above.

(4 marks)

(b) Calculate the present values at 1 January 2004 of Method 1 and of Method 2 for financing the new ferry. Use the specified annual net of tax discount rate of 7%.

(9 marks)

(c) As a consultant, write a memorandum to the Board of TFC which:

   (i) discusses the non-quantitative factors that should be considered when deciding which of the three methods of financing the new ferry is the most appropriate; and

   (ii) evaluates the concerns of the Marketing Director.

(12 marks)
(Total = 25 marks)

Question 12 – Expansion

The directors of XYZ plc wish to expand the company's operations. However, they are not prepared to borrow at the present time to finance capital investment. The directors have therefore decided to use the company's cash resources for the expansion programme.

Three possible investment opportunities have been identified. Only £400,000 is available in cash and the directors intend to limit their capital expenditure over the next 12 months to this amount. The projects are not divisible (i.e. cannot be scaled down) and none of them can be postponed. The following cash flows do not allow for inflation which is expected to be 10% per annum constant for the foreseeable future.

Expected net cash flows (including residual values)

Project	Initial Investment	Year 1	Year 2	Year 3
	£	£	£	£
A	−£350,000	95,000	110,000	200,000
B	−105,000	45,000	45,000	45,000
C	−35,000	−40,000	−25,000	125,000

The company's shareholders currently require a return of 15% nominal on their investment for any project of a similar risk to the current operations.

Ignore taxation for any projects of a similar risk to the current operations.

Requirements

(a) (i) Calculate the expected net present value and profitability indexes of the three projects, and

(ii) comment on which project(s) should be chosen for investment, assuming the company can invest surplus cash in the money market at 10% (*Note*: You should assume that the £400,000 expenditure limit is the absolute maximum the company wishes to spend).

(12 marks)

(b) Discuss whether the company's decision not to borrow, thereby limiting investment expenditure, is in the best interests of its shareholders.

(13 marks)
(Total = 25 marks)

✓ Answers

Question 1 – Machine

Year	Cumulative cash (£'000)
0	(100)
1	(70)
2	(30)
3	30

So payback period is 2½ years

$$\text{Average annual profit} = \frac{(200,000 - 90,000)}{5}$$
$$= 22,000$$

$$\text{ARR (Initial inv)} = \frac{22,000}{100,000} = 22\%$$

$$\text{Average investment} = \frac{(100,000 + 10,000)}{2}$$
$$= 55,000$$

$$\text{ARR (Average inv)} = \frac{22,000}{55,000} = 40\%$$

Time	Cash flow £'000	Discount factor	PV £'000
0	(100)	1	(100)
1	30	0.909	27
2	40	0.826	33
3	60	0.751	45
4	30	0.683	21
5	*50	0.62	31
			NPV = 57

* includes scrap value

Question 2 – IRR

Discount rate (%)	NPV (£)
10	57,000
25	9,000

IRR = 25% + (15% × 9/48) = 27.8%

Using formula:

$$\text{IRR} = 10\% + (25\% - 10\%) \frac{57,000}{57,000 - 9,000}$$

$$= 10\% + (15\% \times 1.1875) = 27.8\%$$

Question 3 – Labour

Skilled = 400 × (8 + 7) = 6,000
Unskilled = 600 × 0   = 0
Relevant cost   = £6,000

Question 4 – RBS

Material X	2,500 kg @ £4 per kg	10,000
Material Y	1,200 kg @ £12 per kg	14,400
Skilled labour	Spare capacity	Nil

Unskilled labour: Alternative project
        Lose SP   (200)
        Save material 60
        Save labour   Nil
        Lost CPU   £140 per unit

An RBS 1 takes 20 hours
An RBS 2 requires 40 hours of unskilled labour

Therefore lose 2 units of RBS 1, losing 2 units × £140 per unit   280
Minimum acceptable price   = 24,680

Question 5 – Money

Money method

	T_0	T_1	T_2	T_3
CFs	(10,000)	5,250	5,513	5,788
DR	1	0.909	0.826	0.751
PV	(10,000)	4,772	4,554	4,347

NPV = 3,673

Question 6 – Taxation

	T_0	T_1	T_2	T_3
CF		5,000	5,000	
Tax @ 30%			(1,500)	(1,500)
Investment	(10,000)			
Scrap			4,000	
WDA		750	563	488
Net CF	(10,000)	5,750	8,063	(1,012)
DR	1	0.909	0.826	0.751
PV	(10,000)	5,227	6,660	(760)

NPV   1,127

			10,000		
31/12/2003	WDA		(2,500)	750	T_1
			7,500		
31/12/2004	WDA		(1,875)	563	T_2
			5,625		
31/12/2005	SCRAP		(4,000)		
			1,625		
	BA		(1,625)	488	T_3
			0		

Question 7 – Cycle

Replace after 1 year			DF	PV	Replace in 2 years	DF	PV
Investment	T_0	(50,000)	1	(50,000)	(50,000)	1	(50,000)
Running costs	T_1	(10,000)	0.909	(9,090)	(10,000)	0.909	(9,090)
Running costs	T_2	N/A			(12,000)	0.826	(9,912)
Scrap	T_1 or T_2	35,000	0.909	31,815	25,000	0.826	20,650
				(27,275)			(48,352)
		AEC		$\dfrac{27,275}{0.909}$			$\dfrac{48,352}{1.735}$
				(30,006)			(27,869)

Therefore, the machine should be replaced every 2 years as the annual equivalent cost is cheaper.

Question 8 – Rationing

Project	A	B	C	D	E
PV of future cash flows	300	120	5	200	84
Investment	100	20	5	40	30
Profitability index	3	6		5	2.8
Ranking	3	1		2	4

So with £100,000, we can undertake B, D and 40% of A.

Question 9 – Indivisible

A alone for £100,000 investment generates £200,000 NPV. B, D and E together use £90,000 to generate £314,000 NPV along with the income generated by the surplus £10,000.

Therefore invest in B, D and E.

Question 10 – ZX rationing

Possible combinations	Investment	NPV
1 and 3	£6.8m	£1.53m
2 and 3	£7.2m	£1.58m

Therefore, as profits are indivisible, we should invest in projects 2 and 3; this will leave £0.3 million excess cash which can be put to the money market for the short term. This is not a long-term option, however, as the return is below that required by shareholders.

As all three projects have positive NPVs, it would be sensible to look for additional funds, or to lift its restrictions, so that all can be undertaken for the additional £3.55 million.

The company has used 14% to assess all three projects, but they might have different risk characteristics which would suggest different required returns.

If the projects had been divisible, the decision would be different:

Project	NPV/£ invested
1	0.22
2	0.21
3	0.23

This would suggest that projects 3 and 1 should be undertaken, with the remaining finance of £0.7 million used to do approximately 16% of project 2, giving an overall NPV of £1.68 million.

Question 11 – TFC

(a) **Pre-tax implicit interest rate**

Rate given by 10m = 3.154m × 4 year Annuity Factor

4 year AF = 3.171

From the tables, this gives the implicit rate as approximately 10% per annum.

(b) **Present values**

Method 1 (long-term lease)

PV of rentals	= 2.8m × 4.1	= (11.48m)
PV of maintenance	= 0.2m × 7.024	= (1.405m)
PV tax relief of rentals	= (11.48 × 0.30)/1.07 =	3.219m
PV tax relief of maintenance	= (1.405 × 0.30)/1.07 =	0.394m
		(9.272m)

Method 2 (short-term lease)

PV of rentals	= 1.7m × (6.515 + 1)	= (12.776m)
PV of tax relief	= (12.776 × 0.30)/1.07 =	3.582m
		(9.194m)

(c)

MEMORANDUM

To: Board of TFC
From: Consultant
Date: xx of xx 2003

Financing considerations

The three methods of financing considered are likely to have similar financial results in a competitive market, but other, non-financial, considerations may be important.

1 *Risk*

   The short-term lease covers the potential breakdown of the ferry, whereas the others do not. The short-term lease is also renewed annually, which means we cannot guarantee that the terms will remain the same, unlike the other two proposals.

   On the other hand, the short-term lease allows TFC to terminate the operation earlier than planned if circumstances change.

2 *Security on assets*

   The bank loan is likely to be secured on other assets of the company in the form of fixed or floating charges. The lease arrangements will only give the lessor the right to reclaim the ferry if the lease payments are not kept up, even if the value of the ferry is exceeded by the amounts owed.

3 *Cash flow*

   The loan is payable over 4 years, while the long-term lease is payable over 5 years and the short-term over the full 10 years. This gives the short-term lease a significant cash-flow advantage. This is despite having to pay annually in advance (the other two are in arrears).

4 *Gearing ratios*

   The long-term lease is probably classified as a finance lease and would therefore be included as an asset and long-term debt, like the bank loan. The short-term lease is probably an operating lease, which would not affect the balance sheet. There could therefore be a difference in the gearing ratios calculated, which can be specified as covenants for debt finance.

5 *Marketing Director's View*

   The Marketing Director feels that internal resources should be used to finance the new ferry. This is sensible if the company has sufficient cash resources as it will involve no arrangement fees and the lost investment income is likely to be lower than the interest rate charged by an outside provider of finance.

   However, internal cash is not costless as it belongs to the company, which in turn belongs to the shareholders; they require a return on the funds used which matches the risk they perceive in the investment.

6 *Conclusion*

   It might be sensible to use some of the company's own resources, leaving some for other opportunities that might present themselves, and some externally. This might suggest the straight loan, rather than leasing, which can be reduced to the amount required. However, this will depend on the confidence of the company in being able to meet the cash-flow commitments and the importance of maintaining a certain gearing ratio.

Question 12 – Expansion

(a)

(i) *PV of future cash flows*

In £'000	A	B	C
t_1	$95 \times 1.1/1.15 = 91$	$45 \times 1.1/1.15 = 43$	$(40) \times (1.1/1.15) = (38)$
t_2	$110 \times (1.1/1.15)^2 = 101$	$45 \times (1.1/1.15)^2 = 41$	$(25) \times (1.1/1.15)^2 = (23)$
t_3	$200 \times (1.1/1.15)^3 = 175$	$45 \times (1.1/1.15)^3 = 39$	$125 \times (1.1/1.15)^3 = 109$
	367	123	43
t_0 Investment	(350)	(105)	(35)
NPV	17	18	13
Profitability Index	1.05	1.17	1.37

(ii) *Decision*

As the shareholders require 15%, it is not worthwhile putting money on deposit at 10% (it would have a negative NPV).

It should therefore be returned to the shareholders in the form of dividends or share buybacks. In practice this may seem unlikely, and it is likely that shareholders would require a substantially lower return on a bank deposit, as it is lower risk, leading to a zero NPV: shareholders would then be indifferent as to the amount on cash put in deposit.

Possibilities	Investment	NPV
A and C	£385,000	£30,000
B and C	£140,000	£31,000

(other possibilities of A, B or C alone will obviously give less)

So invest in projects B and C.

(b) **The interests of the shareholders**

A company has to balance its investment decisions against the financing decision, either using external finance or internal funds, possibly impacting on the dividend policy.

If we assume shareholders' best interests to mean maximising shareholder wealth via the share price, the company would want to undertake all positive NPV projects if it had sufficient finance. This, in theory in an efficient market, would increase the share price; however, raising external finance will involve issue costs which will reduce shareholder value, and reducing the level of dividends might reduce the share price if shareholders were relying on this cash stream.

Whether the company has arrived at the right compromise in committing the expenditure to £400,000 and not borrowing will depend on a number of factors:

- The volatility of the company's operating cash flow; if these are highly volatile, additional gearing will put the returns to shareholders at risk and thus increase the risk perceived and the cost of equity while decreasing the value.
- The current level of gearing, as the company may not be able to manage additional interest payments easily, and it may not be able to raise more if it has no further assets for security.
- The need to respond flexibly to situations as they arise may be important in the industry; debt financing is often long term with structural repayments and interest, which can then affect the operational choices.
- The tax position as debt interest is allowable for tax purposes but a nil tax paying position (possibly due to losses carried forward) would make additional debt finance less attractive.

Risk in Investment Appraisal 12

✎ Exam focus

As far as the exam is concerned, it is important that you can discuss why the investment appraisal methods do not give an exact prediction. You should be able to demonstrate various methods for assessing the risk, particularly sensitivity analysis, and discuss post-investment audits.

🔑 Key points

Uncertainty

All investment appraisal projects have to deal with uncertainty; cash flows have to be forecast, tax rates estimated for the whole project and discount rates have to be estimated.

Such uncertainty can be allowed for by using:

An increased discount rate – to reflect the amount of risk associated with the cash flows.

Certainty equivalents to reduce the value of the cash flows.

Sensitivity analysis to look at how the NPV of the project changes when one factor is changed and hence identify the crucial estimates.

To calculate the sensitivity of a cash-flow estimate:

$$\% \text{ Sensitivity} = \frac{\text{NPV}}{\text{PV cash flow considered}}$$

To calculate the sensitivity to sales volume, use contribution as the denominator in the above formula.

To calculate the sensitivity to the discount rate, calculate the IRR.

Remember it can only deal with one changing variable at a time and the result does not indicate the likelihood of the variable changing, it only quantifies the amount by which the variable can change.

Expected values can be used if probabilities are estimated; alternatively the various possible outcomes can be calculated and the probability of each assessed.

Real options

Traditional NPV only includes predictable cash flows. In some situations this may exclude considerable benefits or costs, often of a strategic nature, which cannot be estimated, such as options on timing or abandonment and other market benefits.

It can be very difficult to value these options, but the NPV clearly does not take account of all the project consequences and needs to be balanced against these more qualitative factors.

Post-implementation audits

As estimates are used in the assessment of projects, it is sensible to monitor performance against estimates, and to introduce greater realism into future estimates.

Questions

Question 1 – Rock (Practice Question)

Rock Ltd invests £100,000, and proposes to make exclusive rocking chairs for 10 years. The company will plan to make 250 chairs per annum, earning a contribution of £151 per chair. Fixed costs are expected to be £17,500 per annum and the scrap value of machinery after 10 years is forecast at £10,000.

Ignore tax and writing down allowances, and use a discount rate of 15%.

Calculate the NPV and the sensitivity to the:

- initial investment
- volume
- contribution
- fixed costs
- scrap.

Question 2 – X training

All of the 100 accountants employed by X Ltd are offered the opportunity to attend six training courses per year. Each course lasts for several days and requires the delegates to travel to a specially selected hotel for the training. The current costs incurred for each course are:

Delegate costs

	£ per delegate per course
Travel	200
Accommodation, food and drink	670
	870

It is expected that the current delegate costs will increase by 5% per annum.

Course costs

	£ per course
Room hire	1,500
Trainers	6,000
Course material	2,000
Equipment hire	1,500
Course administration	750
	11,750

It is expected that the current course costs will increase by 2.5% per annum.

The Human Resources Director of X Ltd is concerned at the level of costs that these courses incur and has recently read an article about the use of the Internet for the delivery of training courses (e-learning). She decided to hire an external consultant at a cost of £5,000 to advise the company on how to implement an e-learning solution. The consultant prepared a report which detailed the costs of implementing and running an e-learning solution:

	Notes	£
Computer hardware	(1)	1,500,000
Software licences	(2)	35,000 pa
Technical Manager	(3)	30,000 pa
Camera and sound crew	(4)	4,000 per course
Trainers and course material	(5)	2,000 per course
Broadband connection	(6)	300 per delegate per annum

Notes

1. The computer hardware will be depreciated on a straight-line basis over 5 years. The scrap value at the end of the 5 years is expected to be £50,000.
2. The company would sign a software licence agreement which fixes the annual software licence fee for 5 years. This fee is payable in advance.
3. An employee working in the IT Department currently earning £20,000 per annum will be promoted to Technical Manager for this project. This employee's position will be replaced. The salary of the Technical Manager is expected to increase by 6% per annum.
4. The company supplying the camera and sound crew for recording the courses for Internet delivery has agreed to hold its current level of pricing for the first 2 years but then it will increase costs by 6% per annum. All courses will be recorded in the first quarter of the year of delivery.
5. The trainers will charge a fixed fee of £2,000 per course for the delivery and course material in the first year and expect to increase this by 6% per annum thereafter. The preparation of the course material and the recording of the trainers delivering the courses will take place in the first quarter of the year of delivery.
6. All of the accountants utilising the training courses will be offered £300 towards broadband costs which will allow them to access the courses from home. They will claim this expense annually in arrears. Broadband costs are expected to decrease by 5% per annum after the first year as it becomes more widely used by Internet users.

X Ltd uses a 14% cost of capital to appraise projects of this nature.

Ignore taxation.

Requirements

As the Management Accountant for X Ltd,

(a) Prepare a financial evaluation of the options available to the company and advise the directors on the best course of action to take, from a purely financial point of view. (Your answer should state any assumptions you have made.)

(16 marks)

(b) (i) Using the annual equivalent technique, calculate the breakeven number of delegates per annum taking each of the six e-learning courses that is required to justify the implementation of the e-learning solution. (Note that you should assume that the number of delegates taking the e-learning courses will be the same in each of the 5 years.)

(6 marks)

(ii) Comment on the implementations of the breakeven number you have calculated in your answer to (b) (i).

(3 marks)
(Total = 25 marks)

Question 3 – HS and IT

HS and IT are both manufacturing companies which trade in similar industries. However, HS is a much larger company with more diversified markets, and trades internationally. By comparison, IT trades solely in its domestic market. Comparative data on these two companies is as follows:

	HS	IT
Sales revenue	US$2.5 billion	US$1.2 million
Gross profit margin	28%	17%
Debt: equity	40%	10%
Shares in issue	200 million	2,000
Number of shareholders	Many	Few
Share price	US$12.60	Not available

Requirement

Compare and evaluate the usefulness or impact of the following variables in the investment appraisal process for these two companies:

1. The use of weighted average cost of capital (WACC) as a discount rate.
2. The use of certainty equivalents compared with using an adjusted discount rate in evaluating the cash flow.
3. The use of payback or accounting rate of return compared with DCF techniques.
4. The influence and effects of taxation on their investment decisions.

(Each item carries up to 7 marks to a maximum of 25 for all four.)

(Total = 25 marks)

Question 4 – SS

SS Ltd is an Internet service provider and also stores and transmits client data over the Internet via its server infrastructure. SS Ltd generates approximately £100,000 in contribution each year from these services to clients.

Because of technical advances in information technology, the existing server infrastructure will shortly become obsolete, and the company is considering what to do. The maintenance of this server infrastructure costs £24,000 per annum and is paid in advance at the beginning of each year. The server infrastructure has been fully written off but has a scrap value of £3,000. A technical consultant hired at a cost of £5,000, prepared a report outlining that two possible replacement server infrastructures are available on the market. The details of each alternative are as follows:

	Alternative 1	Alternative 2
Initial cost	£100,000	£100,000
Estimated useful life	3 years	5 years
Scrap value	£5,000	£3,000
Annual maintenance costs (in advance)	£24,000	£30,000
Annual contributions	£100,000	£105,000

SS Ltd incurs 30% tax on corporate profits. Writing down allowances are allowed at 25% each year on a reducing balance basis. At the end of the server infrastructure's life, a balancing charge or allowance will arise equal to the difference between the scrap proceeds and the tax written down value. Corporation tax is to be paid in two equal instalments: one in the year that profits are earned and the other in the following year.

SS Ltd's after-tax nominal (money) discount rate is 12%.

You can assume that all cash flows occur at the end of each year unless otherwise stated.

Requirements

(a) Calculate for each alternative the net present value and annual equivalent cost. Advise senior management which server infrastructure to purchase, stating any assumptions you have made.

(15 marks)

(b) (i) Briefly explain the purpose and limitations of sensitivity analysis in relation to investment appraisal.

(4 marks)

(ii) Calculate the sensitivity of your recommendation to changes in the contribution generated by Alternative 1, and discuss its relevance to the decision.

(6 marks)
(Total = 25 marks)

✓ Answers

Question 1 – Rock

			15%	
t_0	Invt	(100,000)	1	(100,000)
t_{10}	Scrap	10,000	0.247	2,470
$t_1 - t_{10}$	Cont	37,750	5.019	189,467
$t_1 - t_{10}$	FC	(15,000)	5.019	(87,833)
	NPV			4,104

$$\text{Initial investment} = \frac{4{,}104}{100{,}000} = 4.1\%$$

i.e. the initial investment can increase 4.1% before the NPV becomes zero

$$\text{Volume:} \quad \frac{4{,}104}{189{,}467} = 2.2\%$$

i.e. volume or contribution can fall 2.2% before the NPV becomes zero

$$\text{Fixed costs} = \frac{4{,}104}{87{,}833} = 4.7\%$$

i.e. fixed costs can increase 4.7% before the NPV becomes zero

$$\text{Scrap} = \frac{4{,}104}{2{,}470} = 166\%$$

i.e. the scrap proceeds have to turn negative before the NPV becomes zero!

Question 2 – X training

(a) External training vs e-learning

External training courses

	t_0	t_1	t_2	t_3	t_4	t_5
Delegates		548,100	575,505	604,280	634,494	666,219
Courses		72,263	74,069	75,921	77,819	79,764
		620,363	649,574	680,201	712,313	745,983
DF (14%)		0.877	0.769	0.675	0.592	0.519
PV		544,058	499,522	459,136	421,689	387,165

Total PV of costs = £2,311,570

e-learning

	t_0	t_1	t_2	t_3	t_4	t_5
Hardware	1,500,000					(50,000)
Licence	35,000	35,000	35,000	35,000	35,000	
Manager		30,000	31,800	33,708	35,730	37,874
Crew		24,000	24,000	25,440	26,966	28,584
Trainers		12,000	12,720	13,483	14,292	15,150
Connection		30,000	28,500	27,075	25,721	24,435
	1,535,000	131,000	132,020	134,706	137,709	56,043
DF (14%)	1	0.877	0.769	0.675	0.592	0.519
	1,535,000	114,887	101,523	90,927	81,524	29,086

Total PV of costs = £1,952,947

Therefore, on the basis of these calculations X Ltd should undertake the e-learning option.

Assumptions:

- The delegate and course costs for external training are the current costs and will increase, by the appropriate inflation rate, by next year.
- The consultant's fee is unavoidable and is a sunk cost.
- The Technical Managers' salary is the amount that will be paid in the first year and will inflate thereafter.
- The recording costs are assumed paid at the end of the year, even though the recording takes place in the first quarter.
- As the e-learning investment lasts 5 years, the external training has been evaluated over the same period.

(b) (i) *Breakeven*

If the company changes to e-learning, the fixed costs will be considerably higher. This will only be worthwhile if the variable cost saving more than covers the additional fixed costs.

	Fixed cost (PV)	Variable costs (PV)	
External training	259,048	2,052,524	(delegates)
e-learning	1,858,536	94,411	(broadband)
Difference	1,599,488	1,958,113	
Annual equivalent (divide by 3.432)	466,051	570,546	
		or £5,705	per delegate

Breakeven number of delegates = 466,051/5,705 = 81.7 or 82 delegates.

(ii) *Interpretation*

The company needs at least 82 of the 100 accountants to take up the e-learning in order to make it viable. As this is a high proportion of the 100, it would be sensible to make sure that the accountants were happy to take it up before going ahead.

Question 3 – HS and IT

1 **WACC as a discount rate**

The WACC represents the overall return required from the company's current operations, and should strictly only be used for investment appraisal if the project has the same business risk and is financed in the same proportions as the existing business. However, in a big company, such as HS, a new investment may not be very large compared with the existing operations, so, if no new finance is raised, the WACC might be used as an approximation. IT, being a smaller company, might be looking at relatively larger projects and would need to use an adjusted discount rate, as discussed below, in order to assess the investment accurately.

2 **Certainty equivalents**

Certainty equivalents take account of the risk of the project by reducing the cash flows to those which are reasonably certain, and using a risk-free rate to discount them. The difficulty is in assigning the probabilities, which are highly subjective, to these cash flows. HS might have the expertise available to undertake this, but it is unlikely that IT will.

An adjusted discount rate is a rate which reflects the risk attached to this particular project. Again, this can lead to a subjective risk premium, but one way round this is to look for a company in the same line of business as the project. The cost of capital can then be adjusted for any differences in gearing. This is a more straightforward method and is likely to be used by IT.

3 **Payback and accounting rates return (ARR)**

Payback period and ARR do not use discounted cash flows and are therefore not as theoretically valid as net present value for maximising shareholders' wealth. However, it is difficult to be accurate with a method such as NPV, and so a large company such as HS will probably look at a variety of methods. Often this will be NPV and the payback period. A smaller company, such as IT, will tend to rely on one method, such as payback period.

Payback is easy to use and understand and is a useful screening process to eliminate investments with higher risk. However, it ignores the cash flows after the payback period and so does not give a complete picture.

ARR, by using profits which spread the investment cost over the entire project, and by not discounting, can distort the result, often making the investment appear less viable.

If HS uses a number of methods, it is likely to come to a more informed decision than IT, but this links to its more numerous shareholders and the need for a more structured approach to corporate governance.

4 **Taxation impact on investment decisions**

Tax is a cash flow and also affects the profits generated, so it will have an impact on the investment decision whichever method is used. The impact it has will depend on the extent to which the tax cash flows change. HS is likely to have more scope for relieving taxes as it is a large company, trading internationally, and might be able to take advantage of double taxation treaties, transfer pricing and management charges, and the lower tax rates in some other countries. It might also have tax advisers, although they can be expensive.

Question 4 – SS

(a)

Alternative 1

	t_0	t_1	t_2	t_3	t_4
Contribution		100,000	100,000	100,000	
Maintenance	(24,000)	(24,000)	(24,000)		
	(24,000)	76,000	76,000	100,000	
Tax		(11,400)	(11,400)	(11,400)	
			(11,400)	(11,400)	(11,400)
Investment	(100,000)			5,000	
Tax re: CA's		3,750	2,813	7,687	
			3,750	2,813	7,687
	(124,000)	68,350	59,763	92,700	(3,713)
DF (12%)	1	0.893	0.797	0.712	0.636
PV	(124,000)	61,037	47,631	66,002	(2,361)

NPV = £48,309   so annual equivalent = 48,309/2.402 = £20,112 per annum

Alternative 2

	t_0	t_1	t_2	t_3	t_4	t_5	t_6
Contribution		105,000	105,000	105,000	105,000	105,000	
Maintenance	(30,000)	(30,000)	(30,000)	(30,000)	(30,000)		
	(30,000)	75,000	75,000	75,000	75,000	105,000	
Tax		(11,250)	(11,250)	(11,250)	(11,250)	(11,250)	
			(11,250)	(11,250)	(11,250)	(11,250)	(11,250)
Investment	(100,000)					3,000	
Tax re: CA's		3,750	2,813	2,109	1,582	4,296	
			3,750	2,813	2,109	1,582	4,296
	(130,000)	67,500	59,063	57,422	56,191	91,378	(6,954)
DF (12%)	1	0.893	0.797	0.712	0.636	0.567	0.507
	(130,000)	60,278	47,073	40,884	35,737	51,811	(3,526)

NPV = £102,257   so annual equivalent = 102,257/3.605 = £28,365 per annum

On the basis of these calculations, Alternative 2 will generate the most for the company.

(b)

(i) *Sensitivity analysis*

Sensitivity analysis attempts to identify those variables in which a small change in the estimate would lead to the decision-maker changing their mind. This might mean turning a positive NPV to a negative one, or the ranking of investments changing. Those estimates, which are crucial, can then be re-examined to ensure we are confident about them before deciding to invest.

To calculate the change needed in each variable, we alter one at a time to see how far it must move to give a negative NPV or to change the ranking. Those in which the change needed is small (say less than 10%) will be the crucial estimates.

There are two main limitations of the method. Firstly, only one input is altered at a time even though there might be a much more dramatic impact if a number of estimates proved incorrect at the same time. Secondly, the method gives information on the impact of a change in estimate, but does not attempt to predict how likely this might be.

(ii) *Changes in alternative 1 contribution*

PV of current alternative 1 contribution:
$100{,}000 \times 2.402 = 240{,}200$
$(15{,}000) \times 2.402 = (36{,}030)$ (tax)
$(15{,}000) \times 2.145 = (32{,}175)$ (tax)
£171,995

To change the choice from Alternative 2 to Alternative 1, Annual Equivalent of Alternative 1 must increase to £28,365.

This would give an overall NPV of $28{,}365 \times 2.402 = £68{,}133$

This is an increase in NPV of $68{,}133 - 48{,}309 = £19{,}824$

The contribution must increase by $19{,}824/171{,}995 = 11.53\%$ for this to happen (or by £11,526 pa).

Overseas Investments   13

📝 Exam focus

Many investments made by large companies are now overseas. It is important that you are able to apply a net present value approach to overseas cash flows, although it is unlikely that questions will be particularly complex.

You should ensure that you can calculate the exchange rates and the two discount rates, as well as being able to discuss, and possibly apply, double taxation relief.

🔑 Key points

The investment is assessed from the viewpoint of the UK parent, using sterling cash flows.

However, there are two approaches:

Estimate the cash flows at each point in time and translate them into the home currency using exchange rates derived from Purchasing Power Parity:

$$\text{f/£ Future exchange rate} = \text{f/£ spot rate} \times \frac{1 + \text{foreign inflation rate}}{1 + \text{UK inflation rate}}$$

Then discount the cash flows at the company's discount rate.

Alternatively, discount the overseas cash flows at a discount rate which also reflects the changing exchange rate:

$$(1 + r_f) = (1 + r_£) \frac{\text{f/£ future rate}}{\text{f/£ spot rate}}$$

Where r = discount rate

Then translate all the cash flows at the current exchange rate and total these.

Questions

Question 1 – GH

GH plc is a UK-based retailing company that operates in the USA and UK. The company is evaluating the potential for expansion into Europe, starting in France. A detailed assessment of the costs and likely incremental revenues of opening stores in two major French cities has been carried out. The initial cost of the investment is FFr80 million. The nominal cash flows, all positive and net of all taxes, are summarised below.

	Year 1	Year 2	Year 3
Cash flow (FFr million)	35.50	42.50	45.00

The company's treasurer provides the following information:

- The expected inflation rate in France is 4% each year and in the UK 3% each year.
- Real interest rates in the UK and France are the same. They are expected to remain the same for the foreseeable future.
- The current spot rate is FFr8.5 to £1 sterling.
- The risk-free annual rate of interest in France is 6% and in the UK 5%. These nominal rates are not expected to change in the foreseeable future.
- The company's post-tax weighted average cost of capital (WACC) is 15%, which it uses to evaluate all investment decisions.

The expansion will be financed by a combination of internal funds generated in the UK and long-term fixed interest rate debt raised in France. The company plans to purchase in France the majority of its goods for resale.

Requirements

(a) Calculate the £ Sterling net present value of the project, using both the following methods:

 (i) by discounting annual cash flows in £ sterling;
 (ii) by discounting annual cash flows in FFr, using an adjusted discount rate; and
   explain, briefly, the reasons why the two methods give almost identical answers.
   (9 marks)

(b) Assume that the company's management is considering purchasing from outside France a substantial proportion of its goods to be sold in the French stores. Approximately 50% of total goods for resale might be purchased in the Far East and a further 25% in the UK. Discuss how a decision to change buying patterns might affect the evaluation and funding of the investment.

(8 marks)

(c) Assume that inflation in France turns out to be higher than forecast for the whole period of evaluation, with corresponding impact on the other economic factors. Inflation in the UK is slightly less than forecast. Discuss how the financial returns on the investment might be affected, and advise on a funding strategy that could minimise the impact of such inflationary effects.

(8 marks)

Note: Parts (b) and (c) are independent – that is, part (c) is not dependent upon the answer to part (b).

(Total = 25 marks)

Question 2 – KH

KH is a large food and drink retailer based in the United States of America. To date, the company has operated only in the US but is planning to expand into South America by acquiring a group of stores similar to those operated in the US. Projected cash flows in the US and South America for the first three years of the project, in real terms, are estimated as follows:

	Year 0	Year 1	Year 2	Year 3
Cash flows in USA:				
In US$'000	−10,000	−300	−400	−500
Cash flows in the South American country:				
In SA Currency'000	−1,000,000	+250,000	+350,000	+450,000

US$ cash flows are mainly incremental administration costs associated with the project. SA currency cash flows are cash receipts from sales less all related cash costs and expenses.

The exchange rate for the South American country's currency is extremely volatile. Inflation is currently 40% a year. Inflation in the US is 4% a year. Best estimates by KH's treasurer suggest these rates are likely to continue for the foreseeable future. The current exchange rate is SA currency 30 to US$1.

The following information is relevant:

- KH evaluates all investments using nominal cash flows and a nominal discount rate;
- SA currency cash flows are converted into US$ and discounted at a risk-adjusted US rate;
- All cash flows for this project will be discounted at 20%, a nominal rate judged to reflect its high risk;
- For the purposes of evaluation, assume the year 3 nominal cash flows will continue to be earned each year indefinitely.

Note: Ignore taxation.

Requirements

Assume that you are the Financial Manager of KH. Prepare a report to the Finance Director that evaluates the proposed investment. Include in your report the following:

(a) Calculation of the net present value of the proposed investment and a recommendation as to whether the company should proceed with the investment, supported by your reasons for the recommendation.

(12 marks)

(b) Discussion of the main political risks that might be faced by the company and provision of advice on management strategies that could be implemented to counter those risks.

(13 marks)
(Total = 25 marks)

Question 3 – TMC

TMC is a large cosmetic and toiletries retail organisation based in a country within the European common currency zone. Its current turnover is approximately Euro 1.4 billion and it has an asset base of Euro 750 million.

The company is evaluating opening up to 10 new retail outlets in a country in Asia, to be financed by its existing cash or other highly liquid assets. It proposes to operate these new retail outlets itself for the first two years of operation. After that time, and subject to satisfactory commercial and financial performance, each outlet will be offered as a franchise to either the outlet manager/employees or to a third party.

Forecast nominal cash flows for the first two years of operation for a single outlet are as follows:

	Year 0 Asian $m	Year 1 Asian $m	Year 2 Asian $m
Initial investment	−15		
Pre-tax operating cash flows		4.5	5.5
Exchange rate information is as follows:			
Spot rate as at today Euro/Asian $		0.65	
Forecast inflation rates (% per annum)			
European common currency area		1.50	
Asian country		3.50	

Estimated cash flows beyond year 2 depend on the type of operation. If the company continues to operate the outlet, it assumes zero growth per year on year 2's post-tax Euro operating cash flows until the end of year 10. Cash flows beyond year 10 are ignored. If the outlet is franchised, there will be a one-off taxable payment by the franchisee at the beginning of year 3 of Asian $500,000 plus an annual payment in perpetuity of Asian $3.2 million (both figures in time 3 money), commencing at the end of year 3.

Additional information

- Corporate taxes in the Asian country are 30% per annum, payable or refundable the year in which the liability to tax arises. In the European country, they are 35% payable or refundable the following year. Double taxation agreements are in force between the two countries. Both countries allow 100% writing-down allowance for investments of this type.
- TMC uses 9% as the discount rate in its investment appraisals.
- All operating cash flows may be assumed to occur at the end of each year. The initial capital investment will be made at the beginning of year 1 and written off over 5 years.
- TMC evaluates international investments by converting the foreign currency cash flows to Euros and applying its domestic cost of capital.

Requirement

Evaluate the proposed investment and recommend whether it should proceed. You should include in your evaluation some discussion of the risks that might be associated with the two alternative methods of operation being considered after year 2 and advise on how these risks might be managed.

(Total = 25 marks)

Notes: Up to 10 marks are available for calculations. A report structure is not required for this question.

Question 4 – AB overseas

AB plc manufactures products for children. The company's turnover and earnings last year were £56 million and £3.5 million respectively. Its shares are not listed but they occasionally change hands in private transactions. AB plc's weighted average cost of capital (WACC) is 13% net of tax. The directors believe that an appropriate gearing ratio (debt to debt + equity) for a company such as AB plc is 30%, which is the industry average. Currently, AB plc's gearing ratio is slightly higher than this at 35%. Its debt comprises two secured long-term bank loans and a permanent overdraft, secured by a floating charge on the company's current assets. The current cost of debt to a company such as AB plc is 10% before tax.

The company is considering expansion outside the UK, in particular in an Eastern European (EE) country where its products have become popular. The EE government has offered AB plc a financing deal to establish a manufacturing operation. The financing would take the form of an EE marks 30 million 6-year loan at a subsidised rate of only 2.5% each year interest. The current exchange rate is EE marks 20 to the £ sterling.

Interest would be payable at the end of each year and the principal repaid at the end of 6 years. The exchange rate of EE marks to the £ would be fixed at the current rate for the whole 6-year period of the loan. The marginal corporate tax rate in both countries is 25%.

Requirements

(a) Calculate the company's present cost of equity and the present value of the EE government subsidy implicit in the loan. Comment briefly on the method used and any assumptions you have made in your calculations.

(7 marks)

(b) Discuss the relevance of both the cost of equity you have calculated in answer to (a) above and the WACC given in the scenario, to the company's investment decision. Include comment on an alternative discount rate that could be used appropriately in the scenario's circumstances.

(6 marks)

(c) (i) Discuss the advantages and disadvantages of using the EE government subsidy in AB plc's international investment decision.
    (ii) Recommend alternative methods of financing that might be suitable for AB plc in the circumstances of the scenario.

(12 marks)
(Total = 25 marks)

Answers

Question 1 – GH

(a)

(i)

	t_0	t_1	t_2	t_3
In FFm	(80)	35.50	42.50	45.00
X/R (W1)	8.500	8.583	8.666	8.750
In £m	(9.41)	4.14	4.90	5.14
DF (15%)	1	0.870	0.756	0.658
PV	(9.41)	3.60	3.70	3.38

NPV = £1.27m

(ii)

	t_0	t_1	t_2	t_3
FFm	(80)	35.50	42.50	45.00
DF (W2)	1	0.861	0.742	0.639
PV	(80)	30.57	31.54	28.76

NPV in FFm = 10.87
 At X/R of 8.500 = £1.27m

W1: t_1 X/R = 8.50 × 1.04/1.03 = 8.583
 t_2 X/R = 8.583 × 1.04/1.03 = 8.666
 t_3 X/R = 8.666 × 1.04/1.03 = 8.750

W2: UK risk premium (CAPM) = 15 − 5 = 10%
 FF risk premium = 10% × 1.04/1.03 = 10.097
 FF return required = 6% + 10.097% = 16.1%

These give identical answers as the exchange rates have been estimated using PPP, which links inflation rate differences to interest rates and to exchange rates. The second method adjusts the discount rate to 16.1% and keeps the exchange rate constant at 8.5.

(b) In theory, purchasing power parity says that there will be no effect on the cost to the business, as any change in exchange rates exactly matches the difference in inflation rates in the two countries. However, in practice, there might be substantial impacts on the company because:

- legal restrictions may be imposed on the purchase of goods from the Far East;
- the French revenues will not be matched by costs in the same currency, which means that other hedging techniques may need to be put in place;
- the discount rate may need to be adjusted to allow for the additional risks of dealing in different currencies;
- there might be additional costs, such as transport costs and additional taxes;
- as the French currency is forecast to depreciate against sterling, purchases from the UK might become progressively more expensive.

(c) **Funding strategy**

If inflation rises, interest rates will rise and if PPP and interest rate parity hold, the French currency will depreciate more rapidly than forecast. This means that in sterling terms the NPV will be lower unless the company can raise its prices in line with inflation. It will also be affected by the rate at which the costs in France rise and the source of the goods used.

As finance is to be partly through a French loan, it will be an advantage if the French currency depreciates as it will become cheaper to service the loan as well as the ultimate repayment.

Question 2 – KH

REPORT

To: Finance Director
From: Financial Manager
Date: 30 May 2001

Investment in South America

(a) *Calculation and assessment of viability*

	t_0	t_1	t_2	t_3
SAm (real)	(1,000)	250	350	450
SAm (nominal)	(1,000)	350	686	1,235
X/R (W1)	30	40.38	54.36	73.18
In US$m	(33.33)	8.67	12.62	16.88
US cash flows (nominal)	(10)	(0.31)	(0.43)	(0.56)
US$m	(43.33)	8.36	12.19	16.32
DF (20%)	1	0.833	0.694	0.579
PV	(43.33)	6.96	8.46	9.45

$$\begin{aligned}\text{NPV of above} &= (18.46) \\ t_4 \text{ onwards} = 16.32/0.20 \times 0.579 &= \underline{47.25} \\ &\underline{\$28.79\text{m}}\end{aligned}$$

W1: t_1 X/R = 30 × 1.40/1.04 = 40.38
t_2 X/R = 40.38 × 1.40/1.04 = 54.36 etc

It would therefore seem to be a viable project and the calculations suggest we should go ahead. However, it needs a substantial cash injection at the start of the project and the risk, as looked at later in this report, needs considering carefully.

(b) *Political risks faced and management strategies*

The main political risks faced are as follows:

- repatriation of profits and dividends may be restricted;
- there might be Government interference in the market, ranging from dictating prices or imposing high taxes to expropriating assets;
- there may not be developed capital markets making it difficult to raise finance locally or to hedge currency risks;
- depending on the country under consideration, there might be poor infrastructure with little political will to improve it, social unrest and corruption.

184 Exam Practice Kit: Management Accounting Financial Strategy

Strategies could be developed to mitigate these to some extent, such as:

- assess the extent of the risks by research, discussions with experts and visits;
- purchase in depth analysis of the political and economic prospects that give scores for political risk;
- involve the Government as far as possible, without compromising ethical standards, and try to get commitments on areas such as repatriation of funds;
- take out insurance, where available, against events such as war and riots (although this may be very expensive);
- ensure that purchases are made in the local currency if at all possible.

Conclusion

The political risk should be considered as part of the overall strategic decision-making process, and those residual risks which cannot be mitigated need to be balanced against the strategic benefits.

Question 3 – TMC

First two years:

In A$'000s

	t_0	t_1	t_2	t_3
Operating cash flow		4,500	5,500	
Tax		(1,350)	(1,650)	
Investment and tax	(15,000)	4,500		
	(15,000)	7,650	3,850	
X/rate	0.650	0.637	0.625	0.613
In Euro'000s	(9,750)	4,873	2,406	
Extra tax on op CFs			(143)	(172)
Extra credit on CAs			546	
	(9,750)	4,873	2,809	(172)
DF (9%)	1	0.917	0.842	0.772
PV	(9,750)	4,469	2,365	(133)

NPV for first 2 years = Euro (3,049,000)

Alternative 1
Post-tax Euro operating CF in year 2 = 2,406 − 172 = 2,234
Ignoring the fact that European tax is payable a year in arrears (i.e. the final tax at t_{11}),
PV = 2,234 × (6.418 − 1.759) = 10,408,000
NPV for first 2 years = (3,049,000)
NPV   Euro 7,359,000

Alternative 2
PV of fee = 500,000 × 0.625 × 0.65 × 0.842   = E171,000
PV of payments = (3,200,000 × 0.613 × 0.65)/ 0.09 × 0.842 = E11,929,000
NPV for first 2 years   = (3,049,000)
NPV   = E9,051,000

This also ignores the time lag in the European tax.

Assessment and risks

- Both alternatives, on the basis of these estimates, are viable, with Alternative 2, giving a franchise, giving the most benefit to the company.
- Both assessments are very dependent on the forecasts of cash flows after year 2. These need examining very carefully as the net present value over the first 2 years is negative. It would be sensible to conduct sensitivity analysis on these important cash flows.
- As the investment is overseas, the cash-flow estimates are subject to exchange rate fluctuations, and over 10 years these could be substantial. Hedging is a possibility in the short term but it is unlikely that arrangements could be made for 10 years.
- There is some commercial risk in Alternative 2 in which a franchise is offered as the reputation of the company will depend on the competence of the franchise.
- There may be some credit risk if the franchise is offered as the company is relying on the franchise to make regular payments.
- Political risk will probably be increased by operating in another country. The tax arrangements, particularly the 100% first-year allowances, would impact on the viability if withdrawn; any change in allowing repatriation of profits could also cause problems. However, these risks are reduced if the country has a stable government as there are unlikely to be sudden major changes.
- Overall, the investment changes the risk profile of the company and would be expected to increase the overall risk to an investor and hence the cost of equity. However, as a large company, it is likely that many of its investors are well diversified institutions and so only interested in systematic risk. As such, the overseas venture may be welcomed by them as reducing or diversifying, part of the systematic risk, and the value of the company might rise accordingly.

Question 4 – AB overseas

(a) **Cost of equity**

Given by $(0.65 \times K_e) + (0.35 \times 10 \times 0.75) = 13$

So $K_e = 16\%$

This calculation assumes that the gearing ratio stays at 35%.

Value of subsidised loan given by the loan cash flows (net of tax) discounted at the opportunity cost of capital (in this case the cost of a new commercial loan):

	£	DF at 7.5%	PV
t_0	1,500,000	1	1,500,000
$t_1 - t_6$	(28,125)	4.694	(132,019)
t_6	(1,500,000)	0.6480	(972,000)
		Net PV	£395,981

This has used the current commercial cost of debt to discount, which assumes that by using this loan we have not had to raise a commercial loan. However, it might have been funded from a mix of finance sources, or internally, which would alter the opportunity cost used to discount. The higher the rate, the higher the savings and the benefit (so at the WACC of 13% PV = £667,556).

(b) **Discount rate relevance**

Neither the current cost of equity nor the current WACC are entirely relevant to the investment decision. As the investment is likely to carry a higher business risk than AB's normal operations and the financing structure appears likely to change, AB will need to use a discount rate which has been adjusted to reflect the risk of the project.

One alternative is to find, if possible, a company that operates in the same sector and use its beta, adjusted for the difference in gearing between the companies, to devise a cost of equity via CAPM. However, it will be difficult to find a company that reflects the risk of the operations in the Eastern European country.

(c) **Financing**

1 *Government subsidy*

The advantages of the EE Government subsidy include:

- cheaper finance than commercial rates
- no security is needed for the loan
- the overseas Government will want to help make the project a success.

The disadvantages include:

- the exchange rate may alter, making the repayment of interest and capital more expensive in sterling terms;
- commercial rates may change, making the subsidised loan look less attractive;
- the company is then tied into the loan and the project for 6 years;
- the company will need to establish how trustworthy the foreign Government is, in terms of honouring its commitments.

2 *Alternative methods*

These might include:

Leasing
Finance leases to acquire the main assets for the investment might be available, although there might be some difficulty, given that the assets leased will be overseas.

Equity
£1.5 million is too small for a new issue of shares, but a rights issue would be possible. This rather depends on whether the existing private investors have sufficient funds and the willingness to invest in the project.

Long-term loans
The company already has two loans and an overdraft and its gearing is higher than the industry average (and higher than it would like). Further loans would increase the gearing further and might be considered too risky, especially as it is into a new market.

Venture capital
Venture capitalists might be interested in providing finance, but will require a very high return for the risk envisaged, and are likely to want a sizeable portion of the company's equity. This therefore may not be acceptable to the current owners.

Recommendations
No obvious alternative presents itself unless the existing shareholders have excess funds available for investment. The company itself has no cash (as it runs a permanent overdraft) and the best option may be to accept the foreign Government's offer (subject to the reservations in (c) 1).

Part 5

Case Studies and Exam Papers

Case Study Questions

14

📝 Exam focus

The compulsory case study question takes up 50% of the exam and requires careful planning. The main problem is likely to be poor time management causing you to write very little, or nothing at all, on parts which could have given you easy marks.

The 20 minutes extra reading time at the start of the exam is particularly valuable here. Remember that you cannot write in the answer booklet or use your calculator, but you can use the time profitably to read the question and note in the margin your approach.

You need to break the requirements down into separate questions for timing purposes, but at the same time you don't want to be continually re-reading the scenario.

One approach would be as follows:

Read through all the requirements carefully; they are likely to cover a number of technical areas. Notice any parts that you can answer immediately, or that you have any ideas about and put some notes down on those.

Then scan the scenario quickly. Are there headings which help you find information; what industry and type of company is involved; are there any sections which are only relevant to one requirement?

Get an idea of where the information needed for each requirement is in the scenario (the information for calculating the cost of capital, for example, is likely to be grouped together) and mark it in the margin.

Then go back to the requirements and start working through them, reading the detail in the scenario as you need it. Watch your time carefully in the 3 hours of the actual exam, particularly in the case study question. Even if you haven't finished one requirement, go on to the next if the time is up. You can always come back if you have more time, but it's more important to get the easier marks at the beginning of each question than to make that final point!

On the following questions, be very strict with your time and see if you manage to make a reasonable attempt at all the requirements.

Questions

Question 1 – KL Group

Background of company

KL Group plc provides a range of products and services for sale in the United Kingdom and overseas. Its shares are listed on the London Stock Exchange and are widely held, although institutions hold the majority of shares. The company is structured as a group of wholly owned subsidiaries. Each subsidiary specialises in a particular product or service.

Financial data

Key data for the year to 31 December 2001 is as follows:

Sales revenue	£850m
Earnings	£105m
Shares in issue	250m
Share price as at today (21 May 2002)	331 pence
Weighted Average Cost of Capital (WACC) for the Group	14% (nominal net of tax rate)

Company objectives

The company has two stated objectives:

1. to increase operating cash flow and dividends per share year on year by at least 5%;
2. to increase the wealth of our shareholders whilst respecting the interests of our employees, customers and other stakeholders and operating to the highest ethical standards.

Future plans

The directors are considering establishing a new subsidiary company, KL15, to process industrial waste. The subsidiary will require a factory. The directors have identified that the factory used by a long-established subsidiary, KL3, is currently operating at only 50% capacity. This factory could be converted for use by the new subsidiary at a cost of £1.3 million. KL3's annual net (after-tax) earnings are £1.5 million. This subsidiary's operations would cease immediately after the decision to proceed with KL15 is taken as it will take some months to convert the factory.

However, the company is aware that the government is reviewing the environmental controls currently in operation for waste processing and it is possible that tougher regulations will be introduced. Industry spokesmen are attempting to argue that current controls are adequate. Nevertheless, the directors of the KL Group plc wish to consider the situation should these tougher controls be introduced, and two alternative methods of equipping the new subsidiary have been proposed by the company's technical advisers.

The company has sufficient cash available from a recent disposal to finance the capital costs of the new subsidiary under either alternative.

Alternative 1

This alternative will equip the factory to process waste to the highest environmental standards that the government regulations might impose. This would require the purchase of very expensive, specialised machinery from the USA. This machinery would have to be ordered and delivery time is approximately 6 months, which would coincide with completion of the factory conversion. The cost of this machinery is currently US$12 million but the price of the equipment is likely to rise by 5% over the next 6 months. If an order is placed immediately (year 0), together with a 50% deposit, the supplier will hold today's price. The balance of the purchase price is payable 6 months after installation. The current exchange rate, US$ to £1 sterling, is 1.45. Inflation in the USA is forecast to be 4% over the next 12 months. In the UK it is forecast to be 2.5%.

This equipment is not likely to need replacement for at least 8 years.

Forecast revenues for KL15 under this equipment alternative are as follows. The probabilities are based on forecasts of the economy in the UK and the main overseas trading areas where the KL Group plc hopes to sell its services.

	Year 1 (6 months of operating)			Year 2			Year 3		
Revenues (£m)	0.5	2.5	3.5	8.5	10.5	12.5	10.5	13.5	16.0
Probability	0.4	0.5	0.1	0.4	0.5	0.1	0.4	0.5	0.1
Expected revenues (£m)		1.8			9.9			12.55	

The probabilities of sales for year 2 or 3 and beyond are assumed to be independent of the achievement of the previous year's sales.

The costs are as follows:

- Cash operating costs are expected to have a fixed element of £1.5 million each year starting as soon as the factory starts work, plus a variable element of 30% of sales revenue. A full year's fixed costs will be charged to production in year 1.
- Redundancy payments of £1.2 million will be necessary for staff from the KL3 subsidiary. These would be payable immediately.
- The costs of the factory conversion will be incurred during the 6 months following the decision to proceed but, for simplicity, it can be assumed that these are paid at the end of year 1.
- The availability of capital allowances and other tax reliefs mean that no tax is likely to be payable until year 4. For year 4 onwards a rough estimate suggests 20% of annual net cash flows (revenue less cash operating costs) will be payable in tax.

Alternative 2

To plan for a continuation of, or modest improvement to, current regulations and produce accordingly. This alternative has greater flexibility as there is a much larger market, worldwide, for processing waste at a lower and therefore much cheaper specification. The capital cost to the KL Group plc would also be much lower at £2.5 million. Equipment for this alternative is readily available in the UK and can be bought when the factory conversion is completed. However, the equipment is likely to need to be replaced in 6 years' time from the date of purchase.

The revenues shown below are forecast using similar methods as used in Alternative 1. However, sales will be made to a wider range of customers, many in developing countries.

	Year 1 (6 months of operating)			Year 2			Year 3		
Revenues (£m)	3.5	4.5	5.5	4.5	6.5	7.5	8.5	9.5	11.5
Probability	0.2	0.6	0.2	0.2	0.6	0.2	0.2	0.6	0.2
Expected revenues (£m)		4.5			6.3			9.7	

Costs are as follows:

- Fixed cash operating costs will be £1.2 million each year; variable costs will be 15% of sales revenue.
- With this alternative, there will be fewer redundancies from KL3 and the associated costs will be only 20% of those for Alternative 1.
- Costs of factory conversion are as Alternative 1.
- Tax relief will be similar to Alternative 1, that is, no tax will be payable until year 4 when tax will become payable at 20% of annual net cash flow (revenue less cash operating costs).

Requirements

(a) Calculate net present values for the new subsidiary (KL15) under the two alternatives, using whatever assumptions you think are appropriate. Include brief comments on your assumptions.

(15 marks)

(b) Assume you are the company's financial manager. Write a report to the directors that:

   (i) discusses how the new subsidiary and the two alternatives might contribute to the attainment of the Group's objectives. Refer to the figures you have calculated in answer to part (a) where appropriate.

(10 marks)

   (ii) analyses and discusses the various types of risk and limitation involved in each alternative.

(10 marks)

   (iii) recommends which, if either, of the alternatives should be chosen. Your recommendation should take into account all aspects of your evaluation as discussed in parts (b) (i) and (b) (ii) of this question.

(5 marks)

You should provide any additional calculations that you consider appropriate to support your discussion and analysis.

(Total for part (b) = 25 marks)

(c) Option pricing theory was originally developed to apply to share prices. The theory can also be applied to capital investment options, sometimes known as 'real options'.

Discuss the option features involved in the KL Group plc's decision and explain, briefly, the benefits of including such options in the investment appraisal process.

(10 marks)
(Total = 50 marks)

Question 2 – Dobbs

Background

Dobbs plc is an international publishing company based in the United Kingdom. It has recently sold a subsidiary that publishes technical journals, a field the company considered to be noncore business. The sale raised £30 million in cash. The directors are evaluating what they consider to be a very promising acquisition opportunity and the cash raised from the sale of the subsidiary would be used as part of the financing arrangement.

Potential investment in a new subsidiary

Alice Jain Inc. is an American publisher that has two main divisions. One division publishes books, mainly 'blockbuster' type fiction, and the other publishes 'lifestyle' magazines. Both divisions have seen strong growth over the past 5 years as a result of changes in the public's magazine-buying habits and also because of two high-selling authors whom the company contracted before they became popular. These contracts have between 3 and 5 years to run before they are re-negotiated. Many industry observers think Alice Jain Inc. has been successful because of good luck rather than good judgement and that with stronger management the company could become a major international publisher.

Alice Jain Inc. is privately owned (i.e. it does not have a listing on a stock market). There are approximately 50 shareholders although 60% of the shares are owned by the husband and wife partnership that started the business 25 years ago. Dobbs plc's directors have already made an informal approach to Alice Jain Inc's directors and believe they will be receptive to an offer if terms can be agreed. No announcement has yet been made to the press or to Dobbs plc's shareholders about their intentions.

On the basis of industry information and private sources, Dobbs plc's directors forecast the following cash flows from Alice Jain Inc.:

Year	1	2	3	4
Net cash flows ($m)	35.5	43.5	46.5	52.5

Notes:

1 The spot $US/£ exchange rate is 1.45. Forecast economic data relevant to the USA and the UK is as follows:

	USA	UK
Risk-free rates for each year (%)	3.5	4.5
Inflation rates for each year (%)	2.5	3.2

Assume the theory of interest rate parity applies when forecasting exchange rates.

2 The cash flows are in real terms. Dobbs plc evaluates all its investment decisions at its domestic, post-tax cost of capital, which is a nominal 11%. It evaluates international investments by converting the foreign currency cash flows to sterling and applying its domestic cost of capital of 11%. The cost of capital for Alice Jain Inc. is not known. Dobbs plc's Finance Director has used the capital asset pricing model to assist in the calculation of a discount rate based on the published information about a quoted British company

with a similar commercial and financial profile to Alice Jain Inc. He has calculated that the proxy company's nominal, post-tax cost of capital is 13%.

3   When evaluating investments, Dobbs plc ignores cash flows beyond 4 years and terminal values.

Financing of the acquisition

Dobbs plc's directors are considering offering Alice Jain Inc's shareholders either shares in Dobbs plc or a cash alternative. The two majority shareholders are likely to take 50% shares, 50% cash as there are tax advantages to a share exchange. This will use up most of the cash from the sale of the subsidiary. The cash for the remaining shareholders will have to be raised by Dobbs plc increasing its borrowing. The 'worst case' scenario is that the remaining shareholders (i.e. those except the two major shareholders) will all opt for cash.

Finance Director's concerns

Dobbs plc's long-term debt to equity ratio is relatively high compared with other publishing companies of similar size. The Finance Director thinks some of the cash raised from the sale of the subsidiary should be used to purchase a small British publishing company at an approximate cost of £15 million. The remaining cash should then be used to repay some of Dobbs plc's outstanding debt.

The other directors disagree and believe the financial risk of investing in Alice Jain Inc. will be justified by substantial value enhancement strategies that can be put in place following the acquisition.

Summary financial information on bidder and target companies

	Dobbs plc £m	Alice Jain Inc. $m
Income statement for 12 months to 31 December 2002		
Turnover	251.5	75.8
Operating profit	65.6	20.9
Finance costs	12.0	2.0
Profit before tax	53.6	18.9
Taxation	15.0	7.0
Balance sheet at 31 December 2002		
Fixed assets	195.0	45.0
Net current assets	75.0	25.0
Total assets less current liabilities	270.0	70.0
Long-term debt	125.0	15.0
Net assets	145.0	55.0
Ordinary share capital		
Ordinary shares of £1	45.0	
Common stock of $1		15.0
Total reserves	100.0	40.0
Equity shareholders' funds	145.0	55.0

Current share price for Dobbs plc is 885 pence. High and low share prices for the past 12 months were 925 pence and 755 pence respectively. No share price is available for Alice Jain Inc.

Assume you are a financial manager with Dobbs plc.

Requirements

(a)

    (i) Calculate the present value of the investment/acquisition's cash flows and explain your method of evaluation, including your choice of discount rate.

    (ii) Calculate the number of shares Dobbs plc might need to issue and the amount of debt that might need to be raised in the 'worst case' scenario. Include brief comments to explain your calculations.

(Total for part (a) = 16 marks)

(b) Write a report to the directors of Dobbs plc, evaluating the potential acquisition. You should include in your report:

    (i) a recommendation, with reasons, of whether the investment should proceed and at what price;

    (ii) advice on strategies for enhancing the value of the combined company following the acquisition;

    (iii) discussion of the Finance Director's recommendation to acquire a smaller company and repay some debt;

    (iv) advice on Dobbs plc's directors' responsibilities to ensure fair and equal treatment for all shareholders in accordance with current take-over regulation.

Use additional calculations to support your arguments wherever relevant and appropriate.

Note: Marks are distributed roughly equally between these four sections of the report.

(Total for part (b) = 34 marks)
(Total = 50 marks)

Question 3 – C&C

Background to company

C&C Airlines plc operates a small fleet of aeroplanes from an airport in the United Kingdom. Its business is aimed at low-budget travellers on short-haul flights. The company was formed in 1990 by a group of private investors who continue to own the company. Two of these investors take an active role in the management of the company as executive directors.

The shareholders' objective is long-term capital growth. They have taken relatively low dividends out of the company since its incorporation. The strategy has been to accept low, or no, profits, and build the brand name and market share in its niche market. Their 'exit strategy' is eventually to sell a majority holding in the company following either a stock market flotation or private sale of shares to another company.

Assets and revenue

C&C Airlines plc currently owns 12 planes, mainly Boeing 737s. It has bought all of them second-hand from the major airlines. The company's total net assets are currently, and realistically, valued at £130 million. It is all-equity financed. The revenue in the last full financial year was £85 million. The forecast revenue for the current year is £98 million. Profits after tax are forecast as £18 million.

Proposed investment

The company's directors are examining a proposal for a strategic move into the long-haul market. The initial investment involves the purchase of a 5-year-old Boeing 757, which will be used to fly to and from the Caribbean. Negotiations to buy this plane are already underway. C&C Airlines plc plans to operate the plane for 3 years and replace it at the end of this time with a newer model.

When fully loaded, this type of plane will carry 220 passengers. The company estimates an average return fare of £300 per passenger on this route. All income will be received in £ sterling. The company's estimates of average passenger loading are as follows:

Load	*Probability of load being achieved*	
	Year 1 (%)	Years 2–3 (%)
100% (all seats taken)	10	15
80% full	50	60
50% full	30	20
40% full	10	5

The plane is expected to make 6 return trips every week and be operational 48 weeks of the year.

The capital costs of the purchase of the plane are US$30 million. To date, C&C Airlines plc has spent £500,000 on market research and purchase negotiations. Other financial data associated with the venture are

- Capital allowances are available at 25% on a reducing balance of the total capital cost.
- The estimated resale value of the plane 3 years after purchase, in nominal terms, is $16 million.

Cash operating costs (per annum)

Sterling-denominated costs such as maintenance, insurance, crew wages, salaries and training	£2.9m
US$-denominated fuel costs	US$4.2m

Overheads and other costs (per annum)

Administration and office space (These costs include a £50,000 re-allocation of current head office costs.)	£0.3m
Advertising and promotion	£0.35m

Estimates of increases in income and costs

The figures given above are all in nominal terms as at today. Because this is an increasingly competitive market, the company is unlikely to be able to increase fares in line with inflation. The best estimate is an annual increase of 2%. Operating costs (excluding fuel) are expected to increase by the annual UK rate of inflation (3%). Forecasting fuel costs is very difficult but best estimates are that they will rise by 5% each year over the next 3 years. Assume these inflationary increases commence in the first year of operations. Overheads and other costs are expected to be held constant in nominal terms.

Currency and inflation rates

- current spot exchange rate is US$1.53/£1
- estimated per annum inflation rates are as follows:
  - UK   3%
  - USA   4%

Inflation rates in the UK and USA are expected to remain at these levels.

Allowing for risks

The company evaluates investments by discounting cash flows at 9% per annum nominal and applying certainty equivalents to net after-tax cash flows. The estimates for the proposed investment are shown below:

Year	Certainty equivalent
1	0.90
2	0.85
3	0.80

The company's new Finance Director would prefer to use a risk-adjusted discount rate. A competitor company to C&C Airlines plc has a quoted equity beta of 1.3 and a debt:equity ratio (based on market values) of 1:4. This is unlikely to change in the foreseeable future. The post-tax return on the market is expected to be 12% and the risk-free rate 5%. Assume a debt beta of 0.15.

Assumptions:

- Capital costs are paid immediately but all other cash flows occur at year-end.
- Taxation at 30% is paid or repaid at the end of the year in which the liability/repayment arises (i.e. no time lag).
- The plane is acquired and becomes operational immediately.

Requirements

(a) Calculate the discount rate to be used in the investment decision using the CAPM and comment, briefly, on the limitations of using the CAPM in the circumstances here.

(5 marks)

(b) Calculate the £ sterling NPV of the proposed investment in the new plane using: the discount rate calculated in (a) above, rounded to the nearest 1%; and a discount rate of 9% per annum nominal and adjusting for the company's estimated certainty equivalents, and recommend, briefly, whether to proceed with the investment, based solely on your calculations above.

NPV should be calculated in sterling, converting US$ cash flows to sterling. Assume the theory of purchasing power parity applies when calculating exchange rates.

(Total for part (b) = 20 marks)

(c) Assume you are the assistant to the Finance Director. On his behalf, draft a report to the Board that critically evaluates the following:

  (i) the major economic forces that might impact on, or influence, the success of the investment;
  (ii) commercial aspects of the investment that involve the greatest uncertainty and risk; strategies for managing the risks discussed in parts (c)(i) and (c)(ii).

The report should conclude with a recommendation of a course of action.

(Total for part (c) = 25 marks)
(Total = 50 marks)

Question 4 – Hi-Clean

Background

The Hi-clean Group is a UK-based unlisted company that imports, assembles and distributes laundry and cleaning equipment for hotels and restaurants and for public sector departments, such as hospitals, prisons and the armed forces. The company was formed in 1985 with £24 million start-up capital in ordinary shares of £1. No other capital has been raised since then, except from the venture capital company explained below.

The company has seen growth in turnover and post-tax profits of around 20% each year over the past 3 years in all sectors of its customer base, although sales to the public sector now account for a much higher proportion of the total than 5 years ago: 38% in 2004 compared with 18% in 2000.

Details on major shareholder

A venture capital company owns 20% of the company's shares, bought 3 years ago for £25 million. The venture capital company also provided a £25 million loan with equity warrants attached. The loan carries a variable rate of interest, LIBOR + 3%, and is repayable in 2006. The warrants allow for the venture capital company to buy 1 share at 400 pence for every £10 of debt at the time the loan is repaid. This shareholder is looking to exit from its investment in Hi-clean in 2–3 years time. Unless Hi-clean has obtained a share listing by then, the venture capital company has indicated it is unlikely to exercise its warrants. The venture capital company's usual required return is an average of 50% per annum (dividends plus capital gain as percentage of initial investment) over a 5-year investment period.

Although the venture capital company has a seat on the Hi-clean Group Board, it has taken a very 'hands-off' approach and had little involvement in the company's direction or management.

Forecast results for the year to 31 December 2004

The accounts department has produced the following full-year forecasts for 2004:

Results by sector

	Public sector £m	Hotels and restaurants £m	Total £m
Revenue	83.60	136.40	220.00
Direct costs	45.98	68.20	114.18
Gross profit margin	37.62	68.20	105.82
Fixed overheads *	26.53	43.29	69.82
Operating profit	11.09	24.91	36.00

* Fixed overheads are apportioned to operating sectors on the basis of turnover.

Summary group income statement

	£m
Operating profit	36.00
Finance costs	1.75
Profit before taxation	34.25
Taxation	6.17
Profit after tax	28.08
Ordinary dividends	8.43

Summary group balance sheet

	£m
Fixed assets (net book value)	124.00
Net current assets	48.00
Loan capital	25.00
Assets less liabilities	147.00
Capital and reserves	
Called up share capital (Ordinary shares of £1) (Authorised share capital £35 million)	30.00
Share premium account	18.00
Retained earnings	99.00
Shareholders' funds	147.00

Future funding and request for study

Hi-clean's directors have, for some time, been considering a public listing for the company's shares to raise new finance and provide an exit route for the venture capital company. Assume you are the Financial Manager with Hi-clean. The directors have asked you for a study that includes a forecast of the company's financial situation at 31 December 2005. You have spent the last month obtaining the following information from a variety of sources.

Growth in turnover and profits

You expect growth to continue but not at the high levels seen over the past few years. A complication is that a general election will take place shortly and the outcome will have an effect on Hi-clean's business. If Party A wins, it has promised more money for some public sector departments, which may increase Hi-clean's sales to its public sector customers. However, this increased spending would be paid for by an increase in certain taxes that would adversely impact on some of Hi-clean's private customers. If Party B wins, spending on public services will also increase, but not necessarily in areas serviced by Hi-clean. Opinion polls suggest Party A has a 60% chance of winning and Party B 40%.

Based on your informed opinion about prospects for the economy and the industry, you forecast the following range of sales revenues and probabilities for 2005, by sector, depending on which party wins the election.

		Public sector		Hotels and restaurants
If Party A wins:	Revenue £ million	102.00	112.00	123.00
	Probabilities	0.55	0.45	1
If Party B wins:	Revenue £ million	95.00	110.00	143.00
	Probabilities	0.50	0.50	1

Other information/assumptions

- Corporate tax will be payable at the current percentage level of 18% owing to availability of capital allowances. No capital expenditure is planned for 2005.
- Gross profit margin percentage by sector is expected to remain unchanged irrespective of the election outcome.
- Fixed costs are expected to rise to £71.8 million.
- LIBOR is currently 4%. It is expected to fall to 3% in 2005.
- Average P/E ratio and cost of equity capital for listed companies in this industry are currently 11 and 9% respectively. It is difficult to forecast how P/E ratios will move over the next 12 months but market professionals are expecting an upturn in the market generally, so anything between 12 and 15 is not unreasonable.
- The dividend payout ratio has been constant at 30% since 2001.

Requirements

(a) For 2005, calculate forecasts of the following:

  (i) turnover, gross margin and operating profits by customer sector;
  (ii) a profit and loss account and earnings per share for the Hi-clean Group.

Assume a full-year effect for all the changes forecast for 2005. Provide comments to accompany your forecasts that explain any significant changes between 2004 and 2005.

(10 marks)

(b) As Financial Manager, write a report to the directors of Hi-clean Group. In your report you should:

  (i) Calculate a range of potential values as at the end of 2005 for the entire Group and for the venture capital company's shareholding. Base your calculations on the information you have available and assume the Group remains a private, unlisted company. Accompany your calculations with a brief discussion of each valuation method.
  (ii) Comment on the reasons for potential differences between the value of the entire company and the value of the venture capital company's shares (that is, why the value of the venture capital company's shares might not be strictly proportionate).

(18 marks)

(c) Based on your forecasts, estimate whether the venture capital company will achieve its target return on investment in Hi-clean and identify exit strategies that might be available to the investor in 2006. Evaluate how the venture capital company's situation might affect Hi-clean's future financial strategy.

(10 marks)

(d) Identify the main risks and opportunities facing the company and advise on methods of managing the risks.

(12 marks)
(Total = 50 marks)

Question 5 – JHC Group

Background of company

JHC Group manufactures and distributes a wide range of food products for sale throughout Europe. It also provides advisory services to retailers. Its shares are listed and are widely held, although institutions hold the majority. The company is structured as a group of wholly-owned subsidiaries. Each subsidiary specialises in a particular product or service.

Financial data

Key data for the year to 31 December 2003 is as follows:

Revenue	€1,750 million
Earnings	€215 million
Shares in issue	350 million
Share price as at today	€8.31
Weighted Average Cost of Capital (WACC) for the Group	9% (nominal net of tax rate)

Company objectives

The company has two stated objectives:

- To increase operating cash flow and dividends per share year-on-year by at least 4%, which is 2.5% above the current rate of inflation.
- To increase the wealth of shareholders while respecting the interests of our employees, customers and other stakeholders and operating to the highest ethical standards.

Future plans

The directors are considering establishing a new subsidiary company, SP, to manufacture and distribute health food products. The subsidiary will require a factory. The directors have identified that the factory used by a long-established subsidiary, CC, is currently operating at only 60% capacity. This factory could be converted for use by the new subsidiary at a cost of €2.8 million. CC's annual net (after-tax) earnings are €2.2 million and are expected to remain at this level in nominal terms for the foreseeable future. This subsidiary's operations would cease immediately the decision to proceed with SP is taken as it will take some months to convert the factory.

However, the company is aware that the European parliament is discussing legislation that would introduce more stringent controls on the manufacture of health food products than are currently in operation. Industry spokesmen are attempting to argue that current controls are adequate. Nevertheless, the directors of the JHC Group wish to consider the situation should these tougher controls be introduced and two alternative methods of equipping the new subsidiary have been proposed by the company's technical advisers.

The company has sufficient cash available from a recent disposal to finance the capital costs of the new subsidiary under either alternative.

Alternative 1

This alternative will equip the factory to manufacture to the highest food safety standards that new regulations might impose. It would require the purchase of specialised machinery, which would have to be ordered. Delivery time is approximately 6 months, which would coincide with completion of the factory conversion.

Capital costs
The cost of this machinery is currently €8 million but its price is likely to rise by 5% over the next 6 months. If an order is placed immediately (year 0), together with a 40% deposit, the supplier will hold today's price. The balance of the purchase price is payable 6 months after installation (i.e. 12 months after payment of the initial deposit). This machinery is not likely to need replacement for at least 8 years.

Revenues
Forecast revenues for SP for the first 3 years of operation have been provided by JHC Group's planning department as follows. The probabilities are based on forecasts of the economies of JHC Group's main trading areas.

	Year 1 (6 months of operating)			Year 2			Year 3		
Revenues (€ m)	2.5	4.5	7.4	7.5	12.5	16.5	13.5	18.5	21.5
Probability	0.3	0.5	0.2	0.3	0.5	0.2	0.3	0.5	0.2
Expected revenues (€ m)		4.48			11.80			17.60	

The probabilities of sales for year 2 or 3 and beyond are assumed to be independent of the achievement of the previous year's sales revenues.

Operating and other costs/reliefs

- Cash operating costs are expected to have a fixed element of €2.5 million each year, plus a variable element of 35% of sales revenues. A full year's fixed costs will be charged to production in year 1. Variable costs will be much higher under this alternative because the new regulations are likely to require more expensive ingredients in the products.
- Redundancy payments of €2.1 million will be necessary for staff from the CC subsidiary. These would be payable immediately.

- The costs of the factory conversion will be incurred during the 6 months following the decision to proceed but, for simplicity, it can be assumed that these are paid at the end of year 1.
- The availability of capital allowances and other tax reliefs mean that no tax is likely to be payable until year 4. For year 4 onwards, a rough estimate suggests 20% of annual net cash flows (revenues less cash operating costs) will be payable in tax.

Alternative 2

To plan for a continuation of, or modest improvement to, current controls and regulations. This alternative has greater flexibility, as there is a much larger market, worldwide, for cheaper products.

Capital costs
The capital cost to JHC Group would also be much lower at €4.5 million. Equipment for this alternative is readily available and can be bought when the factory conversion is completed.

However, the equipment is likely to need to be replaced in 6 years' time from the date of purchase.

Revenues
The revenues shown below are forecast using similar methods as used in Alternative 1. However, sales will be made to a wider range of customers, many in developing countries.

	Year 1 (6 months of operating)			Year 2			Year 3		
Revenues (€ m)	4.5	7.5	9.5	7.1	9.4	11.1	9.5	12.5	15.6
Probability	0.1	0.6	0.3	0.1	0.6	0.3	0.1	0.6	0.3
Expected revenues (€ m)		7.80			9.68			13.13	

Costs are as follows:

- Fixed cash operating costs will be €1.5 million each year; variable costs will be 20% of sales revenue.
- With this alternative, there will be fewer redundancies from CC and the associated costs will be only 20% of those for Alternative 1.
- Costs of factory conversion are as Alternative 1.
- Tax relief will be similar to Alternative 1, that is, no tax will be payable until year 4 when tax will become payable at 20% of annual net cash flow (revenue less cash operating costs).

The revenues and costs for both alternatives are in nominal terms.

Requirements

Assume you are JHC Group's financial manager.

(a) (i) Calculate the net present value for the new subsidiary (SP) under each of the two alternatives. Make, and comment on, appropriate assumptions about cash flows beyond year 3, including terminal values, and the discount rate to use in the evaluation.

(15 marks)

(ii) Explain, without doing any additional calculations, the appropriateness and possible advantages of providing modified internal rates of return (MIRRs) for the evaluation of the two alternatives.

(5 marks)

(b) Write a report to the directors that discusses how the new subsidiary and the two alternatives might contribute to the attainment of the Group's objectives and recommends which, if either, of the alternatives should be chosen. Refer to the figures you calculated in part (a) where appropriate. You should provide any additional calculations that you consider relevant to support your discussion and analysis.

(22 marks)

(c) Discuss the option features involved in the JHC Group's decision and explain, briefly, the benefits of including such options in the investment appraisal process.

(8 marks)
(Total marks = 50)

✓ Answers

Question 1 – KL Group

(a) **Net present values**

Alternative 1

In £'000	t_0	t_1	t_2	t_3	$t_4 - t_8$
Equipment (note)	(4,138)	(4,082)			
Revenue		1,800	9,900	12,550	12,550
Variable costs		(540)	(2,970)	(3,765)	(3,765)
Fixed costs		(1,500)	(1,500)	(1,500)	(1,500)
Redundancy	(1,200)				
Conversion		(1,300)			
Tax					(1,457)
Lost earnings		(1,500)	(1,500)	(1,500)	(1,500)
	(5,388)	(7,122)	3,930	5,785	4,328
	1	0.877	0.769	0.675	3.433 × 0.675
	(5,388)	(6,246)	3,022	3,905	10,029

Net present value = £5,322,000 over 8 years

Note: Exchange rate in 1 year estimated as $1.45 \times 1.04/1.025 = 1.47$

Alternative 2

In £'000	t_0	t_1	t_2	t_3	$t_4 - t_6$
Equipment	(2,500)				
Revenue		4,500	6,300	9,700	9,700
Variable costs		(675)	(945)	(1,455)	(1,455)
Fixed costs		(1,200)	(1,200)	(1,200)	(1,200)
Redundancy	(240)				
Conversion		(1,300)			
Tax					(1,409)
Lost earnings		(1,500)	(1,500)	(1,500)	(1,500)
	(2,740)	(175)	2,655	5,545	4,136
	1	0.877	0.769	0.675	3.433 × 0.675
	(2,740)	(153)	2,042	3,743	6,483

Net present value = £9,375,000 over 6 years

These calculations assume:

- The WACC is the appropriate discount rate, but this may not be the case if the business or financial risk changes.
- In alternative 1, we have assumed that we accept the supplier's offer to pay a 50% deposit to secure the price.

- The two alternatives have been assessed over the lives of the machines. They therefore have not considered the loss in earnings from KL3, or any other cash flows, beyond this.
- Cash flows beyond year 3 have been assumed to remain constant but this may not be realistic. The objectives say that KL intend to increase operating cashflows by 5% p.a. but this may be achieved by undertaking new projects or increasing revenues on certain projects, rather than increasing cashflows of all projects across the board. Any increase in cashflows beyond year 3 would clearly increase the net present values.

(b)

REPORT

To: Board of KL Group plc
From: Financial Manager
Date: xx of x 20xx

New subsidiary in KL15

This report will discuss how the new subsidiary might help the group achieve its objectives, look at the risks and limitations involved and make recommendations on the way forward.

(i) *Achievement of objectives*

The two alternatives give different net present values; although both give positive values which would suggest the investment is viable, the greater net present value is achieved under alternative 2 with £9.375 million. In terms of shareholders' wealth, in theory both alternatives should help it to increase, with alternative 2 making the greater contribution. However, the current value of the company is over £800 million so the NPV of approximately £9.4 million will not make a significant impact.

The establishment of KL15 might help the employees and other stakeholders as it will produce employment and demand instead of the subsidiary KL3 which is only operating at 50%.

The company also wants to improve cash flows and dividends by 5% per annum. The cash flows in alternative 1 are greater than those in alternative 2, both inflows and outflows. As the first two years have cash outflows, the group will see a drop in cash flows in the first two years (and a greater drop under alternative 1). The investment will therefore be detrimental to the achievement of this objective, although, as with the first objective, the impact is insignificant in the group context.

(ii) *Risks and limitations*

The risks can be analysed under the areas of commercial, political, operational and financial:

The main commercial risk in alternative 1 is that there are fewer customers, on whom we will be more dependent, while alternative 2 has customers in developing countries, which might cause credit risk problems.

Although there are political uncertainties in the UK relating to safety issues, as mentioned in the scenario, there are further political risks in alternative 2 which include many customers in developing countries.

The main operational risk is that a change in the regulations means that the equipment specified in alternative 2 cannot be used, as it only allows for a modest change in regulations. One possibility is to go for the least-risk option of alternative 1, despite the lower NPV; this could be used in PR and corporate image projection to show the high environmental standards achieved by the group.

The financial risks refer to the calculation of the NPV. The WACC was used as a discount rate but it may not be appropriate to the investment under consideration; we would ideally find a proxy quoted company in the same business and use its beta but this might be difficult in practice.

We have assumed that we will take up the supplier's offer for the equipment purchase; this will protect us against the price rising but means that we pay the cash 6 months earlier than we would otherwise. We therefore need to look at the opportunity cost of this finance.

The revenue estimates have different possible ranges and those in alternative 2 are more likely to be in the mid-range while those under alternative 1 are more likely to be at the lower end. We need to use sensitivity analysis and simulation to establish the likelihood of these outcomes more accurately.

Currency risk is introduced in alternative 2 with diverse overseas customers; it would be sensible to look at the possibilities of hedging these revenues.

The equipment in alternative 2 will need replacing before that in alternative 1 but this is based on current estimates; in a field such as this in which technology is evolving, it is possible that lives may be shorter or alternatively could be extended through adaptive technology.

(iii) *Recommendations*

Maximising shareholders' wealth would suggest alternative 2, as would the employment prospects for the workforce. Alternative 1, however, is environmentally better and therefore may have other, less easily quantifiable, advantages for the group image. The risks discussed above are fairly balanced.

Neither contribute significantly to either objective and as such it is worth seeing if there are any larger scale investments that could be undertaken in preference to this.

(c) **Real options**

KL Group have three possible options relating to this investment – the abandonment option, the delay option and the follow-on option:

Abandonment option

An abandonment option is when a company can decide not to continue with an investment as circumstances change; this can increase the value of a project as there is less risk of being stuck with an unviable investment. Usually this is difficult when expenditure on capital equipment is involved as the main costs have been incurred and abandoning the project will only sacrifice revenues. In this situation alternative 1 could be abandoned if it did not take up the supplier's offer and risked the 5% increase in price; this, along with the redundancies and loss of KL3, seems a high price to pay for this option. In alternative 2 the project could be abandoned up until the factory is fully converted in 6 months' time.

Delay option

There may be scope for delaying the investment until the government decisions and regulations relating to these environmental issues are clearer. This may then allow a much better estimate of revenues and costs and consequently a more reliable decision on the investment. The current NPV has been calculated by using expected values based on subjective probabilities of the different courses of action by the government. We could therefore calculate different NPVs and estimate the probability of us undertaking the investment, based on expected values, but achieving a negative NPV; this would give us an idea of the value of the delay option.

Follow-on option

Sometimes investment decisions give other opportunities even if the original investment was not particularly beneficial in its own right (and possibly even had a negative NPV). In this situation, the knowledge gained in the operation or the reputation of a good environmental record in this area may lead to substantial other work. By its nature this will be difficult to quantify but could be valuable in an industry where safety and environmental concerns are important.

Question 2 – Dobbs

(a)

(i) *Present value of cash flows*

In millions	t_1	t_2	t_3	t_4
US$ cash flows	35.5	43.5	46.5	52.5
Inflated at 2.5%	36.4	45.7	50.1	58.0
Exchange rate (decrease by 1.035/1.045)	1.436	1.422	1.409	1.395
£ cash flows	25.3	32.1	35.5	41.6
Discount factors (13%)	0.885	0.783	0.693	0.613
Present values	22.4	25.1	24.6	25.5

Net present value = £97.6m

Using a discount rate of 11% gives an NPV of £102.3m

The present value of future cash flows over the next 4 years is a reasonable method of estimating the value of the company; asset valuations would not take account of the intellectual capital in the company in the form of the authors' contracts and without any kind of market price other methods could be difficult to apply.

The cash flows could have been discounted at a local cost of capital and then the present value translated at the spot rate, or as here translated at the different exchange rates likely to be ruling and discounting the home currency cash flows at the home country cost of capital.

The discount rate should be appropriate to the risk of the investment and therefore may need to be adjusted for additional currency risks and difference in operations. However, overseas diversification may help to decrease the risk to shareholders. The 11% usually used may not fully incorporate the difference in risk in the

American investment; the 13% from a similar business to Alice Jain is more appropriate, although this is assuming the Finance Director has already adjusted it for the lower gearing in Alice Jain than Dobbs.

(ii) *Shares and debt*

In the worst case scenario the two majority shareholders take 50% in cash and the other shareholders all take cash.

Proportion taking shares = 0.50 × 60% = 30%

Proportion taking cash = 70%

Shares needed in Dobbs = (30% × £97.6m/£8.85 = 3.31m) shares at Dobbs' current share price.

Debt needed = (70% × £97.6m) − £30m = £38.3m

This assumes that the full £30 million is still available from the sale of the other company and that there are no other demands on the money.

(b)

REPORT

To: Board of Dobbs plc
From: Financial Manager
Date: XX of X 20XX

Potential acquisition of Alice Jain

This report will look at the viability of the purchase, strategies for enhancing the value, other recommendations for use of the funds and the directors' responsibilities in respect of fair treatment of all shareholders.

(i) *Viability of purchase*

The present value of the first 4 years' cash flows is approximately £97.6 million; the asset values at today's spot rate are worth approximately £40 million but this does not recognise the intellectual capital in the company in the form of the authors' contracts. Another possibility is to use an earnings multiple approach and use Dobbs' P/E ratio, giving (11.9m × 10.3)/1.45 = £84.5m. However, this again reflects the risk of Dobbs' operations in the UK and the expected growth prospects; the 13% cost of capital calculated by the Finance Director would suggest that the American company has a higher P/E ratio reflecting the higher growth potential often associated with a smaller company. This would therefore lead to the higher value mentioned above.

(ii) *Strategies for enhancing the value after acquisition*

There are a number of actions that could be taken to enhance the value after acquisition, including:

- Review the individual business units for costs that could be cut or assets that could be sold.
- Consider what economies of scale could be enjoyed across the group to reduce costs or improve revenues.

- Ensure that any reorganisation does not demotivate the staff, particularly in the acquired company, by improving and maintaining communication with the workforce.
- To safeguard the revenue stream we should review the contracts with authors and start looking at terms to renew them on expiry.
- Look at marketing the US magazines and books in the UK and vice versa to enhance revenue streams, and generally look at a more aggressive marketing strategy.
- Re-evaluate the group cost of capital which may have changed to reflect the investors' new perception of risk in the shares.

(iii) *Other recommendations for the funds*

The other possibility for the funds was to repay some debt and buy a smaller UK company. Whether it is worthwhile repaying debt depends on the opportunity cost of capital. If the cost of debt is less than 11% (which seems likely) and the group has investment opportunities which give an IRR in excess of 11%, the company should continue to use debt finance to maximise shareholders' wealth, in theory. If the debt is at a floating rate and the group expects an increase in the rate so that the cost rises above 11%, it might be appropriate to repay some debt.

We do not have information on industry averages, but the gearing of 46% by book values in the last balance sheet does not seem excessive and the interest cover was comfortable. Based on market values, the gearing is only $125/(125 + 398) = 24\%$.

The £30 million cash has not been included in this balance sheet and would be used to reduce the debt in the calculation, while the assets sold would reduce the equity. As the sale price would have exceeded the net asset value, this would reduce the gearing calculated.

The smaller UK company identified may or may not be a better acquisition for the group; no information is given about the target or about any potential synergies that might arise. It may reduce the risk associated with an overseas investment, but it may not provide as much in the way of strategic potential.

(iv) *Directors' responsibilities*

The UK Takeover code does not have the force of law but the Takeover Panel can reprimand a listed company, suspend the listing or effectively ensure that no regulated professionals want to work with the company. The objectives are to ensure fair and equal treatment between all shareholders; specifically they forbid:

- Action contrary to shareholders' best interests, such as agreeing or rejecting a bid to suit the managers' interests rather than those of the shareholders.
- Shareholders being treated differently in terms of the price offered.
- Information being restricted in its release and associated manipulation of the share prices.
- Insider dealing (this is also illegal).

Dobbs will also have to obey the US rules on competition.

Question 3 – C&C Airlines

(a) **Discount rate**

Using the competitor's beta we can degear it and calculate the asset beta:

1.3 (4/4.7) + 0.15 (0.7/4.7) = 1.13

Using CAPM, discount rate = 5 + (12 − 5) 1.13 = 12.9 or approximately 13%

(Note that assuming a debt beta of zero gives an asset beta of 1.106 and a discount rate of 12.75% or still approximately 13%.)

Limitations of CAPM are:

- It assumes that all the investors are diversified and that all unsystematic risk has been eliminated in the shareholders' portfolios.
- We have used another company as an approximation, but the listed company is likely to have rather different activities and the shareholders will view an unquoted company as far more risky than a listed company because of the marketability of the shares.
- CAPM gives a return which is valid for the next year (a single period model) but we intend to use it to discount a 3-year project.

(b) **Net present value**

Expected number of passengers:

Year 1 = 220 × (1 × 0.1 + 0.8 × 0.5 + 0.5 × 0.3 + 0.4 × 0.1) = 151.8
Year 2 = 220 × (1 × 0.15 + 0.8 × 0.6 + 0.5 × 0.2 + 0.4 × 0.05) = 165

The revenues generated will be the above 48 × 6 × £300 and inflated at 2%

Predicted exchange rates:

t_0	1.530	
t_1	1.530 × 1.04/1.03	1.545
t_2	1.545 × 1.04/1.03	1.560
t_3	1.560 × 1.04/1.03	1.575

In £'000	t_0	t_1	t_2	t_3
Income		13,378	14,832	15,129
Sterling costs (inflated at 3%)		(2,987)	(3,077)	(3,169)
Overheads		(600)	(600)	(600)
Fuel costs (translated and 5% inflation)		(2,855)	(2,969)	(3,087)
		6,936	8,186	8,273
Tax on operating cash flows		(2,081)	(2,456)	(2,482)
Capital costs	(19,608)			10,159
Tax on capital allowances		1,471	1,103	261
	(19,608)	6,326	6,833	16,211
Discount factor at 13%	1	0.885	0.783	0.693
	(19,608)	5,598	5,351	11,234

(i) Net present value = £2.575m

(ii)

Net cash flows	(19,608)	6,326	6,833	16,211
Certainty equivalents	1	0.90	0.85	0.80
	(19,608)	5,693	5,809	12,969
Discount factor at 9%	1	0.917	0.842	0.772
	(19,608)	5,220	4,891	10,012

Net present value = £0.515m

Based on these calculations, the investment should go ahead. Both methods do depend heavily on the resale value of the plane, however.

(c)

REPORT

To: Board of C&C Airlines plc
From: Assistant to Financial Manager
Date: xx of x 20xx

Investment appraisal of new plane

This report will look at the major economic factors that will impact on the investment decision, the commercial areas of greatest uncertainty and the strategies for dealing with these risks.

1 *Major economic forces*

The major economic forces that might impact on the success of the investment, include:

- The changes in interest rates, both in absolute terms and relatively between those in the Caribbean and the UK. This will affect the borrowing costs, the fuelling costs and the demand.
- Increased interest rate might increase prices in the Caribbean and impact on the tourist business.
- The airline industry is affected by political and safety concerns which can impact on the access to airports and the number of flights, and their timing allowed.

2 *Commercial aspects involving uncertainty*

Those commercial aspects which carry the greatest uncertainty and hence risk to the project are:

- The future state of the tourist trade and estimates of the expansion in demand; are there sufficient numbers of tourists wanting flights only rather than a package holiday?
- Whether there is a realistic demand for a low-cost no-frills airline to fly to an up-market destination.
- The level of competition in the industry and particularly rivals flying to similar destinations.

- The high passenger loading required to be viable.
- The resale value of the plane which will be dependent upon the availability of second-hand planes in 3 years' time.
- The insurance and security costs may increase as airlines come under attack more.

3 *Strategies for dealing with risks*

Dealing with these might include:

- Hedging exchange rates and possibly buying fuel forward to mitigate the effect of rising prices.
- Aim for a mixed demand of tourist and business visitors; in the long term, consider whether an alliance could be made with larger airlines that do not fly to the destination.
- Assess the impact on the viability of the investment of a lower resale value and consider the possibility of agreeing a deal now to take place in 3 years' time.
- Take out insurance and employ security guards to combat the security risks, although this can only mitigate them to a limited extent and can be very expensive.

4 *Recommendations*

- There are large number of estimates and probabilities involved in the calculations. The probabilities attached to the loadings should be reviewed carefully, and all estimates assessed to determine the decision's sensitivity to changes in each. The certainty equivalents are not justified at all and there is an argument for applying different certainties to the operating cash flows and the resale of the plane. The 9% also seems high if the cash flows have been converted into certainty equivalents and there is no justification given for this rate.
- Overall, all the estimates need looking at carefully and sensitivity analysis should be carried out, but based on these calculations the investment should go ahead and the various methods for mitigating the risks identified above implemented.

Question 4 – Hi-Clean

(a) **2005 forecasts**

	Public Sector £m	Hotels/Restaurants £m	Total £m
Sales revenue	104.90	131.00	235.90
Direct costs	57.69	65.50	123.19
Gross profit (45%, 50%)	47.21	65.50	112.71
Fixed overheads (apport'd)	31.93	39.87	71.80
Operating profit	15.28	25.63	40.91
Interest (25m × 0.06)			1.50
			39.41
Taxation (18%)			7.09
Profit after tax			32.32
Dividends (30%)			9.69
Retained earnings			22.63
EPS			107.7p

Sales revenue

Public sector = [(102 × 0.55) + (112 × 0.45)] × 0.6 + [(95 × 0.5) + (110 × 0.5)] × 0.4
= 104.9

Hotels = (123 × 0.6) + (143 × 0.4) = 131

Gross profit is forecast to grow at a faster rate than the fixed costs. As this will lead to an increased operating profit and as interest costs are falling, the constant payout ratio will lead to an increase in dividends of 15%.

(b)

REPORT

To: Board of Hi-clean plc
From: Financial Manager
Date: xx of x 20xx

Company valuation and venture capitalist

This report will look at possible valuations for the company and the stake held by the venture capitalist.

1 *Asset valuation*

We could value the company by adding up the value of all the assets less liabilities of the company. This would give £147 million at the end of 2004 and a further £22.63 million of retained earnings in 2005 giving £169.6 million at the end of 2005. However this does not take account of the value of the future revenue streams, as it makes no allowance for the goodwill that has been generated by the business. In addition, the asset values of buildings, land and other fixed assets may not be up to date in the balance sheet.

2 *Dividend valuation model*

We could value the future projected dividends by discounting the forecasts. The industry cost of capital is 9% and to estimate growth we could look at past growth. As earnings have grown by 20% each year and dividend payout ratio has remained constant at 30%, dividends have also grown by 20% per annum. Even between 2004 and 2005, dividends are forecast to increase by 15%. As both of these are in excess of the return required, it cannot continue at this level indefinitely. To give a base position we could assume a zero growth:

$$\frac{D_1}{(k_e - g)} = \frac{9.69}{0.09} = £107.7m$$

As this is less than the asset valuation, it is not very reliable. With 5% growth, it would give:

$$\frac{(9.69 \times 1.05)}{(0.09 - 0.05)} = £254.4m$$

3 *Earnings capitalisation*

We could assume steady earnings which are all paid out rather than only 30%, giving:

$$\frac{32.32}{0.09} = £359m$$

4 *Earnings multiple*

The industry P/E ratio is forecast to be somewhere between 12 and 15; applying these to post-tax profits gives a variety of estimates:

P/E ratio	12	13	14	15
Value (£32.32 × multiple)	£388m	£420m	£452m	£485m

5 *Summary of valuations*

The venture capitalist owns 20% of the company so the range of values gives:

	Group total £m	VC share (20%) £m
Assets	170	34
Dividends	108	22
Capitalised earnings	359	72
Earnings multiple	388–485	78–97

The highest values are given by the earnings multiple calculated from the industry P/E ratios, even at the lower end of the forecasts.

6 *Venture capitalist's share*

Although the venture capitalist has a seat on the Board, the seat may not be transferable to a new holder, particularly if the shareholding is split up. It therefore does not give control and a 20% stake may be worth substantially less than suggested above; as there is not a stock market listing there is no liquid market in the shares which will also reduce the value of the holding. However, if the venture capitalist exercised the warrants, it would give control of over 26% which could increase its value substantially, as it gives the power to block special resolutions.

(c) **Venture capital return**

The return achieved by the venture capitalist will depend on the price obtained on the sale. If we use the earnings multiple approach based on a P/E ratio of 12 and capitalised earnings:

	P/E ratio	Earnings capitalisation
20% of value	78	72
Investment	25	25
	53	47
Dividends (Working)	7	7
Total return	60	54
Percentage of investment	240%	216%
Annual return (Working)	27.7%	25.9%

218 Exam Practice Kit: Management Accounting Financial Strategy

Working

Working backwards at 20% growth per annum, dividend = 0.20 × (9.69 + 8.43 + 7.02 + 5.85 + 4.88)

Annual return given by $(1 + r)^5$ = 3.40 or 3.16

It can be seen from this that the venture capitalist will not make the required return of 50% per annum. If a simple interest approach had been used instead of compound capital growth, the results would have been 48% and 43% respectively, which are closer. A sale value near the top end of the multiple range would have to be achieved to satisfy this objective.

These calculations also do not take into account the possible downgrading of the value of the stake on sale from a straight 20% of the total value of the company, as discussed above. This would reduce the return further.

Typical exit routes would be to sell them on the open market or privately to a third party. In this case the company is unquoted so the venture capitalist will have to find another private investor; this may be another venture capitalist or the current owners, managers or employees. It is possible that the second group would have difficulty raising the finance required and would try to negotiate an earn-out which would delay payment even longer. The venture capitalist may therefore want the company to float on the stock market as it would give a much easier exit route, probably at a better price and would enable them to exercise their warrants, giving them a greater return.

(d) **Risks and opportunities**

The main risks and opportunities facing the company are:

- The outcome of the election. This will directly affect the sales to the public sector; if party B wins, the company will need to try to increase the sales to the private sector. This may not be easy as all the industry competitors will have the same objective.
- Exchange rate fluctuations. As the company imports equipment a change in the exchange rate could have a dramatic impact on the profitability of the company. The company should consider hedging the risk.
- Interest rate fluctuations. As the loan is a floating rate, an increase in rates could cause a problem. The current rates seem to be lower so it may be an opportunity to refinance the loan (which has to be repaid in 2006) and possibly increase the gearing of the company, which is currently low.
- The change in ownership of the venture capitalist stake. The new owner may want to be more actively involved in the management of the company. This could be an opportunity if they bring additional skills or bring a risk of unwanted interference.
- A listing on the stock market. Flotation would bring greater marketability of shares and the ability to raise finance more easily but also brings greater public scrutiny. The sale of a large stake held by the venture capitalist might also depress the share price.

Question 5 – JHC Group

(a) (i) **Net present values**

Alternative 1

In €'000

	t_0	t_1	t_2	t_3	t_{4-8}
Equipment	(3,200)	(4,800)			
Revenue		4,480	11,800	17,600	17,600
Variable costs		(1,568)	(4,130)	(6,160)	(6,160)
Fixed Costs		(2,500)	(2,500)	(2,500)	(2,500)
Redundancy	(2,100)				
Conversion		(2,800)			
Tax					(1,788)
Lost Earnings		(2,200)	(2,200)	(2,200)	(2,200)
	(5,300)	(9,388)	2,970	6,740	4,952
Discount Factor	1	0.917	0.842	0.772	3.890 × 0.772
	(5,300)	(8,609)	2,501	5,203	14,871

Net present value = €8,666,000 over 8 years

Alternative 2

In €'000

	t_0	t_1	t_2	t_3	t_{4-6}
Equipment	(4,500)				
Revenue		7,800	9,680	13,130	13,130
Variable costs		(1,560)	(1,936)	(2,626)	(2,626)
Fixed Costs		(1,500)	(1,500)	(1,500)	(1,500)
Redundancy	(420)				
Conversion		(2,800)			
Tax					(1,801)
Lost Earnings		(2,200)	(2,200)	(2,200)	(2,200)
	(4,920)	(260)	4,044	6,804	5,003
Discount Factor	1	0.917	0.842	0.772	2.531 × 0.772
	(4,920)	(238)	3,405	5,253	9,776

Net present value = €13,276,000 over 6 years

On the basis of these calculations, it would appear that alternative 2 is the better option.

These calculations assume:

- The WACC is the appropriate discount rate, but this may not be the case if the business or financial risk changes.
- In alternative 1, we have assumed that we accept the supplier's offer to pay a 50% deposit to secure the price.
- The two alternatives have been assessed over the lives of the machines. They, therefore, have not considered the loss in earnings from CC, or any other cashflows, beyond this.

- Cashflows beyond year 3 have been assumed to remain constant but this may not be realistic. The objectives say that JHC intend to increase operating cashflows by 4% pa but this may be achieved by undertaking new projects or increasing revenues on certain projects, rather than increasing cashflows on all projects across the board. Any increase in cashflows beyond year 3 would clearly increase the net present values.

(ii) **MIRR**

The MIRR calculates the Internal Rate of Return, having first converted all cashflows into two single cashflows – the initial investment and a final terminal cashflow. This second cashflow is produced by compounding forward all cashflows, except the initial investment, at the normal cost of capital to the end of the project life. The advantages and disadvantages include

- Having only two cashflows makes the calculation of the IRR straightforward and avoids the possibility of multiple IRRs.
- The MIRR will usually give the same ranking as the NPV.
- However, compounding cashflows at the cost of capital rather than the true IRR (implicit in a "normal" IRR) will understate the value of good projects and overstate poor ones.
- In addition, because of the use of the cost of capital to take cashflows to their terminal value, the longer the project the more approximate it becomes.

In this case, the alternatives have different lives, which makes the MIRR less appropriate.

(b)

REPORT

To: Board of JHC Group
From: Financial Manager
Date: xx of x 20xx

New subsidiary, SP

This report will discuss how the new subsidiary might help the group achieve its objectives, consider other relevant factors and make recommendations on the way forward.

(i) *Achievement of objectives*

The two alternatives give different net present values; although both give positive values which would suggest the investment is viable, the greater net present value is achieved under alternative 2 with €13.276 m. In terms of shareholders' wealth, in theory both alternatives should help it to increase, with alternative 2 making the greater contribution. However, the current value of the company is over €2,900 m so the NPV of approximately €13 m will not make a significant impact. In theory this would add about 4 cents to the current share price of €8.31. In this respect there is little to choose between them.

The establishment of SP might help the employees and other stakeholders as it will produce employment and demand instead of the subsidiary CC which is only operating at 60%.

The company also wants to improve cash flows and dividends by 4% per annum. Under both alternatives, the first two years have cash outflows, so the group will see a drop in cashflows in the first two years (and a greater drop under alternative 1). The investment will, therefore, be detrimental to the achievement of this objective, although, as with the first objective, the impact is insignificant in the group context. There will be little significant impact on dividends.

(ii) *Other factors to consider*

The main commercial risk in alternative 1 is that there are fewer customers, on whom we will be more dependent, while alternative 2 has customers in developing countries, which might cause credit risk problems.

Although there are political uncertainties in the UK relating to safety issues, as mentioned in the scenario, there are further political risks in alternative 2 which includes overseas customers.

The main operational risk is that a change in the regulations means that the equipment specified in alternative 2 cannot be used, as it only allows for a modest change in regulations. One possibility is to go for the least-risk option of alternative 1, despite the lower NPV; this could be used in PR and corporate image projection to show the high environmental standards achieved by the group.

In the calculation of the NPV, the WACC was used as a discount rate but it may not be appropriate to the investment under consideration; we would ideally find a proxy quoted company in the same business and use its beta but this might be difficult in practice.

We have assumed that we will take up the supplier's offer for the equipment purchase; this will protect us against the price rising but means that we pay the cash 6 months earlier than we would otherwise. We, therefore, need to look at the opportunity cost of this finance.

The revenue estimates have different possible ranges; we need to use sensitivity analysis and simulation to establish the likelihood of these outcomes more accurately. Currency risk is introduced in alternative 2 and it would be sensible to look at the possibility of hedging these revenues.

The equipment in alternative 2 will need replacing before that in alternative 1 but this is based on current estimates; in a field such as this in which technology is evolving, it is possible that lives may be shorter or alternatively could be extended through adaptive technology.

(iii) *Recommendations*

Maximising shareholders' wealth would suggest alternative 2, as would the employment prospects for the workforce. Alternative 1, however, is environmentally better and therefore may have other, less easily quantifiable, advantages for the group image. The risks discussed above are fairly evenly balanced.

Neither contribute significantly to either objective and as such it is worth seeing if there are any larger-scale investments that could be undertaken in preference to this.

(c) **Real options**

JHC Group have three possible options relating to this investment – the abandonment option, the delay option and the follow-on option.

Abandonment option

An abandonment option is when a company can decide not to continue with an investment as circumstances change; this can increase the value of a project as there is less risk of being stuck with an unviable investment. Usually this is difficult when expenditure on capital equipment is involved as the main costs have been incurred and abandoning the project will only sacrifice revenues. In this situation, alternative 1 could be abandoned if it did not take up the supplier's offer and risked the 5% increase in price; this, along with the redundancies and loss of CC, seems a high price to pay for this option. In alternative 2 the project could be abandoned up until the factory is fully converted in 6 months' time.

Delay option

There may be scope for delaying the investment until the government decisions and regulations relating to these environmental issues are clearer. This may then allow a much better estimate of revenues and costs and consequently a more reliable decision on the investment. The current NPV has been calculated by using expected values based on subjective probabilities of the different courses of action by the government. We could, therefore, calculate different NPVs and estimate the probability of us undertaking the investment, based on expected values, but achieving a negative NPV; this would give us an idea of the value of the delay option.

Follow-on option

Sometimes investment decisions give other opportunities even if the original investment was not particularly beneficial in its own right (and possibly even had a negative NPV). In this situation, the knowledge gained in the operation or the reputation of a good environmental record in this area may lead to substantial other work. By its nature this will be difficult to quantify but could be valuable in the health food industry.

May 2006 Questions and Answers

15

Strategic Level

Paper P9 – Management Accounting Financial Strategy

Question Paper 224

Examiner's Brief Guide to the Paper 239

Examiner's Answers 241

The answers published here have been written by the Examiner and should provide a helpful guide for both lecturers and students.

Published separately on the CIMA website (www.cimaglobal.com/students) from the end of September 2006 is a Post Examination Guide for this paper, which provides much valuable and complementary material including indicative mark information.

© 2006 The Chartered Institute of Management Accountants. All rights reserved. No part of this publication may be reproduced, stored in a retrieval system, or transmitted, in any form or by any means, electronic, mechanical, photocopying, recorded or otherwise, without the written permission of the publisher.

Financial Management Pillar

Strategic Level Paper

P9 – Management Accounting Financial Strategy

24 May 2006 – Wednesday Morning Session

Instructions to candidates

You are allowed three hours to answer this question paper.
You are allowed 20 minutes reading time **before the examination begins** during which you should read the question paper and, if you wish, make annotations on the question paper. However, you will **not** be allowed, **under any circumstances**, to open the answer book and start writing or use your calculator during the reading time.
You are strongly advised to carefully read ALL the question requirements before attempting the question concerned (that is, all parts and/or sub-questions). The question requirements are highlighted in a dotted box.
Answer the ONE compulsory question in Section A on pages 225 to 228. The question requirements are on page 5, which is detachable for ease of reference.
Answer TWO of the four questions in Section B on pages 229 to 233.
Maths Tables and Formulae are provided on pages 234 to 238. These are detachable for ease of reference.
Write your full examination number, paper number and the examination subject title in the spaces provided on the front of the examination answer book. Also write your contact ID and name in the space provided in the right hand margin and seal to close.
Tick the appropriate boxes on the front of the answer book to indicate which questions you have answered.

SECTION A – 50 MARKS

[the indicative time for answering this section is 90 minutes]

READ THE SCENARIO AND ANSWER THIS QUESTION. THE QUESTION REQUIREMENTS ARE ON PAGE 228

Question One

Scenario

PM Industries plc

Background

PM Industries plc (PM) is a UK-based entity with shares trading on a UK Stock Exchange. It is a long established business with widespread commercial and industrial interests worldwide. It had a modest growth and profitability record until four years ago when a new Chief Executive Officer (CEO) was appointed from the United States of America (US). This new CEO has transformed the business by divesting poor performing, or non-core, subsidiaries or business units and focusing on volume growth in the remaining units. Some of this growth has been internally generated and some has come about because of financially sound acquisitions. A particular area of strength is in non-drug pharmaceutical materials such as packaging. PM now controls the largest share of this market in the UK and Europe.

Financial objectives

PM's current financial objectives are:

- To increase EPS by 5% per annum;
- To maintain a gearing ratio (market values of long-term debt to equity) below 30%;
- To maintain a P/E ratio above the industry average.

Proposed merger

The senior management of PM is currently negotiating a merger with NQ Inc (NQ), a US-based entity with shares trading on a US Stock Exchange. NQ is an entity of similar size to PM, in terms of revenue and assets, with a similar spread of commercial and industrial interests, especially pharmaceutical materials, which is why PM originally became attracted to NQ.

NQ has had a less impressive track record of growth than PM over the last two years because of some poor performing business units. As a result, PM's market capitalisation is substantially higher than NQ's. Although this will, in reality, be an acquisition, PM's CEO refers to it as a "merger" in negotiations to avoid irritating the NQ Board, which is very sensitive to the issue.

NQ holds some software licences to products that the CEO of PM thinks are not being marketed as well as they could be. He believes he could sell these licences to a large software entity in the UK for around £100 million. He does not see the commercial logic in retaining them, as information technology is not a core business. The value of these licences is included in NQ's balance sheet at $US125 million.

Both entities believe a merger between them makes commercial and financial sense, as long as terms can be agreed. The CEO of PM thinks his entity will have the upper hand in negotiations because of the share price performance of PM over the last 12 months and his own reputation in the City. He also believes he can boost the entity's share value if he can convince the market his entity's growth rating can be applied to NQ's earnings.

Summary of relevant financial data

Extracts from the Income Statements for the year ended 31 March 2006

	PM (£m)	NQ ($m)
Revenue	1,560	2,500
Operating profit	546	750
Earnings available for ordinary shareholders	273	300

Extracts from the Balance Sheets as at 31 March 2006

	PM (£m)	NQ ($m)
Total net assets	2,000	2,100
Total equity	850	1,550
Total long term debt	1,150	550

Other data

	PM	NQ
Number of shares in issue		
Ordinary shares of 10 pence	950,000,000	
Common stock of $1		850,000,000
Share price as at today (24 May 2006)	456 pence	450 cents
High/low share price over last 12 months	475/326 pence	520/280 cents
Industry average P/E ratio	14	13
Debt traded within last week at	£105	Par

Five-year revenue and earnings record

	PM (£m)		NQ (US$m)	
Year ended 31 March	Revenue	Earnings	Revenue	Earnings
2002	1,050	225	1,850	250
2003	1,125	231	1,950	265
2004	1,250	245	2,150	280
2005	1,400	258	2,336	290
2006	1,560	273	2,500	300

The two entities' revenue and operating profits are generated in the following five geographical areas, with average figures over the past five years as follows:

	PM		NQ	
Percentage of total	*Revenue*	*Profits*	*Revenue*	*Profits*
UK	30	28	20	17
US	22	23	75	76
Mainland Europe	20	17	5	7
Asia (mainly Japan)	18	20	0	0
Rest of World	10	12	0	0

Economic data

PM's bankers have provided forecast interest and inflation rates in the two main areas of operation for the next 12 months as follows:

	Interest rates *Current forecast*	*Inflation rate* *Current forecast*
UK	4.5%	2.0%
US	2.5%	1.5%

Terms of the merger

PM intends to open the negotiations by suggesting terms of 1 PM share for 2 NQ stock units. The Finance Director of PM, plus the entity's professional advisors, have forecast the following data, post-merger, for PM. They believe this is a "conservative" estimate as it excludes their estimate of value of the software licences. The current spot exchange rate is $US1.85 = £1.

Market capitalisation	£6,905 million
EPS	31.65 pence

A cash offer as an alternative to a share exchange is unlikely, although the CEO of PM has not ruled it out should the bid turn hostile. However, this would require substantial borrowing by PM, even if only 50% of NQ's shareholders opt for cash.

Except for the potential profit on the sale of the licences, no savings or synergies from the merger have as yet been identified.

Requirements

Assume you are one of the financial advisors working for PM.

(a)
- (i) Explain, with supporting calculations, how the Finance Director and advisors of PM have arrived at their estimates of post-merger values.

    (10 marks)

- (ii) Calculate and comment briefly on the likely impact on the share price and market capitalisation for each of PM and NQ when the bid terms are announced. Make appropriate assumptions based on the information given in the scenario.

    (4 marks)

- (iii) If NQ rejects the terms offered, calculate
    - the maximum total amount and price per share to be paid for the entity; and
    - the resulting share exchange terms PM should be prepared to agree without reducing PM's shareholder wealth.

    (6 marks)
    (Total for part (a) = 20 marks)

(b)

Write a report to the Board of PM that evaluates and discusses the following issues:

- (i) How the merger might contribute to the achievement of PM's financial objectives, assuming the merger goes ahead on the terms you have calculated in (a) (iii). If you have not managed to calculate terms, make sensible assumptions;

    (12 marks)

- (ii) External economic forces that might help and/or hinder the achievement of the merger's financial objectives. Comment also on the policies the merged entity could consider to help reduce adverse effects of such economic forces;

    (8 marks)

- (iii) Potential post-merger value enhancing strategies that could increase shareholder wealth.

    (10 marks)
    (Total for part (b) = 30 marks)

Up to 4 marks are available for structure and presentation in Question One.

(Total for Question One = 50 marks)

SECTION B – 50 MARKS

[the indicative time for answering this section is 90 minutes]

ANSWER *TWO* ONLY OF THE FOUR QUESTIONS

Question Two

MNO is a private toy distributor situated in the United States of America (US) with a US customer base and local suppliers. There is a central manufacturing base and several marketing units spread across the US. The marketing units are encouraged to adapt to local market conditions, largely acting independently and free from central control. These units are responsible for all aspects of local sales, including collecting sales revenues, which are paid across to Head Office on a monthly basis. Funding is provided by Head Office as required.

Figures for last year to 31 December 2005 were as follows:

Revenue	$10 million
Gross profit margin	40% of revenue
Accounts receivable days	minimum 20, maximum 30 days
Accounts payable days	minimum 40, maximum 50 days
Inventories	minimum 50, maximum 80 days
Non-current assets	$8 million

Accounts receivable, accounts payable and inventories can all be assumed to be the same on both 31 December 2004 and 31 December 2005, but fluctuate between those dates.

The Financial Controller is carrying out an analysis of MNO's working capital levels, as requested by the Treasurer. He is assuming that the peak period for accounts receivable coincides with the peak period for inventories and the lowest level of accounts payable.

MNO is currently in consultation with a potentially significant new supplier in Asia, who will demand payment in its local currency.

Requirements

(a)
  (i) Calculate the minimum and maximum working capital levels based on the Financial Controller's assumption regarding the timing of peaks and troughs in working capital variables and discuss the validity of that assumption.

  (6 marks)

  (ii) Using the figures calculated in (i) above, calculate and draw a chart in your answer book to show the short-term and long-term (permanent) financing requirements of MNO under each of the following working capital financing policies:

  - moderate policy, where long-term financing matches permanent net current assets;
  - aggressive policy, where 30% of permanent net current assets are funded by short-term financing;
  - conservative policy, where only 40% of fluctuating net current assets are funded by short-term financing.

  (7 marks)

(b) Discuss the advantages and disadvantages of an aggressive financing policy and advise whether or not such a policy would be appropriate for MNO.

  (6 marks)

(c) Advise MNO whether a profit or cost centre structure would be more appropriate for its treasury department.

  (6 marks)
  (Total for Question Two = 25 marks)

Question Three

EFG is a South American entity specialising in providing information systems solutions to large corporates. It is going through a period of rapid expansion and requires additional funds to finance the long-term working capital needs of the business.

EFG has issued one million $1 ordinary shares, which are listed on the local stock market at a current market price of $15, with typical increases of 10% per annum expected in the next five-year period. Dividend payout is kept constant at a level of 10% of post-tax profits. EFG also has $10 million of bank borrowings.

It is estimated that a further $3 million is required to satisfy the funding requirements of the business for the next five-year period beginning 1 July 2006. Two major institutional shareholders have indicated that they are not prepared to invest further in EFG at the present time and so a rights issue is unlikely to succeed. The directors are, therefore, considering various forms of debt finance. Three alternative structures are under discussion as shown below:

- Five-year unsecured bank loan at a fixed interest rate of 7% per annum;
- Five-year unsecured bond with a coupon of 5% per annum, redeemable at par and issued at a 6% discount to par;
- A convertible bond, issued at par, with an annual coupon of 4.5% and a conversion option in five years' time of five shares for each $100 nominal of debt.

There have been lengthy boardroom discussions on the relative merits of each instrument and you, as Finance Director, have been asked to address the following queries:

Sr. A: "The bank loan would seem to be more expensive than the unsecured bond. Is this actually the case?"

Sr. B: "Surely the convertible bond would be the cheapest form of borrowing with such a low interest rate?"

Sr. C: "If we want to increase our equity base, why use a convertible bond, rather than a straight equity issue?"

Requirements

(a) Write a response to Sr. A, Sr. B and Sr. C, directors of EFG, discussing the issues raised and advising on the most appropriate financing instrument for EFG. In your answer, include calculations of:

- expected conversion value of the convertible bond in five years' time;
- yield to maturity (redemption yield) of the five-year unsecured bond. Ignore tax.

(18 marks)
(including up to 8 marks for calculations)

(b) Advise a prospective investor in the five-year unsecured bond issued by EFG on what information he should expect to be provided with and what further analysis he should undertake in order to assess the creditworthiness of the proposed investment.

(7 marks)
(Total for Question Three = 25 marks)

Question Four

GHI is a mobile phone manufacturer based in France with a wide customer base in France and Germany, with all costs and revenues based in euro (€). GHI is considering expanding into the UK market and has begun investigating how to break into this market and is designing a new phone specifically for it. A small project committee has been formed to plan and control the project.

After careful investigation, the following project cash flows have been identified:

Year	£million
0	(10)
1	5
2	5
3	4
4	3
5	3

The project is to be funded by a loan of €16 million at an annual interest rate of 5% and repayable at the end of five years. Loan issue costs amount to 2% and are tax deductible.

GHI has a debt–equity ratio of 40:60 based on market values, a pre-tax cost of debt of 5.0% and a cost of equity of 10.7%.

Tax on entity profits in France can be assumed to be at a rate of 35%, payable in the year in which it arises. UK tax at 25% is deductible in full against French tax in the same time period under the terms of the double tax treaty between the UK and France. The initial investment of £10 million will not qualify for any tax relief.

Assume the current spot rate is £1 = €1.60 and sterling (£) is expected to weaken against the euro by 3% per annum (so that in year 1 it is worth only 97% of its value in euro (€) in year 0).

Requirements

(a) Advise GHI on whether or not to proceed with the project based on a calculation of its adjusted present value (APV) and describe the limitations of an APV approach in this context.

(15 marks)

(b) Explain the function of the project committee of GHI in the following stages of the project:

　(i) determining customer requirements and an appropriate product design for the UK market; and

(5 marks)

　(ii) controlling the implementation stage of the project.

(5 marks)
(Total for Question Four = 25 marks)

Question Five

RST is a publicly owned and funded health organisation based in the Far East. It is reviewing a number of interesting possibilities for new development projects in the area and has narrowed down the choice to the five projects detailed below. RST is aware that government budget restrictions may be tighter in a year's time and so does not want to commit to a capital budget of more than $30 million in Year 1. In addition, any project cash inflows in Year 1 may be used to fund capital expenditure in that year. There is sufficient capital budget remaining in Year 0 to enable all projects to be undertaken. Under government funding rules, any unused capital in Year 0 cannot be carried over to Year 1 and no interest may be earned on unused capital. No borrowings are permitted.

RST assesses capital projects at a hurdle rate of 15% based on the equity beta of health-based companies in the private sector.

Project	Cash outflows Year 0 $ million	Year 1 $ million	Cash inflows $ million
A	9	16	4 from Year 1 in perpetuity
B	10	10	4 from Year 2 in perpetuity
C	10	12	5 in Years 1 to 10
D	8	5	6 in Years 3 to 7
E	9	8	{2 in Years 1 to 5 / 5 in Years 6 to 15}

Notes:
- the projects are not divisible
- each project can be undertaken only once
- ignore tax.

Requirements

(a) Advise RST on the best combination of projects based on an evaluation of each project on the basis of both:

(i) NPV of cashflows;
(ii) a profitability index for use in this capital rationing analysis.

(15 marks)

(b) Discuss

(i) whether or not capital rationing techniques based on NPV analysis are appropriate for a publicly owned entity such as RST.

(5 marks)

(ii) as a publicly owned entity, what other factors RST should consider and what other analysis it should undertake before making a final decision on which project(s) to accept.

(5 marks)
(Total for Question Five = 25 marks)

Maths Tables and Formulae

Present value table

Present value of 1.00 unit of currency, that is $(1 + r)^{-n}$ where r = interest rate; n = number of periods until payment or receipt.

Periods (n)	Interest rates (r)									
	1%	2%	3%	4%	5%	6%	7%	8%	9%	10%
1	0.990	0.980	0.971	0.962	0.952	0.943	0.935	0.926	0.917	0.909
2	0.980	0.961	0.943	0.925	0.907	0.890	0.873	0.857	0.842	0.826
3	0.971	0.942	0.915	0.889	0.864	0.840	0.816	0.794	0.772	0.751
4	0.961	0.924	0.888	0.855	0.823	0.792	0.763	0.735	0.708	0.683
5	0.951	0.906	0.863	0.822	0.784	0.747	0.713	0.681	0.650	0.621
6	0.942	0.888	0.837	0.790	0.746	0.705	0.666	0.630	0.596	0.564
7	0.933	0.871	0.813	0.760	0.711	0.665	0.623	0.583	0.547	0.513
8	0.923	0.853	0.789	0.731	0.677	0.627	0.582	0.540	0.502	0.467
9	0.914	0.837	0.766	0.703	0.645	0.592	0.544	0.500	0.460	0.424
10	0.905	0.820	0.744	0.676	0.614	0.558	0.508	0.463	0.422	0.386
11	0.896	0.804	0.722	0.650	0.585	0.527	0.475	0.429	0.388	0.350
12	0.887	0.788	0.701	0.625	0.557	0.497	0.444	0.397	0.356	0.319
13	0.879	0.773	0.681	0.601	0.530	0.469	0.415	0.368	0.326	0.290
14	0.870	0.758	0.661	0.577	0.505	0.442	0.388	0.340	0.299	0.263
15	0.861	0.743	0.642	0.555	0.481	0.417	0.362	0.315	0.275	0.239
16	0.853	0.728	0.623	0.534	0.458	0.394	0.339	0.292	0.252	0.218
17	0.844	0.714	0.605	0.513	0.436	0.371	0.317	0.270	0.231	0.198
18	0.836	0.700	0.587	0.494	0.416	0.350	0.296	0.250	0.212	0.180
19	0.828	0.686	0.570	0.475	0.396	0.331	0.277	0.232	0.194	0.164
20	0.820	0.673	0.554	0.456	0.377	0.312	0.258	0.215	0.178	0.149

Periods (n)	Interest rates (r)									
	11%	12%	13%	14%	15%	16%	17%	18%	19%	20%
1	0.901	0.893	0.885	0.877	0.870	0.862	0.855	0.847	0.840	0.833
2	0.812	0.797	0.783	0.769	0.756	0.743	0.731	0.718	0.706	0.694
3	0.731	0.712	0.693	0.675	0.658	0.641	0.624	0.609	0.593	0.579
4	0.659	0.636	0.613	0.592	0.572	0.552	0.534	0.516	0.499	0.482
5	0.593	0.567	0.543	0.519	0.497	0.476	0.456	0.437	0.419	0.402
6	0.535	0.507	0.480	0.456	0.432	0.410	0.390	0.370	0.352	0.335
7	0.482	0.452	0.425	0.400	0.376	0.354	0.333	0.314	0.296	0.279
8	0.434	0.404	0.376	0.351	0.327	0.305	0.285	0.266	0.249	0.233
9	0.391	0.361	0.333	0.308	0.284	0.263	0.243	0.225	0.209	0.194
10	0.352	0.322	0.295	0.270	0.247	0.227	0.208	0.191	0.176	0.162
11	0.317	0.287	0.261	0.237	0.215	0.195	0.178	0.162	0.148	0.135
12	0.286	0.257	0.231	0.208	0.187	0.168	0.152	0.137	0.124	0.112
13	0.258	0.229	0.204	0.182	0.163	0.145	0.130	0.116	0.104	0.093
14	0.232	0.205	0.181	0.160	0.141	0.125	0.111	0.099	0.088	0.078
15	0.209	0.183	0.160	0.140	0.123	0.108	0.095	0.084	0.079	0.065
16	0.188	0.163	0.141	0.123	0.107	0.093	0.081	0.071	0.062	0.054
17	0.170	0.146	0.125	0.108	0.093	0.080	0.069	0.060	0.052	0.045
18	0.153	0.130	0.111	0.095	0.081	0.069	0.059	0.051	0.044	0.038
19	0.138	0.116	0.098	0.083	0.070	0.060	0.051	0.043	0.037	0.031
20	0.124	0.104	0.087	0.073	0.061	0.051	0.043	0.037	0.031	0.026

Cumulative present value of 1.00 unit of currency per annum

Receivable or Payable at the end of each year for n years $\left[\dfrac{1-(1+r)^{-n}}{r}\right]$

Periods (n)	Interest rates (r)									
	1%	2%	3%	4%	5%	6%	7%	8%	9%	10%
1	0.990	0.980	0.971	0.962	0.952	0.943	0.935	0.926	0.917	0.909
2	1.970	1.942	1.913	1.886	1.859	1.833	1.808	1.783	1.759	1.736
3	2.941	2.884	2.829	2.775	2.723	2.673	2.624	2.577	2.531	2.487
4	3.902	3.808	3.717	3.630	3.546	3.465	3.387	3.312	3.240	3.170
5	4.853	4.713	4.580	4.452	4.329	4.212	4.100	3.993	3.890	3.791
6	5.795	5.601	5.417	5.242	5.076	4.917	4.767	4.623	4.486	4.355
7	6.728	6.472	6.230	6.002	5.786	5.582	5.389	5.206	5.033	4.868
8	7.652	7.325	7.020	6.733	6.463	6.210	5.971	5.747	5.535	5.335
9	8.566	8.162	7.786	7.435	7.108	6.802	6.515	6.247	5.995	5.759
10	9.471	8.983	8.530	8.111	7.722	7.360	7.024	6.710	6.418	6.145
11	10.368	9.787	9.253	8.760	8.306	7.887	7.499	7.139	6.805	6.495
12	11.255	10.575	9.954	9.385	8.863	8.384	7.943	7.536	7.161	6.814
13	12.134	11.348	10.635	9.986	9.394	8.853	8.358	7.904	7.487	7.103
14	13.004	12.106	11.296	10.563	9.899	9.295	8.745	8.244	7.786	7.367
15	13.865	12.849	11.938	11.118	10.380	9.712	9.108	8.559	8.061	7.606
16	14.718	13.578	12.561	11.652	10.838	10.106	9.447	8.851	8.313	7.824
17	15.562	14.292	13.166	12.166	11.274	10.477	9.763	9.122	8.544	8.022
18	16.398	14.992	13.754	12.659	11.690	10.828	10.059	9.372	8.756	8.201
19	17.226	15.679	14.324	13.134	12.085	11.158	10.336	9.604	8.950	8.365
20	18.046	16.351	14.878	13.590	12.462	11.470	10.594	9.818	9.129	8.514

Periods (n)	Interest rates (r)									
	11%	12%	13%	14%	15%	16%	17%	18%	19%	20%
1	0.901	0.893	0.885	0.877	0.870	0.862	0.855	0.847	0.840	0.833
2	1.713	1.690	1.668	1.647	1.626	1.605	1.585	1.566	1.547	1.528
3	2.444	2.402	2.361	2.322	2.283	2.246	2.210	2.174	2.140	2.106
4	3.102	3.037	2.974	2.914	2.855	2.798	2.743	2.690	2.639	2.589
5	3.696	3.605	3.517	3.433	3.352	3.274	3.199	3.127	3.058	2.991
6	4.231	4.111	3.998	3.889	3.784	3.685	3.589	3.498	3.410	3.326
7	4.712	4.564	4.423	4.288	4.160	4.039	3.922	3.812	3.706	3.605
8	5.146	4.968	4.799	4.639	4.487	4.344	4.207	4.078	3.954	3.837
9	5.537	5.328	5.132	4.946	4.772	4.607	4.451	4.303	4.163	4.031
10	5.889	5.650	5.426	5.216	5.019	4.833	4.659	4.494	4.339	4.192
11	6.207	5.938	5.687	5.453	5.234	5.029	4.836	4.656	4.486	4.327
12	6.492	6.194	5.918	5.660	5.421	5.197	4.988	7.793	4.611	4.439
13	6.750	6.424	6.122	5.842	5.583	5.342	5.118	4.910	4.715	4.533
14	6.982	6.628	6.302	6.002	5.724	5.468	5.229	5.008	4.802	4.611
15	7.191	6.811	6.462	6.142	5.847	5.575	5.324	5.092	4.876	4.675
16	7.379	6.974	6.604	6.265	5.954	5.668	5.405	5.162	4.938	4.730
17	7.549	7.120	6.729	6.373	6.047	5.749	5.475	5.222	4.990	4.775
18	7.702	7.250	6.840	6.467	6.128	5.818	5.534	5.273	5.033	4.812
19	7.839	7.366	6.938	6.550	6.198	5.877	5.584	5.316	5.070	4.843
20	7.963	7.469	7.025	6.623	6.259	5.929	5.628	5.353	5.101	4.870

FORMULAE

Valuation models

(i) Irredeemable preference share, paying a constant annual dividend, d, in perpetuity, where P_0 is the ex-div value:

$$P_0 = \frac{d}{k_{pref}}$$

(ii) Ordinary (equity) share, paying a constant annual dividend, d, in perpetuity, where P_0 is the ex-div value:

$$P_0 = \frac{d}{k_e}$$

(iii) Ordinary (equity) share, paying an annual dividend, d, growing in perpetuity at a constant rate, g, where P_0 is the ex-div value:

$$P_0 = \frac{d_1}{k_e - g} \quad \text{or} \quad P_0 = \frac{d_0[1+g]}{k_e - g}$$

(iv) Irredeemable (undated) debt, paying annual after-tax interest, $i[1-t]$, in perpetuity, where P_0 is the ex-interest value:

$$P_0 = \frac{i[1-t]}{k_{dnet}}$$

or, without tax:
$$P_0 = \frac{i}{k_d}$$

(v) Total value of the geared firm, V_g (based on MM):

$$V_g = V_u + TB_c$$

(vi) Future value of S, of a sum X, invested for n periods, compounded at $r\%$ interest:

$$S = X[1+r]^n$$

(vii) Present value of 1.00 payable or receivable in n years, discounted at $r\%$ per annum:

$$PV = \frac{1}{[1+r]^n}$$

(viii) Present value of an annuity of 1.00 per annum, receivable or payable for n years, commencing in one year, discounted at $r\%$ per annum:

$$PV = \frac{1}{r}\left[1 - \frac{1}{[1+r]^n}\right]$$

(ix) Present value of 1.00 per annum, payable or receivable in perpetuity, commencing in one year, discounted at $r\%$ per annum:

$$PV = \frac{1}{r}$$

(x) Present value of 1.00 per annum, receivable or payable, commencing in one year, growing in perpetuity at a constant rate of g% per annum, discounted at r% per annum:

$$PV = \frac{1}{r-g}$$

Cost of capital

(i) Cost of irredeemable preference capital, paying an annual dividend, d, in perpetuity, and having a current ex-div price P_0:

$$k_{\text{pref}} = \frac{d}{P_0}$$

(ii) Cost of irredeemable debt capital, paying annual net interest, $i[1-t]$, and having a current ex-interest price P_0:

$$k_{\text{d net}} = \frac{i[1-t]}{P_0}$$

(iii) Cost of ordinary (equity) share capital, paying an annual dividend, d, in perpetuity, and having a current ex-div price P_0:

$$k_e = \frac{d}{P_0}$$

(iv) Cost of ordinary (equity) share capital, having a current ex-div price, P_0, having just paid a dividend, d_0, with the dividend growing in perpetuity by a constant g% per annum:

$$k_e = \frac{d_1}{P_0} + g \quad \text{or} \quad k_e = \frac{d_0[1+g]}{P_0} + g$$

(v) Cost of ordinary (equity) share capital, using the CAPM:

$$k_e = R_f + [R_m - R_f]\beta$$

(vi) Cost of ordinary (equity) share capital in a geared firm (no tax):

$$k_{eg} = k_0 + [k_0 - k_d]\frac{V_D}{V_E}$$

(vii) Cost of ordinary (equity) share capital in a geared firm (with tax):

$$k_{eg} = k_{eu} + [k_{eu} - k_d]\frac{V_D[1-t]}{V_E}$$

(viii) Weighted average cost of capital, k_0:

$$k_0 = k_{eg}\left[\frac{V_E}{V_E + V_D}\right] + k_d\left[\frac{V_D}{V_E + V_D}\right]$$

(ix) Adjusted cost of capital (MM formula):

$$k_{adj} = k_{eu}[1 - tL] \quad \text{or} \quad r^* = r[1 - T^*L]$$

In the following formulae, β_u is used for an ungeared β and β_g is used for a geared β:

(x) β_u from β_g, taking β_d as zero (no tax):

$$\beta_u = \beta_g \left[\frac{V_E}{V_E + V_D} \right]$$

(xi) If β_d is not zero:

$$\beta_u = \beta_g \left[\frac{V_E}{V_E + V_D} \right] + \beta_d \left[\frac{V_D}{V_D + V_E} \right]$$

(xii) β_u from β_g, taking β_d as zero (with tax):

$$\beta_u = \beta_g \left[\frac{V_E}{V_E + V_D[1 - t]} \right]$$

(xiii) Adjusted discount rate to use in international capital budgeting using interest rate parity:

$$\frac{1 + \text{annual discount rate C\$}}{1 + \text{annual discount rate Euro}} = \frac{\text{Exchange rate in 12 month's time C\$/Euro}}{\text{Spot rate C\$/Euro}}$$

Other formulae

(i) Interest rate parity (international Fisher effect):

$$\text{Forward rate US\$/£} = \text{Spot US\$/£} \times \frac{1 + \text{nominal US interest rate}}{1 + \text{nominal UK interest rate}}$$

(ii) Purchasing power parity (law of one price):

$$\text{Forward rate US\$/£} = \text{Spot US\$/£} \times \frac{1 + \text{US inflation rate}}{1 + \text{UK inflation rate}}$$

(iii) Link between nominal (money) and real interest rates:

$$[1 + \text{nominal (money) rate}] = [1 + \text{real interest rate}][1 + \text{inflation rate}]$$

(iv) Equivalent annual cost:

$$\text{Equivalent annual cost} = \frac{PV \text{ of costs over } n \text{ years}}{n \text{ year annuity factor}}$$

(v) Theoretical ex-rights price:

$$\text{TERP} = \frac{1}{N + 1} [(N \times \text{cum rights price}) + \text{issue price}]$$

(vi) Value of a right:

$$\text{Value of a right} = \frac{\text{Rights on price} - \text{issue price}}{N + 1}$$

or

$$\frac{\text{Theoretical ex rights price} - \text{issue price}}{N}$$

where N = number of rights required to buy one share.

The Examiner for Financial Strategy offers to future candidates and to tutors using this booklet for study purposes, the following background and guidance on the questions included in this examination paper.

Section A – Compulsory

Question One This question concerns a proposed merger between a UK-based company and a US-based company. They are of similar size in terms of revenue and net assets, but the UK-based company has a higher growth rating measured by its P/E ratio. The CEO of the UK-based company believes he can improve profitability and market capitalisation by selling some intangible assets and by "bootstrapping" the US-based company's earnings.

The question requires calculations of likely share price movements for both companies, the maximum price the bidder should pay and terms of a share exchange. It further requires evaluation and discussion of how the merger would contribute to the bidder's financial objectives, how these objectives might be affected by external economic forces and post-merger value enhancing strategies.

The question addresses learning outcomes in three sections of the syllabus: Section A – Formulation of financial strategy; Section B – Financial management; and Section C – Business valuations and acquisitions.

Section B – Choice of two from four questions

Question Two Parts (a) and (b) relate to different policies for financing working capital. Candidates are required to calculate the minimum and maximum levels between which the working capital of the entity fluctuates and draw a chart to illustrate how the working capital requirement would be financed under three different financing policies cited in the question. In part (c), candidates are asked to advise the entity on whether a profit or cost centre would be more appropriate for its treasury department.

Question Three This question concerns a South American entity which is going through a period of rapid expansion and requires additional funding. Three alternative debt instruments are proposed and candidates are asked to evaluate these instruments and advise the directors of the entity on the most appropriate financing instrument to use. Calculations of the expected conversion value of a convertible bond and the yield to maturity of an unsecured bond are required as part of the evaluation. Candidates are also required to write a response to queries from the directors about the different instruments under consideration. In the final part, candidates are required to advise on what information is needed by an investor in order to assess the creditworthiness of a proposed investment in EFG.

Question Four Part (a) is a standard appraisal question using an adjusted present value (APV) approach and requiring candidates to describe the limitations of using APV in the context of the scenario given. Part (b) looks at the project in a broader context, asking candidates to explain the function of the project committee at various stages of the project, including product design and pricing structure and implementation. It is based on a topic area that is new to the syllabus and has not been examined before in this manner. Candidates are expected to draw on information provided in the CIMA Study System and also to use general financial and business knowledge when examining the given scenario in order to put together a suitable response.

Question Five This question focuses on capital rationing, testing candidates' computation skills and their understanding of the wider issues involved. Part (a) requires an evaluation of a range of projects using both NPV and profitability index methods in order to advise on the best combination of projects for RST. There are a couple of new twists here: first, capital rationing occurs in year 1, rather than year 0, and, second, candidates are required to calculate the NPV of the cash flows for each project, rather than these being provided. Part (b) contains two discursive sections. First, a discussion of whether capital rationing is appropriate for a publicly owned entity such as RST and, second, consideration of what other factors RST should think about, and what other analysis it should undertake, before making a final decision on which project(s) to accept.

May 2006 Questions and Answers **241**

Examiner's Answers

SECTION A

> **Examiner's Note:**
> The answer to **Question One** is fuller than was expected from a well-prepared candidate. It has been provided for future candidates, and tutors, for study and revision purposes.

Question One

(a)

(i) *Preliminary calculations*

It is useful to convert some of NQ's figures from US$ to £ at spot of 1.85:

Earnings	$300 m/1.85	=	£162.2 m
Share price	450 cents/1.85	=	243 pence
Market capitalisation	243 pence × 850 m shares	=	£2,065 m

The Finance Director and advisors of PM have assumed that PM's own pre-merger P/E ratio will be applied by the market to the combined earnings of the merged entity, as follows:

Pre-merger	PM	NQ	PM + NQ	
Earnings (£m)	273	162.2	435.2	
Number of shares (million)	950	850	1,375	(950 + 850/2)
EPS (pence)	28.74	19.08	31.65	
P/E ratio	15.87	12.73	15.87	
Share price (pence)	456	243	502	
Market value (£m)	4,332	2,065	6,903	(502p × 1,375 m shares)

Post-merger

Proportion of merged entity owned by the present shareholders of:

PM	(950/1,375 × 100)	69.1%		
NQ	(425/1,375 × 100)		30.9%	
Market value (proportion × 6,903)		4,770	2,133	6,903
Number of shares pre-merger (m)		950	850	
Post-merger share price per existing share (pence)		502	251	

PM has assumed its own P/E ratio of 15.87 will be applied to the combined earnings of the merged entity. The combined total of the current market capitalisation of PM and NQ in sterling is £6,397 m (£4,332 m + £2,065 m). The difference between the estimated post-merger value and the current value is £506 m. This is the "bootstrapping" effect – the difference between the P/E ratios is 3.14 (15.87 − 12.73) × NQ's earnings of £162.2 m.

Note: Precise reconciliation is difficult because of roundings.

(ii) In the absence of any synergy, and assuming the market is unaware of PM's estimate of the value of the software licences, there is no reason why the stock market value of the merged entity should be any different from £6,397 m. This would suggest post-merger prices per existing share of:

PM – £6,397 × 69.1% = £4,420 or 465 pence per share compared with 456 pence now

NQ – £6,397 × 30.9% = £1,977 or 233 pence per share compared with 243 pence now

This implies a transfer of wealth from NQ's shareholders to PM's as the share exchange offered is more generous to PM than the ratio of old share prices. Pre-merger share prices would suggest 456:243 or 1 for 1.88 not 1 for 2.

(iii) If PM genuinely believes it can bootstrap NQ's earnings and also believes the software licences are worth £100 million, it could offer the following:

	£m
Value of merged entity	6,903
Plus: Sale of licences	100
Less: Current value of PM	4,332
	2,671

Maximum price £2,671 m, or 314 pence per share

If a share exchange, this suggests a maximum offer in the region of 1 PM for 1.5 NQ.

(b)

REPORT

To: Board of PM

From: Financial Advisor

Date: 24 May 2006

Subject: Evaluation of merger with NQ

Introduction

The purpose of this report is to evaluate the proposed merger between PM and NQ. In accordance with the terms of reference, the following issues are discussed:

- The contribution of the merger to the achievement of PM's financial objectives;
- The external economic forces that might help or hinder the achievement of the merger's financial objectives. Some comments are also provided on the policies that the merged entity could consider to help reduce the adverse effects of such economic forces;
- Potential post-merger value enhancing strategies that could increase our shareholders' wealth.

The report proceeds as follows:

In sections (i), (ii) and (iii) each of the above issues is discussed followed by a short conclusion.

An appendix is provided that shows figures to support the discussion in section (i).

Section (i) – How the merger might contribute to the achievement of PM's financial objectives

Increase EPS by 5% per annum

- PM has demonstrated steady growth in both revenue and earnings since 2002 (this could be supported by growth percentages as shown in appendix 1), although earnings as a percentage of revenue is declining – which might suggest the entity is aggressively reducing prices to obtain market share, but is also managing to control costs to allow earnings growth.
- If PM acquires NQ immediately, the effect would be to increase revenue in the first full year of operations. Earnings per share have been projected as 31.65 pence per share. Assuming around 567 m new shares are issued (850 m old NQ shares in issue/1.5) this would mean 1,517 bn in total. This implies earnings of £480 m. Clearly, as a percentage increase on only PM's 2005 earnings this is an increase well above 5%. On the combined earnings it is an increase of 10%.
- If the more realistic projections are taken, it is unlikely PM will "grow" earnings at the rate expected, at least in the first full year of operations. Assuming both entities' earnings grow at the same rate as 2005/06, this would imply earnings of £457 m [PM's 2005/06 earnings of £273 m × 1.058 plus NQ's 2005/06 earnings of £162.2 m × 1.034]. This is an increase of just 5% (£457 m compared with combined earnings of £435.2 m in 2005/06].
- On the positive side, no real savings or synergies have yet been identified and these might help boost earnings. It is, therefore, quite possible PM's management will be able to increase NQ's earnings sufficiently more than 3.4% to more easily clear the 5% hurdle, so the merger could make a greater contribution to the achievement of this objective.
- There will, of course, be an impact on future earnings of the sale of the licences. There is insufficient information in the scenario to quantify this.

Maintain a gearing ratio below 30%

- Current gearing is 28% [market value of debt is £1,207 m [£1,150 m × £105/100 as percentage of market capitalisation of £4,332 m];
- If the merger is on the basis of a share exchange, and assuming a market capitalisation of the merged entity of £6,903 m, the ratio falls to 21.8% [PM's debt of £1,207 m as calculated above plus NQ's debt of £297 m ($550 m/1.85) as percentage of £6,903];
- If a cash alternative is offered and 50% or 100% of NQ's shareholders accept, the gearing would clearly rise well in excess of 30% (*Note:* calculations could be provided here, but are not expected.);
- All these calculations ignore movements in the market prices of debt and equity and the exchange rate, but they are unlikely to be substantially different unless there is a major market crash.

Maintain a P/E ratio above the industry average

- Future growth rating by the market depends on how the merger is received by the market. Typically, bidders overpay for their acquisitions and as a result are downgraded by the market. However, PM does appear to have a better track record than NQ and if it is an agreed merger there is less likelihood of PM overpaying.

- Unlikely PM's P/E ratio will maintain for the merged entity, at least in the immediate future. The P/E is more likely to be a weighted average as follows:

    PM   15.87 × 69.1% = 11
    NQ   12.73 × 30.9% = 3.9
    Say, 15.

This is still above the industry average of 14, but ignores potential downside risks, such as problems with integration and exchange rate volatility affecting the increased percentage of the business now conducted overseas.

Section (ii) – External economic forces that might affect the achievement of the entity's objectives

The success of the merger depends on a number of factors:

- The NQ shareholders' willingness to accept sterling denominated shares (and dividends);
- The movement of the exchange rate between sterling and the US$. A merger such as this may take between 6 and 12 months to complete. Well over 40% of the merged entity's profits will be generated in the US and exchange rates in countries in the rest of the world may be pegged to the US$. However, interest rate parity suggests the £ will depreciate against the US$ by around 2% a year, which implies a net exchange rate benefit. Nevertheless, parity theories have not held recently in the US$–£ relationship so there is still a risk.
- External factors such as unforeseen changes in interest and/or inflation rates in any of the two entity's major areas of operation.
- PM could use the capital and money markets to hedge $ and other currency denominated transactions, but it is difficult to do this on all operations long term. Internal or informal methods may be preferable here, and may already exist.
- Competition controls – unlikely here, but it is possible certain areas of the entity's operations might attract the attention of the competition authorities, for example the pharmaceutical materials sector referred to. PM is already market leader in UK and Europe, acquiring NQ would increase this even further.
- A general crash in the stock market – this would affect the second and third objective, but probably not the first. Little can be done about the P/E ratio, but if the second objective were to be restated so that gearing is measured in book value terms not market value terms, the volatility of stock markets can be overcome.
- While not strictly an "economic" force, the integration of the two entities could be a challenge. It is already stated that the NQ board is "sensitive" to whether this is termed a merger or an acquisition, so there is clearly scope for disagreements. How these issues are managed is mentioned in the next part of this report.

Section (iii) – Post-merger value enhancing strategies

- Position audit – need to understand NQ's entity culture, its staff, products and other stakeholders.
- The integration strategy must be in place before the merger is finalised.
- Improve efficiency – Synergies have not yet been identified, but there are bound to be some administrative savings. If these involve redundancies – and they surely must – the effect on the workforce in both the UK and the US must be considered together with the need to recognise local employment laws and sensitivities.

- Improve profitability/earnings – undertake a comprehensive, but realistic and time-bound action plan.
- Review and improve marketing strategy, especially for key areas such as pharmaceutical materials.
- Asset sales – already considered in respect of the software licences, but there may be other assets that will be surplus to requirements.
- The entity's cost of capital should be re-evaluated: the level of diversification obtained by merging two different income streams might reduce this and therefore increase the value of the entity.

Conclusion and summary

This report has shown that the merger will meet at least two of the entity's three objectives. Earnings will increase by 5% per annum, at least in the first full year of operations. On the positive side no real savings or synergies have as yet been identified, which would help boost earnings. On the negative side, the effect on earnings of the disposal of the licenses has not yet been quantified. PM's P/E ratio is likely to be maintained above the industry average, but there are potential downside risks.

The effect on gearing is difficult to predict with accuracy as the proportion of NQ's shareholders who will opt for cash, necessitating additional borrowings, is unknown.

A number of economic forces were identified that could help or hinder the achievement of the objectives. These include exchange rate movements, changes in interest and inflation rates, competition controls and stock market volatility.

Post-merger value enhancing strategies were identified as the need for a position audit, marketing and integration strategies, and strategies to improve efficiency and profitability. Also considered are the sale of surplus assets and the need to re-evaluate the cost of capital.

In summary, the merger has potential, but is not without its downside risks.

Appendix 1

Year end	PM Revenue £m	%	PM Earnings £M	% Growth	Earnings as % of Revenue	NQ Revenue $m	% Growth	NQ Earnings $m	% Growth	Earnings as % of Revenue
2002	1,050		225		21.4	1,850		250		13.5
2003	1,125	7.1	231	2.7	20.5	1,950	5.4	265	6.0	13.6
2004	1,250	11.1	245	6.1	19.6	2,150	10.3	280	5.7	13.0
2005	1,400	12.0	258	5.3	18.4	2,336	8.7	290	3.6	12.4
2006	1,560	11.4	273	5.8	17.5	2,500	7.0	300	3.4	12.0

SECTION B

Question Two

(a)

(i) *Calculation of working capital*

		$m
Accounts receivable:		
minimum	20/365 × $10 m	= 0.55
maximum	30/365 × $10 m	= 0.82
Accounts payable:		
minimum	40/365 × $6 m	= 0.66
maximum	50/365 × $6 m	= 0.82
Inventories:		
minimum	50/365 × $6 m	= 0.82
maximum	80/365 × $6 m	= 1.32
Working capital:		
minimum	0.55 − 0.82 + 0.82	= 0.55
maximum	0.82 − 0.66 + 1.32	= 1.48

Discussion of the validity of the assumption re peaks and troughs in working capital variables

The peak period for accounts receivable is unlikely to coincide with that for inventories. Indeed, inventories would generally be lower following a period of high sales unless products have been immediately replaced. Similarly, large levels of purchases are likely to result in high levels of inventories to store the items purchased as well as a high level of accounts payable until invoices have been settled.

The pattern of working capital levels will be determined by factors such as the nature of the business and the frequency of sales. A more accurate picture would be obtained by monitoring working capital levels throughout the year to identify cyclical patterns.

(ii) *Calculation of short- and long-term financing*

	Moderate re financing ($m)	Aggressive ($m)	Conservative ($m)
Short-term, variable financing	Surplus WC, if any	Surplus WC plus 30% of minimum WC i.e. 0.16 minimum	Any surplus, if any
Long term, permanent financing	0.55 (= 100% × 0.55) That is, 100% min WC	0.39 (= 70% × 0.55) that is, 70% min WC	1.11 (= 0.55 + 60% × 0.93) that is, min WC plus 60% of the min/max difference
Total	Minimum 0.55	Minimum 0.55	Exceeds 0.55 min WC

Alternative approach:

	Moderate ($m)	Aggressive ($m)	Conservative ($m)
Short-term variable financing	0.93 (= 1.48 − 0.55)	1.09 (= (30% × 0.55) + 0.93)	0.37 (= 40% × 0.93)
Long term permanent financing	8.55 (= 0.55 + 8)	8.39 (= 8 + 70% × 0.55)	9.11 (= 8 + 0.55 + 60% × 0.93)
Total	9.48	9.48	9.48

Graphical illustration:

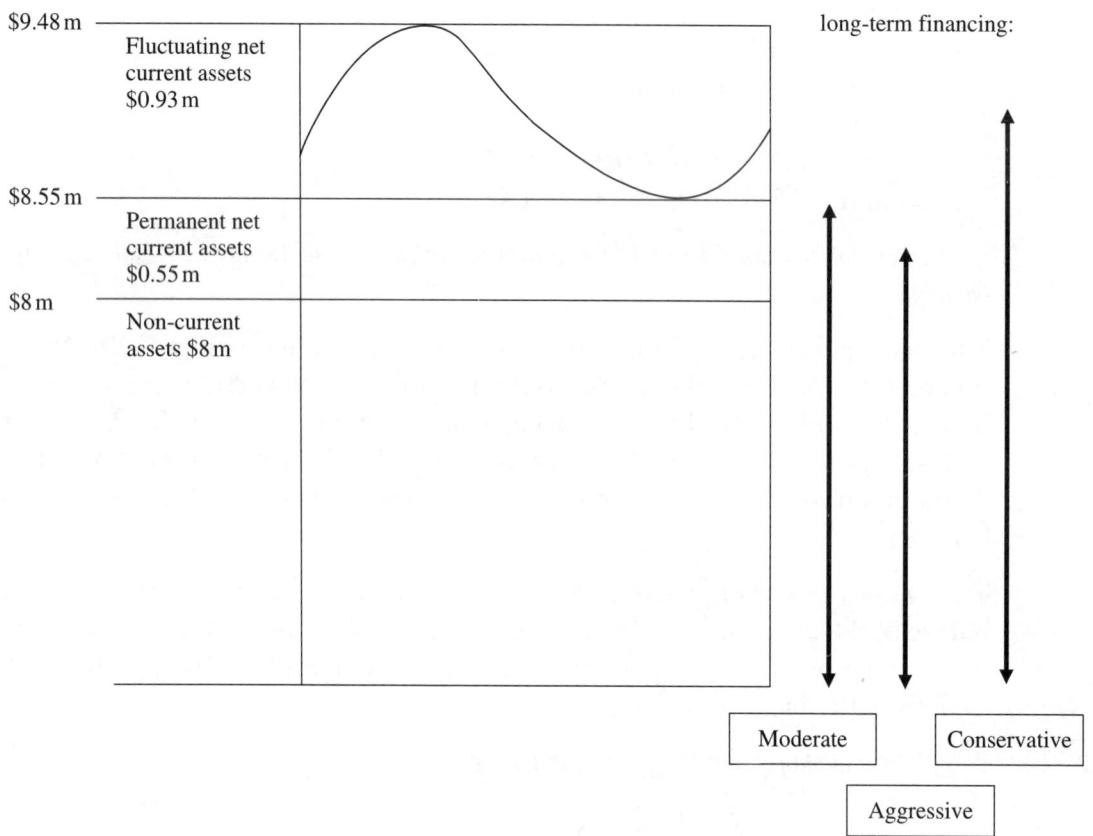

(b)

Aggressive financing policy

- Advantages

  - provides the greatest returns;
  - reason: short-term financing is cheaper than long-term financing due to the compensation required by lenders for loss of liquidity preference and greater credit risk of longer term finance;
  - greater flexibility;
  - reason: even if net current assets fall below expected "permanent" levels, MNO would not be over-financed.

- Disadvantages
  - carries a higher risk of illiquidity;
  - involves greater management time to manage and renew short-term financing sources.
- Appropriateness for MNO
  - MNO faces potentially large fluctuations in net current asset levels and would benefit from the flexibility that an aggressive financing policy provides.

(c) **Profit or cost centre**

- "profit" is made by a treasury department by
  - charging individual business units a market rate for services which can be provided at a lower cost;
  - aggregating and netting bank positions and exposures across different business units and thereby reducing interest expense and bank spreads lost on foreign exchange conversions.
- there is limited scope for a treasury department in MNO to make a "profit" since
  - the entity is relatively small, so the potential savings are also small;
  - the entity has no foreign exchange dealings at present, but would have such dealings in the future if the Asian supplier is adopted. However, these would be "one-way" purchases of the required currency and so a centralised treasury could not make a profit by co-ordinating the netting of currency flows or aggregating requirements from different parts of the entity;
  - the entity has a strong de-centralised culture, making it harder to operate uniform central policies. However, MNO does appear to already operate a system of centralised cash management and may be able to make some contribution towards its costs from these activities.
- conclusion: a cost centre structure with some limited contribution towards costs from its centralised cash management activities would be appropriate for MNO.

Question Three

(a) **Response to Board members**

Response to Sr. A:

- the redemption yield (YTM) allows the cost of the loan and bond to be compared on the same basis;
- the redemption yield is effectively the IRR of the cash flows under the debt instrument and so takes into account the time value of money;
- the bond is slightly cheaper than the loan, with a redemption yield of 6.45% instead of 7%;
- this result would be expected, since the bond is marketed to a wider investor base and so finer rates can be obtained;
- issue costs must also be taken into account; no information is provided in the question, but costs can be expected to be significantly higher for the bond because of the publicity and underwriting required.

Response to Sr.B:

- looking at coupon rates in isolation, the convertible bond appears to cost less than the bond; certainly the interest cost would be lower over the five-year period;
- however, if the share price rises by 10% a year as predicted, each convertible bond worth $100 on redemption will convert to 5 shares worth $120.80. This capital gain is equivalent to a compound yield of 3.85% per annum. This is in addition to the 4.5% coupon on the convertible, making it overall significantly more expensive than the unsecured bond (*Workings* $3.85\% = (120.80/100)^{1/5} - 1$);
- in addition, from year 6 onwards, the entity will need to pay dividends on the shares created on conversion which is likely to increase the cost of capital since the cost of equity is generally higher than the cost of debt.

Response to Sr.C:

- investors may have concerns about the future growth of the entity and be reluctant to subscribe to shares at the present time, as indicated by the two major institutional shareholders;
- the convertible bond gives investors the opportunity to acquire new shares, but they have the assurance that they do not need to convert the bond into shares unless the entity performs well in the next five-year period;
- in the meantime, the entity benefits from lower financing costs for five years.

Recommendation

For a rapidly expanding entity such as EFG, the convertible bond may be the most appropriate. The convertible bond provides low cost finance for five years and may result in the desired equity base at the end of the five year period.

Appendix: Calculations and workings

Calculation of the expected conversion value of the convertible on 1 July 2011:

Share price now:	$15
Share price in five years' time:	$24.16 (=15 \times (1 + 10\%)^5$)
So conversion value is:	$120.80 per $100 nominal (= 5 \times $24.16)
Capital gain is:	$24.16 - $15 = $9.16

Yield to maturity (YTM) calculations:

Loan: The YTM for the bank loan is equal to the annual coupon of 7%.

Bond:

Based on $100 nominal for simplicity:

Using a 6% discount rate:

Year	Cashflow $	Discount factor	PV (5cashflow 3 discount factor) $
0	94	1.000	94.00
1–5	(5)	4.212	(21.06)
5	(100)	0.747	(74.70)
TOTAL NPV			(1.76)

Using a 7% discount rate:

Year	Cashflow $	Discount factor	PV (5 cashflow 3 discount factor) $
0	94	1.000	94.00
1–5	(5)	4.100	(20.50)
5	(100)	0.713	(71.30)
TOTAL NPV			2.20

So, by interpolation, the YTM of the bond is approximately:

$$6\% + 1\% \times \frac{1.76}{(1.76 + 2.20)} = 6.44\%$$

Alternative approach based on actual cashflows:

Using a 6% discount rate:

Year	Cashflow $m	Discount factor	PV (5 cashflow 3 discount factor) $m
0	3.00	1.000	3.000
1–5	(0.16)	4.212	(0.674)
5	(3.19)	0.747	(2.383)
TOTAL NPV			(0.057)

Using a 7% discount rate:

Year	Cashflow $m	Discount factor	PV (5 cashflow 3 discount factor) $m
0	3.00	1.000	3.000
1–5	(0.16)	4.100	(0.656)
5	(3.19)	0.713	(2.274)
TOTAL NPV			0.070

So, by interpolation, the YTM of the bond is approximately:

$$6\% + 1\% \times \frac{0.057}{(0.057 + 0.070)} = 6.45\%$$

Workings:

- Borrowings needed of $3 m;
- The bond is issued at a 6% discount, so issue nominal of $3 m/0.94 = $3.19 m in order to raise $3 m;
- Annual interest at 5% on a nominal value of $3.19 m is $3.19 m × 5% = $0.16 m.

(b) In assessing creditworthiness, a prospective investor should be provided with the following information:

- financial statements for the last three years;
- cash flow forecasts;
- long- and short-term ratings from rating agencies of this and similar entities' bonds;
- business prospects;
- prospects for the market sector.

and undertake the following analyses:

- calculate ratios (gearing, interest cover, dividend cover, working capital ratios);
- analyse free cash flow;
- carry out a risk assessment of the business and the market sector.

Question Four

(a) **APV calculation**

Using the formula:

$$k_{eg} = k_{eu} + [k_{eu} - k_d] \frac{V_D(100 - t)\%}{V_E}$$

$$10.7\% = k_{eu} + [k_{eu} - 5\%] \times \frac{4 \times (100 - 35)\%}{6}$$

therefore, $10.7\% = k_{eu} + 0.433 k_{eu} - 2.167\%$

therefore, $k_{eu} = 12.867\%/1.433 = 8.98\%$, or, approximately, 9%.

Alternative approach

Using $k_{adj} = k_{eu}[1 - tL]$

Where k_{adj} = WACC = $10.7 \times \frac{60}{100} + 5(1 - 0.35) \times \frac{40}{100} = 7.72$

So $7.72 = k_{eu}[1 - 0.35 \times \frac{40}{100}]$

So $K_{eu} = 8.99\%$ or 9% as previously

Exchange rate calculation $/€m

Year	Rate	Workings	Alternative Exchange rates €m
0	1.6	Spot rate	0.625
1	1.552	1.6 × 0.97	0.644
2	1.505	1.552 × 0.97	0.664
3	1.460	1.505 × 0.97	0.685
4	1.416	1.460 × 0.97	0.706
5	1.374	1.416 × 0.97	0.728

Year	0	1	2	3	4	5
	£m	£m	£m	£m	£m	£m
Project cash flows	−10	5	5	4	3	3
Tax on cash flows at 25%		−1.25	−1.25	−1	−0.75	−0.75
Net £ cash flows	−10	3.75	3.75	3	2.25	2.25
Exchange rate	1.6	1.55	1.51	1.46	1.42	1.37
	€m	€m	€m	€m	€m	€m
€ cash flows	−16.00	5.82	5.64	4.38	3.19	3.09
Additional tax at 10% On UK profits		−0.78	−0.76	−0.58	−0.43	−0.41
Post tax cash flows	−16.00	5.04	4.88	3.80	2.76	2.68
Discount factor (9%)	1	0.917	0.842	0.772	0.708	0.650
Discounted cashflow	−16	4.62	4.11	2.93	1.95	1.74

Cumulative NPV = a loss of €0.65 million

Alternative approach (assuming French tax is based on remittances rather than UK profits):

Year	0	1	2	3	4	5
	£m	£m	£m	£m	£m	£m
Project cash flows	−10	5	5	4	3	3
Tax on cash flows at 25%		−1.25	−1.25	−1	−0.75	−0.75
Net £ cash flows	−10	3.75	3.75	3	2.25	2.25
Exchange rate	1.6	1.55	1.51	1.46	1.42	1.37
	€m	€m	€m	€m	€m	€m
€ cash flows	−16.00	5.82	5.64	4.38	3.19	3.09
Tax at 35%		−2.04	−1.98	−1.53	−1.12	−1.08
Add back UK tax		1.94	1.88	1.46	1.06	1.03
Post tax cash flows	−16.00	5.72	5.54	4.31	3.13	3.04
Discount factor (9%)	1	0.917	0.842	0.772	0.708	0.650
Discounted cashflow	−16	5.25	4.66	3.33	2.22	1.98

Cumulative NPV at 9%: €1.440 million

Tax shield on debt:

Tax relief on debt interest	= €280,000 each year for five years	
	(= €16 million × 5% × 35%)	
PV of tax relief on debt interest at 5% (cost of debt)	= €1,212,120	(= €280,000 × 4.329)

Issue costs:

Issue costs	= €320,000	(= €16 million × 2%)
Tax relief on issue costs	=€112,000	(= €320,000 × 0.35)

Adjusted present value	First tax basis	Alternative tax basis	If tax relief on interest discounted at Ke:	
	€'000	€'000	€'000	or: €'000
Base cost PV	(650)	1,440	(650)	1,440
PV of tax relief on debt interest	1,212	1,212	1,089	1,089
Issue costs	(320)	(320)	(320)	(320)
Tax relief on issue costs	112	112	112	112
Adjusted present value	354	2,444	231	2,321

Advice

Base PV is negative, but becomes marginally positive after taking into account the tax relief on debt. GHI is unlikely to proceed with the project with such a marginal result.

Limitations of APV:

- determining the costs and benefits involved in the financing method to be used can be difficult (especially where they are based on an estimate of the enhanced debt capacity provided by the project as in this case);
- the example of GHI assumes that the whole debt of €16 million will be needed for the project or can be used elsewhere in the business for the full five years (under NPV calculations, it is implicit that the debt is repaid over the period of the project as cash flows allow);
- finding a suitable cost of equity for the base NPV calculation is subjective and may not truly reflect the risk associated with the new project.

(b)

(i) *Customer requirements and product design*

Gather external information: full market research required specific to the UK to assess UK customer requirements.

Consider strategic market position: for example unique features required to break into saturated UK phone market, such as:

- tariff package differentiation: undercut competitors (for example, free text messages);
- design differentiation: cutting edge design that attracts new users;
- service differentiation: ease of use features.

Note that the planning stage is crucial to the success of the project – and product design is key to the success of this project.

(ii) *Control of implementation*

Prepare plan of implementation
Carry out implementation

- trial implementation
- nationwide implementation

Evaluate performance

- collect statistics of costs incurred on a regular basis
- monitor sales volumes and sales prices against budget

Feedback mechanism

- investigate deviations from budget (in both the trial and nationwide implementation)
- carry out a post-completion appraisal

Question Five

(a)

Evaluating projects is on the next page.

Selecting projects:

Consider all possible combinations of projects within the $30 million capital constraint in year 1:

			Cumulative NPV $m	Net cash outflow in year 1 $m
Ranking by NPV:	C, B, A, E, D Accept:	C, B, A	12.90	29
Ranking by PI:	C, D, E, B, A Accept:	C, D, E, B	15.22	28
Best combination	C, D, E, B		15.22	28

Conclusion: accept projects B, C, D and E on the basis of capital rationing analysis
Justification: This is the combination of projects which offers the highest overall NPV return;

(b)

(i) Discussion of whether such analysis is appropriate for public bodies:

- Publicly-owned bodies may be subject to absolute spending constraints, unlike private entities who could normally borrow to fund an attractive project that falls outside its capital spending budget for the year. Effective allocation of capital is therefore, arguably, even more important for publicly-owned bodies than for private entities;
- The key objective of a private entity is to maximise shareholders' wealth and NPV calculations are a useful measure of the increase in shareholders' wealth created by a project; however, publicly-owned bodies will have other priorities and objectives and so a model of capital rationing based on maximising NPV may not be appropriate.

(ii) Discussion of what other factors should be considered and analysis undertaken:

- Sensitivity analysis of the impact of changes in key underlying variables to the outcome;
- Consideration of non-financial factors such as:
  - Government or self-imposed targets and priorities on such issues as type of patient care to be provided or geographic locations that are in greatest need of improved health care;
  - environmental issues;
  - staffing issues.

Evaluating projects:

Project A

		$m	d.f.	NPV
Outflows	Year 0	−9	1.000	−9.00
	Year 1	−16	0.870	13.92
Inflows	Years 1 to inf	4	6.667 (W1)	26.67
Year 1 net outflow:		−12		

Profitability index against year 1 net cashflow: (W6)   **0.31**
- second figure is based upon discounted year 1 cashflows   *or 0.36*

Project B

		$m	d.f.	NPV
Outflows	Year 0	10	1.000	−10.00
	Year 1	10	0.870	−8.70
Inflows	Years 2 to inf	4	5.797 (W2)	23.19
				4.49

Year 1 net outflow: −10

Profitability index against year 1 net cashflow: **0.45**
     or 0.52

Project C

		$m	d.f.	NPV
Outflows	Year 0	−10	1.000	−10.00
	Year 1	−12	0.870	−10.44
Inflows	Years 1–10	5	5.019 (W3)	25.10
				4.66

Year 1 net outflow: −7

Profitability index against year 1 net cashflow: **0.67**
     or 0.77

Project D

		$m	d.f.	NPV
Outflows	Year 0	−8	1.000	−8.00
	Year 1	−5	0.870	−4.35
Inflows	Years 3–7	6	2.534 (W4)	15.20
Year 1 net outflow:		−5		2.85

Profitability index against year 1 net cashflow: **0.57**
     or 0.66

Project E

		$m	d.f.	NPV
Outflows	Year 0	−9	1.000	−9.00
	Year 1	−8	0.870	−6.96
Inflows	Years 1–5	2	3.352	6.70
	Years 6–15	5	2.495 (W5)	12.48
Year 1 net outflow:		−6		
Profitability index against year 1 net cashflow:				**0.54**
				or **0.62**

Workings:
- W1: $6.667 = 1/0.15$
- W2: $5.797 = (1/0.15)/1.15$
- W3: $5.019 = af\,(t = 10, r = 15)$
- W4: $2.534 = 4.160 - 1.626$
  $= af\,(t = 7, r = 15) - af\,(t = 2, r = 15)$
- W5: $2.495 = 5.847 - 3.352$
  $= af\,(t = 15, r = 15) - af\,(t = 5, r = 15)$
- W6: $0.31 = 3.75/12$
  Or: $0.36 = 3.75/(12/1.15)$

Nov 2006 Questions and Answers

16

Strategic Level

Paper P9 – Management Accounting – Financial Strategy

Question Paper 260

Examiner's Brief Guide to the Paper 277

Examiner's Answers 278

The answers published here have been written by the Examiner and should provide a helpful guide for both tutors and students.

Published separately on the CIMA website (www.cimaglobal.com/students) from mid-February 2007 is a Post Examination Guide for this paper, which provides much valuable and complementary material including indicative mark information.

© 2006 The Chartered Institute of Management Accountants. All rights reserved. No part of this publication may be reproduced, stored in a retrieval system, or transmitted, in any form or by any means, electronic, mechanical, photocopying, recorded or otherwise, without the written permission of the publisher.

Financial Management Pillar

Strategic Level Paper

P9 – Management Accounting Financial Strategy

22 November 2006 – Wednesday Morning Session

Instructions to candidates

You are allowed three hours to answer this question paper.

You are allowed 20 minutes reading time **before the examination begins** during which you should read the question paper and, if you wish, make annotations on the question paper. However, you will **not** be allowed, **under any circumstances**, to open the answer book and start writing or use your calculator during the reading time.

You are strongly advised to carefully read ALL the question requirements before attempting the question concerned (that is, all parts and/or sub-questions). The question requirements are highlighted in a dotted box.

Answer the ONE compulsory question in Section A on pages 261 to 263.

Answer TWO of the four questions in Section B on pages 264 to 271.

Maths Tables and Formulae are provided on pages 272 to 276.

Write your full examination number, paper number and the examination subject title in the spaces provided on the front of the examination answer book. Also write your contact ID and name in the space provided in the right hand margin and seal to close.

Tick the appropriate boxes on the front of the answer book to indicate which questions you have answered.

SECTION A – 50 MARKS

[the indicative time for answering this Section is 90 minutes]

READ THE SCENARIO AND ANSWER THIS QUESTION. THE QUESTION REQUIREMENTS ARE ON PAGE 263

Question One Scenario

SHINE

Business background
SHINE is a publicly owned multinational group based in Germany with its main business centred on the production and distribution of gas and electricity to industrial and domestic consumers. It has recently begun investing in research and development in relation to renewable energy, exploiting solar, wave or wind energy to generate electricity.

Corporate objectives
Developing renewable energy sources is an important non-financial objective for the SHINE Group in order to protect and enhance the group's reputation. Renewable energy projects have been given a high profile in recent investor communications and television advertising campaigns.

Wind farm investment project
The latest renewable energy project under consideration is the development of a wind farm in the USA. This would involve the construction of 65 wind powered electricity generators which would be owned and operated by a new, local subsidiary entity and electricity that is generated by the farm would be sold to the local electricity grid. A suitable site, subject to planning permission, has been located.

Forecast operating cash flows for the project are as follows:

	Year(s)	US$ million
Initial investment (including working capital)	0	200
Residual value	4	50
Pre-tax operating net cash inflows	1 to 4	70

Other relevant data and assumptions:

- The initial investment is expected to be made on 30 November 2006 and cash flows will arise at any point in the year;

- However, in any net present value (NPV) exercise, all cash flows should be assumed to arise on 31 December of each year;

- The local tax rate in the USA for this industry is set at a preferential rate of 10% to encourage environmentally-friendly projects rather than the normal rate of 25%;

- Tax is payable in the year in which it arises;

- No tax depreciation allowances are available;

- No additional tax is payable in Germany under the terms of the double tax treaties with the USA;

- Net cash flows are to be paid to the German parent entity as dividends at the end of each year.

Uncertainties affecting the outcome of the project

There is some uncertainty over the US tax rate over the period of the project, with extensive discussion at local government level about raising the tax rate to 25% with immediate effect. A vote will be taken in the next six months to decide whether to retain the preferential 10% tax rate, or to increase it to 25%. Once the vote has been taken and a decision made, the tax rate will not be open for debate again for at least four years.

Economic forecasters expect the value of the euro to either stay constant against the value of the US dollar for the next four years or to strengthen by 7% per annum. Assume that there is an equal probability of each of these two different exchange rate forecasts.

There is also significant risk to the project from strong objections to the wind farm scheme from local farmers in the USA who are concerned about the impact of acid water run-off from boring holes for the 65 windmills. In addition, there are a number of executive holiday homes nearby whose owners are objecting to the visual impact of the windmills.

Investment criteria

The SHINE Group evaluates foreign projects of this nature based on a euro cost of capital of 12% which reflects the risk profile of the proposed investment.

Extracts from the forecast financial statements for the SHINE Group at 31 December 2006, the end of the current financial year:

	€ million	€ million
ASSETS		
Total assets		28,000
EQUITY AND LIABILITIES		
Equity		
Share capital	3,000	
(3,000 million €1 ords)		
Retained earnings	8,300	
		11,300
Non-current liabilities		
Floating rate borrowings		4,000
Current liabilities		12,700
		28,000

Alternative financing methods

The SHINE Group aims to maintain the group gearing ratio (debt as a proportion of debt plus equity) below 40% based on book values.

The following alternative methods are being considered by the SHINE parent entity for financing the new investment:

- Long-term borrowings denominated in euro;

- Long-term borrowings denominated in US dollars.

Required:

(a) Calculate the NPV of the cash flows for the proposed investment for **each** of the following four possible scenarios:

- Constant exchange rate and a tax rate of 10%;
- Constant exchange rate and a tax rate of 25%;
- The euro to strengthen against the US dollar by 7% a year and a tax rate of 10%;
- The euro to strengthen against the US dollar by 7% a year and a tax rate of 25%.

In each case, assume that the exchange rate at year 0 is US$1·10 = €1·00.

(12 marks)

(b) Prepare the forecast balance sheet of the SHINE Group on 31 December 2006, incorporating the project under each of the two alternative financing structures and each of the following two exchange rate scenarios A and B:

Date	Exchange rates under scenario A	Exchange rates under scenario B
30 November 2006 (date of the initial investment and arrangement of financing)	US$1·10 = €1·00	US$1·10 = €1·00
31 December 2006 (financial reporting/balance sheet date)	US$1·10 = €1·00 (no change)	US$1·40 = €1·00

Assume that no other project cash flows occur until 2007.

(8 marks)

(c) Write a report addressed to the Directors of the SHINE Group in which you, as Finance Director, address the following issues relating to the evaluation and implementation of the proposed wind farm project:

(i) Discuss the internal and external constraints affecting the investment decision and advise the SHINE Group how to proceed. In your answer, include reference to your calculations in part *(a)* above.

(9 marks)

(ii) Discuss the comparative advantages of each of the two proposed alternative financing structures and advise the SHINE group which one to adopt. In your answer include reference to your results in part *(b)* above, and further analysis and discussion of the impact of each proposed financial structure on the group's balance sheet.

(9 marks)

(iii) Discuss the differing roles and responsibilities of the treasury department and finance department in evaluating and implementing the US project and the interaction of the two departments throughout the process.

(8 marks)

Marks available for structure and presentation in Question One. *(4 marks)*

(Total for Question One = 50 marks)

(Total for Section A = 50 marks)

End of Section A

SECTION B – 50 MARKS

[the indicative time for answering this Section is 90 minutes]

ANSWER *TWO* ONLY OF THE FOUR QUESTIONS

Question Two

AB is a telecommunications consultancy based in Europe that trades globally. It was established 15 years ago. The four founding shareholders own 25% of the issued share capital each and are also executive directors of the entity. The shareholders are considering a flotation of AB on a European stock exchange and have started discussing the process and a value for the entity with financial advisors. The four founding shareholders, and many of the entity's employees, are technical experts in their field, but have little idea how entities such as theirs are valued.

Assume you are one of AB's financial advisors. You have been asked to estimate a value for the entity and explain your calculations and approach to the directors. You have obtained the following information.

Summary financial data for the past three years and forecast revenue and costs for the next two years is as follows:

Income Statement for the years ended 31 March

	Actual			Forecast	
	2004	2005	2006	2007	2008
	€ million	€ million	€ million	€ million	€ million
Revenue	125·0	137·5	149·9	172·0	198·0
Less:					
Cash operating costs	37·5	41·3	45·0	52	59
Depreciation	20·0	22·0	48·0	48	48
Pre-tax earnings	67·5	74·2	56·9	72	91
Taxation	20·3	22·3	17·1	22	27

Balance Sheet at 31 March

	2004	2005	2006
	€ million	€ million	€ million
ASSETS			
Non-current assets			
Property, plant and equipment	150	175	201
Current assets	48	54	62
	198	229	263
EQUITY AND LIABILITIES			
Equity			
Share capital (Shares of €1)	30	30	30
Retained earnings	148	179	203
	178	209	233
Current liabilities	20	20	30
	198	229	263

Note: The book valuations of non-current assets are considered to reflect current realisable values.

Other information/assumptions

- Growth in after tax cash flows for 2009 and beyond (assume indefinitely) is expected to be 3% per annum. Cash operating costs can be assumed to remain at the same percentage of revenue as in previous years. Depreciation will fluctuate but, for purposes of evaluation, assume the 2008 charge will continue indefinitely. Tax has been payable at 30% per annum for the last three years. This rate is expected to continue for the foreseeable future and tax will be payable in the year in which the liability arises.

- The average P/E ratio for telecommunication entities' shares quoted on European stock exchanges has been 12·5 over the past 12 months. However, there is a wide variation around this average and AB might be able to command a rating up to 30% higher than this;

- An estimated cost of equity capital for the industry is 10% after tax;

- The average pre-tax return on total assets for the industry over the past 3 years has been 15%.

Required:

(a)

Calculate a range of values for AB, in total and per share, using methods of valuation that you consider appropriate. Where relevant, include an estimate of value for intellectual capital.

(12 marks)

(b)

Discuss the methods of valuation you have used, explaining the relevance of each method to an entity such as AB. Conclude with a recommendation of an approximate flotation value for AB, in total and per share.

(13 marks)

(Total for Question Two = 25 marks)

A report format is **not** required for this question.

Question Three

VCI is a venture capital investor that specialises in providing finance to small but established businesses. At present, its expected average pre-tax return on equity investment is a nominal 30% per annum over a five-year investment period.

YZ is a typical client of VCI. It is a 100% family owned transport and distribution business whose shares are unlisted. The company sustained a series of losses a few years ago, but the recruitment of some professional managers and an aggressive marketing policy returned the company to profitability. Its most recent accounts show revenue of $105 million and profit before interest and tax of $28·83 million. Other relevant information is as follows:

- For the last three years dividends have been paid at 40% of earnings and the directors have no plans to change this payout ratio;

- Taxation has averaged 28% per annum over the past few years and this rate is likely to continue;

- The directors are forecasting growth in earnings and dividends for the foreseeable future of 6% per annum;

- YZ's accountants estimated the entity's cost of equity capital at 10% some years ago. The data they worked with was incomplete and now out of date. The current cost could be as high as 15%.

Extracts from its most recent balance sheet *at 31 March 2006* are shown below.

	$ million
ASSETS	
Non-current assets	
Property, plant and equipment	35·50
Current assets	4·50
	40·00
EQUITY AND LIABILITIES	
Equity	
Share capital (Nominal value of 10 cents)	2·25
Retained earnings	18·00
	20·25
Non-current liabilities	
7% Secured bond repayable 2016	15·00
Current liabilities	4·75
	19·75
	40·00

Note: The entity's vehicles are mainly financed by operating leases.

YZ has now reached a stage in its development that requires additional capital of $25 million. The directors, and major shareholders, are considering a number of alternative forms of finance. One of the alternatives they are considering is venture capital funding and they have approached VCI. In preliminary discussions, VCI has suggested it might be able to finance the necessary $25 million by purchasing a percentage of YZ's equity. This will, of course, involve YZ issuing new equity.

Required:

(a)

Assume you work for VCI and have been asked to evaluate the potential investment.

(i) Using YZ's forecast of growth and its estimates of cost of capital, calculate the number of new shares that YZ will have to issue to VCI in return for its investment and the percentage of the entity VCI will then own. Comment briefly on your result.

(9 marks)

(ii) Evaluate exit strategies that might be available to VCI in five years' time and their likely acceptability to YZ.

(6 marks)

Note: Use sensible roundings in your calculations.

(Total for Requirement (a) = 15 marks)

(b)

Discuss the advantages and disadvantages to an established business such as YZ of using a venture capital entity to provide finance for expansion as compared with long term debt. Advise YZ about which type of finance it should choose, based on the information available so far.

(10 marks)

(Total for Question Three = 25 marks)

A report format is **not** required for this question.

Question Four

CD is a furniture manufacturer based in the UK. It manufactures a limited range of furniture products to a very high quality and sells to a small number of retail outlets worldwide.

At a recent meeting with one of its major customers it became clear that the market is changing and the final consumer of CD's products is now more interested in variety and choice rather than exclusivity and exceptional quality.

CD is therefore reviewing two mutually exclusive alternatives to apply to a selection of its products:

Alternative 1
To continue to manufacture, but expand its product range and reduce its quality. The net present value (NPV), internal rate of return (IRR) and modified internal rate of return (MIRR) for this alternative have already been calculated as follows:

NPV	=	£1·45 million using a nominal discount rate of 9%
IRR	=	10·5%
MIRR	=	Approximately 13·2%

Alternative 2
To import furniture carcasses in "flat packs" from the USA. The imports would be in a variety of types of wood and unvarnished. CD would buy in bulk from its US suppliers, assemble and varnish the furniture and re-sell, mainly to existing customers. An initial investigation into potential sources of supply and costs of transportation has already been carried out by a consultancy entity at a cost of £75,000.

CD's Finance Director has provided estimates of net sterling and US$ cash flows for this alternative. These net cash flows, in *real* terms, are shown below.

Year	0	1	2	3
US$m	-25·00	2·60	3·80	4·10
£m	0	3·70	4·20	4·60

The following information is relevant:

- CD evaluates all its investments using nominal Sterling cash flows and a nominal discount rate. All non-UK customers are invoiced in US$. US$ nominal cash flows are converted to Sterling at the forward rate and discounted at the UK nominal rate;

- For the purposes of evaluation, assume the entity has a three year time horizon for investment appraisals;

- Based on recent economic forecasts, inflation rates in the US are expected to be constant at 4% per annum. UK inflation rates are expected to be 3% per annum. The current exchange rate is £1 = US$1·6.

Note: Ignore taxation.

The requirement for Question Four is on the next page

Required:

Assume that you are the Financial Manager of CD.

(i) Calculate the net present value (NPV), internal rate of return (IRR) and (approximate) modified internal rate of return (MIRR) of alternative 2.

(12 marks)

(ii) Briefly discuss the appropriateness and possible advantages of providing MIRRs for the evaluation of the two alternatives.

(4 marks)

(iii) Evaluate the two alternatives and recommend which alternative the entity should choose. Include in your answer some discussion about what other criteria could or should be considered before a final decision is taken.

(9 marks)

(Total for Question Four = 25 marks)

A report format is **not** required for this question.

Question Five

(a)

CCC is a local government entity. It is financed almost equally by a combination of central government funding and local taxation. The funding from central government is determined largely on a *per capita* (per head of population) basis, adjusted to reflect the scale of deprivation (or special needs) deemed to exist in CCC's region. A small percentage of its finance comes from the private sector, for example from renting out City Hall for private functions.

CCC's main objectives are:

- To make the region economically prosperous and an attractive place to live and work;
- To provide service excellence in health and education for the local community.

DDD is a large, listed entity with widespread commercial and geographical interests. For historic reasons, its headquarters are in CCC's region. This is something of an anomaly as most entities of DDD's size would have their HQ in a capital city, or at least a city much larger than where it is.

DDD has one financial objective: To increase shareholder wealth by an average 10% per annum. It also has a series of non-financial objectives that deal with how the entity treats other stakeholders, including the local communities where it operates.

DDD has total net assets of $1·5 billion and a gearing ratio of 45% (debt to debt plus equity), which is typical for its industry. It is currently considering raising a substantial amount of capital to finance an acquisition.

Required:

Discuss the criteria that the two very different entities described above have to consider when setting objectives, recognising the needs of each of their main stakeholder groups. Make some reference in your answer to the consequences of each of them failing to meet its declared objectives.

(13 marks)

(b)

MS is a private entity in a computer-related industry. It has been trading for six years and is managed by its main shareholders, the original founders of the entity. Most of the employees are also shareholders, having been given shares as bonuses. None of the shareholders has attempted to sell shares in the entity so the problem of placing a value on them has not arisen. Dividends have been paid every year at the rate of 60 cents per share, irrespective of profits. So far, profits have always been sufficient to cover the dividend at least once but never more than twice.

MS is all-equity financed at present although $15 million new finance is likely to be required in the near future to finance expansion. Total net assets as at the last balance sheet date were $45 million.

The requirement for Question Five part (b) is on the next page

Required:

Discuss and compare the relationship between dividend policy, investment policy and financing policy in the context of the small entity described above, MS, and DDD, the large listed entity described in part *(a)*.

(12 marks)

(Total for Question Five = 25 marks)

(Total for Section B = 50 marks)

End of Question Paper

Maths Tables & Formulae are on pages 272-276

MATHS TABLES AND FORMULAE

Present value table

Present value of 1.00 unit of currency, that is $(1 + r)^{-n}$ where r = interest rate; n = number of periods until payment or receipt.

Periods (n)	Interest rates (r)									
	1%	2%	3%	4%	5%	6%	7%	8%	9%	10%
1	0.990	0.980	0.971	0.962	0.952	0.943	0.935	0.926	0.917	0.909
2	0.980	0.961	0.943	0.925	0.907	0.890	0.873	0.857	0.842	0.826
3	0.971	0.942	0.915	0.889	0.864	0.840	0.816	0.794	0.772	0.751
4	0.961	0.924	0.888	0.855	0.823	0.792	0.763	0.735	0.708	0.683
5	0.951	0.906	0.863	0.822	0.784	0.747	0.713	0.681	0.650	0.621
6	0.942	0.888	0.837	0.790	0.746	0705	0.666	0.630	0.596	0.564
7	0.933	0.871	0.813	0.760	0.711	0.665	0.623	0.583	0.547	0.513
8	0.923	0.853	0.789	0.731	0.677	0.627	0.582	0.540	0.502	0.467
9	0.914	0.837	0.766	0.703	0.645	0.592	0.544	0.500	0.460	0.424
10	0.905	0.820	0.744	0.676	0.614	0.558	0.508	0.463	0.422	0.386
11	0.896	0.804	0.722	0.650	0.585	0.527	0.475	0.429	0.388	0.350
12	0.887	0.788	0.701	0.625	0.557	0.497	0.444	0.397	0.356	0.319
13	0.879	0.773	0.681	0.601	0.530	0.469	0.415	0.368	0.326	0.290
14	0.870	0.758	0.661	0.577	0.505	0.442	0.388	0.340	0.299	0.263
15	0.861	0.743	0.642	0.555	0.481	0.417	0.362	0.315	0.275	0.239
16	0.853	0.728	0.623	0.534	0.458	0.394	0.339	0.292	0.252	0.218
17	0.844	0.714	0.605	0.513	0.436	0.371	0.317	0.270	0.231	0.198
18	0.836	0.700	0.587	0.494	0.416	0.350	0.296	0.250	0.212	0.180
19	0.828	0.686	0.570	0.475	0.396	0.331	0.277	0.232	0.194	0.164
20	0.820	0.673	0.554	0.456	0.377	0.312	0.258	0.215	0.178	0.149

Periods (n)	Interest rates (r)									
	11%	12%	13%	14%	15%	16%	17%	18%	19%	20%
1	0.901	0.893	0.885	0.877	0.870	0.862	0.855	0.847	0.840	0.833
2	0.812	0.797	0.783	0.769	0.756	0.743	0.731	0.718	0.706	0.694
3	0.731	0.712	0.693	0.675	0.658	0.641	0.624	0.609	0.593	0.579
4	0.659	0.636	0.613	0.592	0.572	0.552	0.534	0.516	0.499	0.482
5	0.593	0.567	0.543	0.519	0.497	0.476	0.456	0.437	0.419	0.402
6	0.535	0.507	0.480	0.456	0.432	0.410	0.390	0.370	0.352	0.335
7	0.482	0.452	0.425	0.400	0.376	0.354	0.333	0.314	0.296	0.279
8	0.434	0.404	0.376	0.351	0.327	0.305	0.285	0.266	0.249	0.233
9	0.391	0.361	0.333	0.308	0.284	0.263	0.243	0.225	0.209	0.194
10	0.352	0.322	0.295	0.270	0.247	0.227	0.208	0.191	0.176	0.162
11	0.317	0.287	0.261	0.237	0.215	0.195	0.178	0.162	0.148	0.135
12	0.286	0.257	0.231	0.208	0.187	0.168	0.152	0.137	0.124	0.112
13	0.258	0.229	0.204	0.182	0.163	0.145	0.130	0.116	0.104	0.093
14	0.232	0.205	0.181	0.160	0.141	0.125	0.111	0.099	0.088	0.078
15	0.209	0.183	0.160	0.140	0.123	0.108	0.095	0.084	0.079	0.065
16	0.188	0.163	0.141	0.123	0.107	0.093	0.081	0.071	0.062	0.054
17	0.170	0.146	0.125	0.108	0.093	0.080	0.069	0.060	0.052	0.045
18	0.153	0.130	0.111	0.095	0.081	0.069	0.059	0.051	0.044	0.038
19	0.138	0.116	0.098	0.083	0.070	0.060	0.051	0.043	0.037	0.031
20	0.124	0.104	0.087	0.073	0.061	0.051	0.043	0.037	0.031	0.026

Cumulative present value of 1.00 unit of currency per annum

Receivable or Payable at the end of each year for n years $\left[\dfrac{1-(1+r)^{-n}}{r}\right]$

Periods (n)	\multicolumn{10}{c}{Interest rates (r)}									
	1%	2%	3%	4%	5%	6%	7%	8%	9%	10%
1	0.990	0.980	0.971	0.962	0.952	0.943	0.935	0.926	0.917	0.909
2	1.970	1.942	1.913	1.886	1.859	1.833	1.808	1.783	1.759	1.736
3	2.941	2.884	2.829	2.775	2.723	2.673	2.624	2.577	2.531	2.487
4	3.902	3.808	3.717	3.630	3.546	3.465	3.387	3.312	3.240	3.170
5	4.853	4.713	4.580	4.452	4.329	4.212	4.100	3.993	3.890	3.791
6	5.795	5.601	5.417	5.242	5.076	4.917	4.767	4.623	4.486	4.355
7	6.728	6.472	6.230	6.002	5.786	5.582	5.389	5.206	5.033	4.868
8	7.652	7.325	7.020	6.733	6.463	6.210	5.971	5.747	5.535	5.335
9	8.566	8.162	7.786	7.435	7.108	6.802	6.515	6.247	5.995	5.759
10	9.471	8.983	8.530	8.111	7.722	7.360	7.024	6.710	6.418	6.145
11	10.368	9.787	9.253	8.760	8.306	7.887	7.499	7.139	6.805	6.495
12	11.255	10.575	9.954	9.385	8.863	8.384	7.943	7.536	7.161	6.814
13	12.134	11.348	10.635	9.986	9.394	8.853	8.358	7.904	7.487	7.103
14	13.004	12.106	11.296	10.563	9.899	9.295	8.745	8.244	7.786	7.367
15	13.865	12.849	11.938	11.118	10.380	9.712	9.108	8.559	8.061	7.606
16	14.718	13.578	12.561	11.652	10.838	10.106	9.447	8.851	8.313	7.824
17	15.562	14.292	13.166	12.166	11.274	10.477	9.763	9.122	8.544	8.022
18	16.398	14.992	13.754	12.659	11.690	10.828	10.059	9.372	8.756	8.201
19	17.226	15.679	14.324	13.134	12.085	11.158	10.336	9.604	8.950	8.365
20	18.046	16.351	14.878	13.590	12.462	11.470	10.594	9.818	9.129	8.514

Periods (n)	\multicolumn{10}{c}{Interest rates (r)}									
	11%	12%	13%	14%	15%	16%	17%	18%	19%	20%
1	0.901	0.893	0.885	0.877	0.870	0.862	0.855	0.847	0.840	0.833
2	1.713	1.690	1.668	1.647	1.626	1.605	1.585	1.566	1.547	1.528
3	2.444	2.402	2.361	2.322	2.283	2.246	2.210	2.174	2.140	2.106
4	3.102	3.037	2.974	2.914	2.855	2.798	2.743	2.690	2.639	2.589
5	3.696	3.605	3.517	3.433	3.352	3.274	3.199	3.127	3.058	2.991
6	4.231	4.111	3.998	3.889	3.784	3.685	3.589	3.498	3.410	3.326
7	4.712	4.564	4.423	4.288	4.160	4.039	3.922	3.812	3.706	3.605
8	5.146	4.968	4.799	4.639	4.487	4.344	4.207	4.078	3.954	3.837
9	5.537	5.328	5.132	4.946	4.772	4.607	4.451	4.303	4.163	4.031
10	5.889	5.650	5.426	5.216	5.019	4.833	4.659	4.494	4.339	4.192
11	6.207	5.938	5.687	5.453	5.234	5.029	4.836	4.656	4.486	4.327
12	6.492	6.194	5.918	5.660	5.421	5.197	4.988	7.793	4.611	4.439
13	6.750	6.424	6.122	5.842	5.583	5.342	5.118	4.910	4.715	4.533
14	6.982	6.628	6.302	6.002	5.724	5.468	5.229	5.008	4.802	4.611
15	7.191	6.811	6.462	6.142	5.847	5.575	5.324	5.092	4.876	4.675
16	7.379	6.974	6.604	6.265	5.954	5.668	5.405	5.162	4.938	4.730
17	7.549	7.120	6.729	6.373	6.047	5.749	5.475	5.222	4.990	4.775
18	7.702	7.250	6.840	6.467	6.128	5.818	5.534	5.273	5.033	4.812
19	7.839	7.366	6.938	6.550	6.198	5.877	5.584	5.316	5.070	4.843
20	7.963	7.469	7.025	6.623	6.259	5.929	5.628	5.353	5.101	4.870

FORMULAE

Valuation models

(i) Irredeemable preference shares, paying a constant annual dividend, d, in perpetuity, where P_0 is the ex-div value:

$$P_0 = \frac{d}{k_{pref}}$$

(ii) Ordinary (equity) shares, paying a constant annual dividend, d, in perpetuity, where P_0 is the ex-div value:

$$P_0 = \frac{d}{k_e}$$

(iii) Ordinary (equity) shares, paying an annual dividend, d, growing in perpetuity at a constant rate, g, where P_0 is the ex-div value:

$$P_0 = \frac{d_1}{k_e - g} \quad \text{or} \quad P_0 = \frac{d_0[1+g]}{k_e - g}$$

(iv) Irredeemable bonds, paying annual after-tax interest, $i[1-t]$, in perpetuity, where P_0 is the ex-interest value:

$$P_0 = \frac{i[1-t]}{k_{dnet}}$$

or, without tax:

$$P_0 = \frac{i}{k_d}$$

(v) Total value of the geared firm, V_g (based on MM):

$$V_g = V_u + TB_c$$

(vi) Future value of S, of a sum X, invested for n periods, compounded at $r\%$ interest:

$$S = X[1+r]^n$$

(vii) Present value of 1·00 payable or receivable in n years, discounted at $r\%$ per annum:

$$PV = \frac{1}{[1+r]^n}$$

(viii) Present value of an annuity of 1·00 per annum, receivable or payable for n years, commencing in one year, discounted at $r\%$ per annum:

$$PV = \frac{1}{r}\left[1 - \frac{1}{[1+r]^n}\right]$$

(ix) Present value of 1·00 per annum, payable or receivable in perpetuity, commencing in one year, discounted at $r\%$ per annum:

$$PV = \frac{1}{r}$$

(x) Present value of 1·00 per annum, receivable or payable, commencing in one year, growing in perpetuity at a constant rate of $g\%$ per annum, discounted at $r\%$ per annum:

$$PV = \frac{1}{r-g}$$

FORMULAE CONTINUE ON THE NEXT PAGE

Cost of capital

(i) Cost of irredeemable preference shares, paying an annual dividend, d, in perpetuity, and having a current ex-div price P_0:

$$k_{pref} = \frac{d}{P_0}$$

(ii) Cost of irredeemable bonds, paying annual net interest, $i[1-t]$, and having a current ex-interest price P_0:

$$k_{d\,net} = \frac{i[1-t]}{P_0}$$

(iii) Cost of ordinary (equity) shares, paying an annual dividend, d, in perpetuity, and having a current ex-div price P_0:

$$k_e = \frac{d}{P_0}$$

(iv) Cost of ordinary (equity) shares, having a current ex-div price, P_0, having just paid a dividend, d_0, with the dividend growing in perpetuity by a constant $g\%$ per annum:

$$k_e = \frac{d_1}{P_0} + g \quad \text{or} \quad k_e = \frac{d_0[1+g]}{P_0} + g$$

(v) Cost of ordinary (equity) shares, using the CAPM:

$$k_e = R_f + [R_m - R_f]\beta$$

(vi) Cost of ordinary (equity) shares in a geared firm (no tax):

$$k_{eg} = k_0 + [k_0 - k_d]\frac{V_D}{V_E}$$

(vii) Cost of ordinary (equity) share capital in a geared firm (with tax):

$$k_{eg} = k_{eu} + [k_{eu} - k_d]\frac{V_D[1-t]}{V_E}$$

(viii) Weighted average cost of capital, k_0:

$$k_0 = k_{eg}\left[\frac{V_E}{V_E + V_D}\right] + k_d\left[\frac{V_D}{V_E + V_D}\right]$$

(ix) Adjusted cost of capital (MM formula):

$$K_{adj} = k_{eu}[1 - tL] \quad \text{or} \quad r^* = r[1 - T^*L]$$

In the following formulae, β_u is used for an ungeared β and β_g is used for a geared β:

(x) β_u from β_g, taking β_d as zero (no tax):

$$\beta_u = \beta_g\left[\frac{V_E}{V_E + V_D}\right]$$

(xi) If β_d is not zero:

$$\beta_u = \beta_g\left[\frac{V_E}{V_E + V_D}\right] + \beta_d\left[\frac{V_D}{V_D + V_E}\right]$$

(xii) β_u from β_g, taking β_d as zero (with tax):

$$\beta_u = \beta_g\left[\frac{V_E}{V_E + V_D[1-t]}\right]$$

(xiii) Adjusted discount rate to use in international capital budgeting using interest rate parity:

$$\frac{1 + \text{annual discount rate C\$}}{1 + \text{annual discount rate euro}} = \frac{\text{Exchange rate in 12 months' time C\$/euro}}{\text{Spot rate C\$/euro}}$$

Other formulae

(i) Interest rate parity (international Fisher effect):

$$\text{Forward rate US\$/£} = \text{Spot US\$/£} \times \frac{1 + \text{nominal US interest rate}}{1 + \text{nominal UK interest rate}}$$

(ii) Purchasing power parity (law of one price):

$$\text{Forward rate US\$/£} = \text{Spot US\$/£} \times \frac{1 + \text{US inflation rate}}{1 + \text{UK inflation rate}}$$

(iii) Link between nominal (money) and real interest rates:

$$[1 + \text{nominal (money) rate}] = [1 + \text{real interest rate}][1 + \text{inflation rate}]$$

(iv) Equivalent annual cost:

$$\text{Equivalent annual cost} = \frac{PV \text{ of costs over } n \text{ years}}{n \text{ year annuity factor}}$$

(v) Theoretical ex-rights price:

$$\text{TERP} = \frac{1}{N+1} [(N \times \text{cum rights price}) + \text{issue price}]$$

(vi) Value of a right:

$$\text{Value of a right} = \frac{\text{Rights on price} - \text{issue price}}{N+1}$$

or

$$\frac{\text{Theoretical ex rights price} - \text{issue price}}{N}$$

where N = number of rights required to buy one share.

The Examiner for Financial Strategy offers to future candidates and to tutors using this booklet for study purposes, the following background and guidance on the questions included in this examination paper.

Section A – Compulsory

Question One considers various issues surrounding a proposed investment in a wind farm in the US by SHINE, a multinational energy entity based in Germany. The question falls into three sections and requires an answer, in report format, addressed to the Directors of the SHINE group.

There are a number of internal and external constraints and uncertainties surrounding the success of the project and these are the focus of the investment appraisal exercise and ensuing discussion.

The centre of attention then shifts to the choice of currency for long-term borrowings to finance the project. An analysis is required of the impact of each proposed financial structure on the group balance sheet and discussion of the results of this analysis and of the wider issues involved in the choice of currency for the long-term borrowings. A recommendation is also required.

Finally, the question considers some broader organisational issues relating to the evaluation and implementation of the wind farm project. The emphasis here is on the differing roles and responsibilities of the treasury and finance departments and their interaction throughout the evaluation and implementation process.

The question tests topics across the syllabus in sections A, B and D covering investment decisions (section D), impact of constraints on financial strategy (section A), and the evaluation of alternative financing structures and the role of treasury (section B).

Section B – Choice of two from four questions

Question Two concerns a telecommunications consultancy based in Europe, but which trades globally. It is privately owned by the founding shareholders, who are also directors and now considering a flotation. The financial advisor has been asked to provide a range of possible values for the entity using suitable methods of valuation. The advisor has been asked to explain the methods of valuation to the directors and to make a recommendation of a course of action, including a possible flotation value. The question tests topics in section C of the syllabus – *business valuations and acquisitions*.

Question Three involves a venture capital entity that specialises in providing finance to small, but established, businesses. The entity is examining a potential equity investment in a medium-sized family owned transport and distribution business that is looking for additional capital to expand its operations. The question requires calculation of the number of shares the transport and distribution entity would need to issue to the venture capital entity to raise the necessary finance and what price these shares need to achieve to satisfy the venture capitalist's return requirement. A discussion of the possible exit strategies available to the venture capital entity and their likely acceptability to the transport and distribution entity is also required.

The question further requires discussion of the advantages and disadvantages to an established business such as the one in the scenario of using a venture capital entity compared with raising the necessary finance through long term debt. The question tests topics in section C of the syllabus – *business valuations and acquisitions*.

Question Four concerns a manufacturing entity based in the UK. Consumer tastes and demands are changing and the entity needs to reconsider its products and how they are manufactured and sourced. The question requires an evaluation of two alternative approaches to the continuation of how it supplies its main retailing customers with some of its products. As part of this evaluation, calculations are required of NPV, IRR and MIRR. Finally, a recommendation, with reasons, of which alternative the entity should choose is required. The question tests topics in Section D of the syllabus – *investment decisions and project control*.

Question Five is in two separate parts. Part (a) examines the objectives of a local government entity and a large, listed entity. The requirement is a discussion of the main criteria that these two very different entities need to consider when setting objectives.

The second part of the question compares the large, listed entity described in part (a) and a small private entity. The requirement is to discuss the relationship between dividend policy, investment policy and financing policy in the context of the two entities. The question tests topics in section A of the syllabus – *formulation of financial strategy*.

Strategic Level

P9 – Management Accounting Financial Strategy

Examiner's Answers

SECTION A

> *Examiner's Note:*
> The answer to **Question One** is fuller than would be expected from a well-prepared candidate. It has been provided for future candidates, and tutors, for study and revision purposes.

Answer to Question One

(a)

Tables showing separate workings for each year

	millions	millions	millions	millions	millions	
Years	0	1	2	3	4	
1. Constant exchange rate and 10% tax rate						
Net operating cash flows ($)	-	70·00	70·00	70·00	70·00	
Less tax at 10%	-	(7·00)	(7·00)	(7·00)	(7·00)	
Initial/residual investment	(200·00)				50·00	
Net $ cashflows	(200·00)	63·00	63·00	63·00	113·00	
Convert to € at rate of:	1·10	1·10	1·10	1·10	1·10	
Net $ cashflows	(181·82)	57·27	57·27	57·27	102.73	
Discount factor	1	0·893	0·797	0·712	0·636	
PV of € cashflows	(181·82)	51·14	45·65	40·78	65·34	**TOTAL 21·09**
2. Constant exchange rate and 25% tax rate						
Net operating cash flows ($)	-	70·00	70·00	70·00	70·00	
Less tax at 10%	-	(17·50)	(17·50)	(17·50)	(17·50)	
Initial/residual investment	(200·00)				50·00	
Net $ cashflows	(200·00)	52·50	52·50	52·50	102·50	
Convert to € at rate of:	1·10	1·10	1·10	1·10	1·10	
Net $ cashflows	(181·82)	47·73	47·73	47·73	93.18	
Discount factor	1	0·893	0·797	0·712	0·636	
PV of € cashflows	(181·82)	46·62	38·04	33·98	59·26	**TOTAL (7·92)**

	millions	millions	millions	millions	millions
Years	0	1	2	3	4
3. Euro strengthening and 10% tax rate					
Net operating cash flows ($)	–	70.00	70.00	70.00	70.00
Less tax at 10%	–	(7.00)	(7.00)	(7.00)	(7.00)
Initial/residual investment	(200.00)				50.00
Net $ cashflows	(200.00)	63.00	63.00	63.00	113.00
Convert to € at rate of:	1.1000	1.1770	1.2594	1.3476	1.4419
Net $ cashflows	(181.82)	53.53	50.02	46.75	78.37
Discount factor	1	0.893	0.797	0.712	0.636
PV of € cashflows	(181.82)	47.80	39.87	33.29	49.84

TOTAL (11.02)

	millions	millions	millions	millions	millions
4. Euro strengthening and 25% tax rate					
Net operating cash flows ($)	–	70.00	70.00	70.00	70.00
Less tax at 25%	–	(17.50)	(17.50)	(17.50)	(17.50)
Initial/residual investment	(200.00)				50.00
Net $ cashflows	(200.00)	52.50	52.50	52.50	102.50
Convert to € at rate of:	1.1000	1.1770	1.2594	1.3476	1.4419
Net $ cashflows	(181.82)	44.60	41.69	38.96	71.09
Discount factor	1	0.893	0.797	0.712	0.636
PV of € cashflows	(181.82)	39.83	33.23	27.74	45.21

TOTAL (35.81)

Workings: exchange rates

Year 1	1.10 x 1.07	=	1.177
Year 2	1.177 x 1.07	=	1.2594
Year 3	1.2594 x 1.07	=	1.3476
Year 4	1.3476 x 1.07	=	1.4419

Examiner's Notes:

1. These figures were based on the discount factors quoted in the tables provided. Candidates who used calculators to obtain discount factors would have obtained slightly different answers due to rounding differences.
2. Candidates who used a correctly adjusted discount rate (approximately 20%) instead of applying forward rates in the two scenarios where the Euro is strengthening against the $ would have gained full credit.

Summary of results	NPV
	€ million
Constant exchange rate and tax rate of 10%	21.1
Constant exchange rate and tax rate of 25%	(7.9)
Euro strengthening against the dollar by 7% pa and tax rate of 10%	(11.0)
Euro strengthening against the dollar by 7% pa and tax rate of 25%	(35.8)
Expected average NPV at tax rate of 10%	5.0
Expected average NPV at tax rate of 25%	(21.9)

Alternative approach using aggregate cash flows for constant exchange rate scenarios:

Years	0	1 to 4	4
1. Constant exchange rate and 10% tax			
Net operating cash flows ($)	–	70.00	
Less tax at 10%	–	(7.00)	
Initial/residual investment	(200.00)		50.00
Net $ cashflows	(200.00)	63.00	50.00
Convert to € at rate of:	1.10	1.10	1.10
Net $ cashflows	(181.82)	57.27	45.45
Discount factor	1	3.037	0.636
PV of € cashflows	(181.82)	173.93	28.91

TOTAL 21.02

2. Constant exchange rate and 25% tax			
Net operating cash flows ($)	–	70.00	
Less tax at 10%	–	(17.50)	
Initial/residual investment	(200.00)		50.00

Net $ cashflows	(200·00)	52·50	50·00
Convert to € at rate of:	1·10	1·10	1·10
Net $ cashflows	(181·82)	47.73	45.45
Discount factor	1	3·037	0·636
PV of € cashflows	(181·82)	144·96	28·91

TOTAL (7·96)

Examiner's Note: This alternative approach produces slightly different answers due to rounding differences.

(b)

	SCENARIO A		SCENARIO B	
	borrowings denominated in euro €millions	borrowings denominated in US dollars $millions	borrowings denominated in euro €millions	borrowings denominated in US dollars $millions
Assets	28,182 (W1)	28,182 (W1)	28,143 (W3)	28,143 (W3)
Non-current liabilities	4,182 (W2)	4,182 (W2)	4,182 (W2)	4,143 (W4)
Current liabilities	12,700	12,700	12,700	12,700
Equity	11,300 (balance)	11,300 (balance)	11,261 (balance)	11,300 (balance)
Total liabilities and equity	28,182	28,182	28,143	28,143

W1	28,182	=	28,000 + 200/1·1
W2	4,182	=	4,000 + 200/1·1
W3	28,143	=	28,000 + 200/1·40
W4	4,143	=	4,000 + 200/1·40

(c)

To: The Directors of the SHINE Group

From: Finance Director

Date: 22 November 2006

Report on proposed wind farm project

Purpose

This report considers the financial viability of the proposed wind farm project and whether or not it would be in the best interests of the group to proceed with the project. Alternative financing structures are also evaluated. The report concludes with a review of the different roles of the treasury and finance departments in the implementation process.

(i) **Discussion of the internal and external constraints**

External constraints
Uncertainty over the tax rate

- The tax rate is highly significant to the success of the project. The "expected" NPV is negative (€22·15 million) at a tax rate of 25%, but positive at a tax rate of 10%.

- If a tax rate of 25% is voted in by the local government, SHINE must take account of the risk of loss from the project and weigh that risk against the public relations benefits that would arise from undertaking the project.

- SHINE could also choose to wait until the tax rate is known before deciding whether or not to proceed with the project.

Uncertainty over the exchange rate

- Exchange rate movements are also key to the profitability of the project.

- Assuming that SHINE only proceeds with the project if the tax rate is fixed at 10%, exchange rate movements could make the difference between a positive NPV of €21·1 million at constant exchange rates to a negative NPV of €7·9 million if the euro were to strengthen against the US dollar by 7% per annum.

- The "expected" NPV result at a tax rate of 10% is positive at €5·0 million.

- SHINE would be well advised to use forward contracts to fix the exchange rate on future cash flows. If forward rates reflect current exchange rate expectations, it could then "lock into" a positive NPV result.

Objections from local holiday home owners and farmers

- The project may not be permitted at all if local holiday home owners and farmers succeed in their objections to the project.

- SHINE should take these objections seriously and employ local lawyers and a public relations organisation to assist them in defending the project.

- The main motivation of the wind farm project is to boost the reputation of the group and SHINE needs to assess the risk that negative publicity from local holiday home owners and farmers might significantly reduce the potential public relations benefit of the project.

Internal constraints

The decision on whether to proceed, even with a 25% tax rate, will largely depend on whether a suitable alternative project can be found that meets the group's public relations requirements and gives a positive NPV result.

However, the corporate objective to enhance the group's reputation by engaging in projects involving renewable energy is regarded as an important objective and may override any doubts about the potential profitability of the project.

Note that the 40% gearing ratio target is not perceived as a constraint since the project has very little impact on group gearing levels and is currently well within the 40% limit.

Conclusion
- The decision on whether or not to proceed will be largely dependent on how important the project is considered to be from a public relations viewpoint. If it is seen as regarded as very important and there are no suitable alternative projects, SHINE should proceed with the project regardless of the tax rate. If not, SHINE should hold back until the actual tax rate is known and only accept the project if a 10% tax rate is adopted.

- It is strongly recommended that exchange rates should be fixed by using forward contracts.

(ii) **Financing the project**

A large multinational group such as SHINE would be able to borrow from both domestic banks and international banks and financial markets in either euro or US dollar, who would be largely indifferent to the choice of currency.

Euro borrowings
- Euro borrowings have the disadvantage that they do not provide a natural hedge of the US$ assets. The value of equity would fall from €11,300 million to €11,261 million as a direct result of a rise in the value of the euro from US$ 1·10 = €1·00 to US$ 1·40 = €1·00.

- Gearing is likely to increase slightly with a rise in the value of the euro. However, the impact is negligible.

US dollar borrowings
- The dollar borrowings, however, provide a natural hedge against the dollar denominated investment, protecting the value of equity at €11,300 million despite a significant rise in the value of the euro.

- They may also enable US dollar net revenue streams to be netted against interest payments in US dollars.

- However, gearing levels are still slightly affected by changes in exchange rate movements. In this case, gearing improves marginally from 27.0% to 26.8% as a result of a rise in the value of the euro.

Conclusion:
- The project is so small in comparison in relation to the size of the SHINE group, that the type of financing has no major impact on either gearing levels or exposure of equity to exchange rate movements.

Workings:

Gearing:	Scenario A	Scenario B	Workings:
Euro borrowing	27·0%	27·1%	27·0% = 100 × 4,182/(4,182 + 11,300)
US dollar borrowings	27·0%	26·8%	

These figures compare to a pre-project gearing of 26·1%
Workings: 26·1% = 100% × 4,000/(4,000 + 11,300)

(iii) **Differing roles and responsibilities of the treasury department and finance department**

	Treasury	Finance
Evaluating the project	Quantify risks and look for ways of hedging or managing risks such as exchange rate and interest risk. Advise on an appropriate discount factor to be used in the investment appraisal evaluation.	Assess costs and revenues. Analyse risk factors. Evaluate the project.
Evaluating financing options	Treasury department to investigate alternative sources of finance.	Liaise with treasury on wider implications of financing options.
Arranging finance	Treasury to liaise with the banks and other intermediaries to arrange finance.	
Implementation of the project	Provide liquidity, and so on, as required. Prepare cash forecasts. Arrange interest rate and exchange rate hedging.	Set the budget and timetable. Monitor and control costs and revenues against the budget. Oversee the implementation.

Conclusion

The financial viability of the project is highly dependent on the final tax rate. At 10%, the project is highly attractive, but at 25% it is no longer financially viable, and we have to consider whether the public relations benefits outweigh the financial cost. We could also choose to delay the project until the final tax rate is known.

In terms of financing the project, the currency of any loan is insignificant from the group's perspective as the project is so small. The choice of currency would only affect overall cost of the project after taking the type of financing into account.

Both the treasury and finance departments would play an important and distinctive role in the implementation of the project and it is important that the departments work closely together throughout the process.

SECTION B

Answer to Question Two

(a)

Calculations

Methods that could be considered are:

- Asset value
- Market capitalisation
- Dividend/earnings valuation model
- NPV

Each method is calculated as follows:

Asset value

The balance sheet for 2006 shows net assets of €233 million. However, this entity clearly has substantial intellectual capital, which the value of tangible assets in the balance sheet does not reflect. An estimate of the value of an intangible asset can be attempted as follows. This method involves taking the excess returns on tangible assets and uses this figure as a basis for determining the proportion of return attributable to intangible assets.

1. *Calculation of average pre-tax earnings for three years:*
   (€67·5 million + €74·2 million + €56·9 million)/3 = €66·2 million

2. *From the balance sheet the average year end tangible assets over the last three years is calculated as:*
   (€198 million + €229 million + €263 million)/3 = €230 million

3. *The return on assets is calculated by dividing earnings by average assets as follows:*
   (€66·2 million/€230 million) x 100 = 28·8%

4. *The industry's return on assets for this same three years is 15% (as per the scenario)*

5. *Multiply the industry average pre-tax return on assets by the entity's average tangible assets to show what the average telecoms entity would earn from that amount of tangible assets:*
   €230 million x 15% = €34·5 million

   Subtract this from the entity's pre-tax earnings: €66·2 million - €34·5 million = €31·7 million
   This figure shows how much more AB earns from its assets than the average telecommunications company.

6. *The after tax premium attributable to intangible assets is calculated as follows:*

(i)	Three-year average income tax rate	=	30%
(ii)	Excess return	=	€31·7 million
(iii)	Multiply (i) by (ii)	=	€9·5 million
(iv)	(ii) – (iii)	=	€22·2 million

7. *The NPV of the premium is calculated by dividing the premium by the entity's cost of capital as follows:*
   €22·2 million/0·08 = €277·5 million ≈ €277 million

If the NPV of the estimated value of intellectual capital is added to the value of net tangible assets we get €263 million + €277 million = €540 million, less current liabilities gives a net figure of €510 million.

Examiner's Note: This estimate is based on the method shown in the CIMA Study System. Candidates would have gained credit for any valid attempt to place a value on intellectual capital.

Market capitalisation
If we use the industry average P/E of 12·5 the potential value is €497·5 million. If AB can command a rating up to 30% higher, this value rises to €646·7 million.

Examiner's Note: € 497·5 is calculated as €56·9 (2006 pre-tax earnings) less €17·1 (taxation) multiplied by 12·5 (industry average P/E)

Dividend/earnings model
There is insufficient information to use the DVM, although earnings could be used as a proxy. However, as the future growth rate is not constant the simplified model cannot be used. The NPV approach would give broadly similar results.

NPV

Year:	2007	2008
	€ million	€ million
After tax profit	50	64
Add: Depreciation	48	48
Cash flow	98	112
DF @ 10%	0·909	0·826
DCF	89	93

DCF of cash flows for 2009 and beyond are €112 million x 1·03 x 0·826/(0·10 − 0·03) = €1·361 million

NPV = €89 million + €93 million + €1,361 million = €1,543 million

Examiner's Note: The calculations here use the industry average cost of capital. An acceptable alternative would use 8%, the earnings yield (reciprocal of P/E ratio of 12·5). In this case the NPV would be €2,164 million.

	Total	Per share
	€ million	€
Asset value	233	7·7
Asset value including intellectual capital	455	15·17
Market capitalization	497 – 647	16·57 – 21·57
NPV	1,543	51·43

(b)

Discussion of methods and recommendation

Asset value
Asset value has little relevance except in specific circumstances such as a liquidation or disposal of parts of a business. Asset value is of even more limited usefulness in an entity such as AB, which earns a substantial proportion of its income from intellectual capital that generally does not feature in the balance sheet.

Market capitalisation

The P/E basis of valuation has the advantage that it bases value on the future earnings of the entity. In a listed entity the P/E ratio is used to describe the relationship between the share price (or market capitalisation) and earnings per share (or total earnings). It is calculated by dividing the price per share by the earnings per share. Market capitalisation is the share price multiplied by the number of shares in issue. Market capitalisation is not necessarily the true value of a entity as it can be affected by a variety of extraneous factors but for a listed entity it provides a benchmark that cannot be ignored in, say, a take-over situation.

In the case of an unlisted entity, a P/E ratio that is representative of similar quoted entities might be used as a starting point for arriving at an estimated market value, based upon the present earnings of the unlisted entity. The potential market capitalisation would be the entity's latest earnings multiplied by the benchmark P/E ratio.

AB is an unlisted entity so does not have a market capitalisation or a quoted P/E ratio. Applying the industry average P/E provides a benchmark but not a very good one. As noted in the scenario, there is a wide variation around this average. Also, although not stated, the definition of the industry is likely to be very broad. A better approach might be to find an entity similar to AB and apply its P/E. Again, this is very rough and ready. As AB is unlisted there are arguments for both lowering and raising the P/E as compared with either a proxy entity or the industry average. The Financial Advisor's estimate is that AB could command a rating 30% higher than the industry average. It is not clear how this estimate was made, as an argument could be made for lowering the P/E ratio to reflect the higher risk and lower liquidity of such entities. It would be more appropriate to use the NPV method and adjust the discount rate – as discussed below.

NPV/Earnings method

Forecasting cash flows and discounting at a specific risk adjusted discount rate is the theoretically correct valuation method. The valuation here uses the industry average cost of equity. Using an industry average suffers from the problems noted above. Also, the cost of equity will include an element of return for financial risk if entities have debt in their capital structure. Many entities included in the industry average will have substantial debt finance.

What is needed here is an exercise to calculate a more accurate cost of capital. As with using the P/E ratio approach, discussed above, finding a proxy entity may be more reliable than using an industry average.

Recommendation

As shown in the summary table in part (a), the likely market value ranges from €233 million (net tangible assets) to €1,543 million (NPV). The NPV valuation is substantially higher than any of the others. While this method is theoretically correct, the reliability of the results does of course depend on the accuracy of the forecast cash flows and the discount rate used. Using growth in perpetuity (although a sensible simplification for examination purposes) is unrealistic.

None of the figures produced by this exercise is wholly reliable, neither is it expected to be as this is simply an estimate based on incomplete information. The main recommendation must be to conduct a more detailed evaluation involving other advisors such as the entity that will be responsible for the flotation. It needs also to be established what percentage of their shareholding each director wishes to sell on flotation and how many new shares will need to be reissued. The calculations have been made on the current number of shares in issue to the directors/founding shareholders.

However, if a recommendation has to be made, a flotation value in the region of €600 million or €20 per share would be conservative. [*Examiner's Note:* Any sensible recommendation, or argument for not making one on the evidence available, would gain credit.]

A secondary recommendation would be to split the shares in readiness for a flotation. The share prices produced by all valuation methods, except asset value, are "heavy" – that is buyers would not get many shares for their money. More shares would need to be in issue to allow a reasonably liquid market in them.

Answer to Question Three

(a)

(i) – **Calculations**

Calculation of dividends and retained earnings:

	$ million
Revenue	105·00
Profit before interest and tax	28·83
Interest (15·0 x 7%)	1·05
Profit after interest before tax	27·78
Tax at 28%	7·78
Earnings	20·00
Dividends at 40%	8·00
Retained earnings	12·00

Valuation assuming constant growth of 6%

Value = D1/(ke – g)

Ke @	10%	15%
=	($8·00m x 1·06)/(0·10 - 0·06)	($8·00m x 1·06)/(0·15 - 0·06)
≈	$212 million	$94 million
Value per share $ (22,500,000 shares in issue)	9·42	4·19
Shares to issue to VCI	2,653,928 ($25m/9·42)	5,966,587 ($25m/4·19)
Total shares in issue after new issue	25,153,928	28,466,587
Percentage owned by VCI	10·6 (2·654/25·154 x 100)	21·0 (5·967/28·467 x 100)

The calculations suggest YZ would need to issue between approximately 2·7 and 6 million new shares depending on the valuation accepted. This would result in VCI owning between around 11% and 21% of YZ. Even 21% is not a particularly high percentage, assuming this does not give VCI the highest single shareholding. If this were the case, then YZ is vulnerable to the level of control VCI could exert on its management.

(ii)

Exit strategies

- Sell back to YZ shareholders, perhaps via a MBO. As founding shareholders they may value the business more highly than a third party investor. This is an advantage for VCI and provides VCI with a good base to negotiate a higher price. This might be a disadvantage to YZ shareholders, who also might not be in a position to raise the finance.

- Push YZ to apply for a stock market listing – YZ is too small for a main market listing, so it would have to be on the secondary market – and then sell on the open market. This can be an administratively lengthy and expensive process. Also, YZ may not wish to make available the percentage of shares necessary to allow a market in its shares. However, there would be many advantages of a listing at this stage in YZ's development.

- If VCI is seeking a quick sale, it may be easier to sell to a ready buyer, for example a trade sale, although this might infer a lower price for this speed and ease of disposal. YZ may not be happy with the new shareholder unless it has some right of veto built into the initial deal with VCI.

Some comment that VCI is unlikely to achieve its required rate of return given YZ's growth rate would gain credit.

Some calculations are also possible, for example at the 15% cost of equity, $25 million buys VCI a 21% stake in the company. If the pre-tax earnings for the year to 31 March 2007 are $27·78 million x 1·06 = $29·45 million, less 21% of this figure is VCI's, that is $6·18 million. This would be a 6·18/25 = 25% return, less than the 30% sought. At the 10% cost of capital share valuation, VCI would only attract 11% of the earnings, $3·24 million, and a return of 13%.

(b)

VCI financing versus long term debt

Advantages

- Money appears to be readily available.
- VCI may bring useful management expertise and, possibly, take a seat on the board (could also be seen as a disadvantage/interference by YZ).
- Reduces rather than increases gearing.

Disadvantages

- VCI may want more control than management wish to give and may push for higher risk strategies than YZ is comfortable with to allow for its required rate of return.
- It may ask for a seat on the board (which could be an advantage, as noted above).
- VCI may eventually sell shares to an unwanted (to YZ) buyer, or push for an early flotation.
- No tax advantages on dividend payments, compared with debt.
- Difficulty of valuing shares: in the circumstances here we are valuing only part of the entity and estimates of value might need to be adjusted for a part-sale. Any adjustment will inevitably be subjective, but in some ways it is no different from flotation where founding shareholders issue less than 50% in order to retain control.
- There may be higher set up fees.

YZ has high gearing based on book values and appears dangerously illiquid, with a current ratio of less than 1. Borrowing from a bank is likely to be difficult and expensive in these circumstances. However, although YZ is "well established", which meets one of VCI's investment criteria, it has lower growth than would normally be expected by venture capitalists. New finance from either route might therefore be problematic. Putting its finances in order might be a pre-requisite for additional funding from any source.

Answer to Question Four

(i) **Calculations of NPV, IRR and MIRR for alternative 2**

Forward rates

Spot	=	1·6
1 year forward	=	1·616 (1·6 x (1·04/1·03))
2 years forward	=	1·631 (1·615 x (1·04/1·03))
3 years forward	=	1·647 (1·631 x (1·04/1·03))

Calculation of NPV

Year:	0	1	2	3

All figures in millions

	0	1	2	3
US$ cash flows	-25·00	2·60	3·80	4·10
Inflated at 4% per annum	-25·00	2·70	4·11	4·61
Converted to £ at	1·600	1·616	1·631	1·647
£	-15·63	1·67	2·52	2·80
£ cash flows		3·70	4·20	4·60
Inflated at 3% per annum		3·81	4·46	5·03
Total cash flows £	15·63	5·48	6·98	7·83
DF @ 9%	1	0·917	0·842	0·772
DCFs	-15·63	5·03	5·88	6·04

NPV = £1·32 million

Calculation of IRR

	0	1	2	3
DF @ 14%	1	0·877	0·769	0·675
DCFs	-15·63	4·81	5·37	5·29

NPV = £-0·16 million

IRR by interpolation is calculated as follows:

$$9\% + \left[\frac{1 \cdot 32}{(1 \cdot 32 + 0 \cdot 16)} \times (14\% - 9\%) \right]$$

≈ 9% + 4·5% = 13·5%

However, the spread between the two rates is a long way apart for the result to be interpreted with accuracy.

Calculation of MIRR

At 9% reinvestment rate

Year	Cash flow	Factor	£m
1	5·48	1·1881	6·51
2	6·98	1·090	7·61
3	7·83	1	7·83
Total			21·95

MIRR = 15·63/21·95 = 0·712
From tables this is 12%

(ii) **Comments on MIRR**

The process for calculating MIRR is:

- An outflow in year 0 and a single inflow at the end of the project life is assumed;
- Cash flows after the initial investment are converted to a single cash inflow by assuming that the cash flows are reinvested at, usually, the cost of capital.
- MIRR is calculated by dividing the outflow by the single inflow, using PV tables and interpolation to arrive at the discount rate, or MIRR.

MIRR is intended to address some of the deficiencies of IRR, for example:

- It eliminates the possibility of multiple rates of return;
- It addresses the reinvestment issue;
- MIRR rankings are consistent with the NPV rule, which is not always the case with IRR.

However, there are weaknesses:

- If the reinvestment rate is greater than the cost of capital, then MIRR will underestimate the project's true return;
- The determination of the life of the project can have a significant effect on the actual MIRR if the difference between the project's IRR and the entity's cost of capital is large;
- The MIRR, like IRR, is biased towards projects with short payback periods;
- It does not appear to be understood or used extensively in practice;
- In the case here, we are evaluating two mutually exclusive projects. The argument for using MIRR is therefore weak.

Examiner's Note: The above discussion of MIRR was more than expected from a candidate, but some indication of an understanding of the key criteria for MIRR was expected.

(iii) **Recommendation**

Summary:

	Alternative 1	Alternative 2
NPV	£1·45m	£1·32m
IRR	10·5%	13·5%
MIRR	13·2%	12·0%

On the basis of NPV and MIRR the choice is for alternative 1. On the basis of IRR, alternative 2 is more advantageous. The main points to consider in respect of these criteria are:

- Theoretically, NPV is superior as shareholder wealth will increase by this amount. This criterion alone should recommend alternative 1.

- IRR has certain technical difficulties, although in reality these have little significance. Its advantage is that is it more easily understood by non-finance managers. This is not an argument for using it in preference to NPV.

- MIRR overcomes some of the technical difficulties of IRR, as explained below, but is little used and more difficult to understand.

Other criteria to consider are:

- Has a real evaluation of the market/customer requirements been carried out? Only one customer has been consulted as far as we know.

- Cash flows beyond three years need to be estimated – also, how has the FD made his estimates?

- What is the effect on other stakeholders if alternative 2 was chosen, for example employees and local suppliers?

- Is the investment consistent with the entity's objectives?

- Theory of interest rate parity has its weaknesses in practice. Some sensitivity analysis of the effect of different forward exchange rates, and therefore discount rate for alternative 2, could be attempted.

- Payback could also be considered. The information in the question is insufficient to make comparisons between the two alternatives.

The recommendation on purely financial grounds is marginal, so if using NPV as the main criterion the choice should be for alternative 1, but other criteria, including non-financial considerations, should be taken into account before a final decision is made.

Answer to Question Five

(a)

Objectives

The main issues to consider when determining objectives are:

Who are the main stakeholders?
In the case of CCC, it is the local population who are the main stakeholders, irrespective of whether or not they are taxpayers. The concept of "universal service" means a local government body must allow all inhabitants equal access to services. The government is also a major stakeholder as it provides much of the finance.

In the case of DDD, the main stakeholders are the shareholders who provide the risk capital of the business. The entity needs to recognise the needs of this group, in respect of the risk/return relationship and the attitude to dividends versus capital growth.

Both entities have other groups of stakeholders, such as employees and suppliers, but nowadays there is likely to be little difference in how the two entities recognise these groups when setting objectives. An interesting fact about DDD is that it chooses to maintain its HQ in a relatively small town. This suggests the company takes seriously its responsibilities to "minor" stakeholders, such as employees and the local community and makes it even more comparable with CCC than many large listed companies. There could also be implications of this decision for shareholders, although whether it is favourable (lower costs of an HQ) or otherwise (distance from City and major shareholders perhaps) is hard to say.

Where is the financing coming from, and in what proportions?
CCC is financed almost equally by central government and the local population. As central government's funding comes from taxpayers, then many of CCC's stakeholders and financiers will fall into both categories. DDD is financed mainly by its shareholders, who are therefore its main stakeholders, as noted.

Are there other, higher level, objectives that will supersede those set by the public sector entity, for example political aims/goals set by the government?
In the case of CCC, the government's objectives cannot be ignored, although the political persuasion of the elected council might influence the extent to which the central and local objectives complement each other.

Does the objective need to be measurable?
The objectives of both entities are difficult to measure, but it is easier to interpret whether DDD has achieved its objective than CCC. Setting a financial objective has the main advantage of being measurable. If CCC were to have a financial objective it could be benchmarked against the performance of similar entities. Both public sector and private sector entities should have measurable objectives to aid comparison with other similar entities.

Will information on the two entities' performance be subject to public scrutiny?
In both cases, the entities' performance will be public information. CCC has to provide annual reports, as well as a substantial amount of other information for its population. DDD has to provide annual reports and accounts, but is not legally obliged to provide information beyond what is required by Company law and International Financial Reporting Standards. The difference might be that those who scrutinise DDD's accounts and publicly announced information are better able to absorb and analyse it than those who receive CCC's information.

If DDD fails to meet its financial objective, the consequences may simply be that shareholders sell their shares. If they choose to take an active part in the management of their company they may force the removal of one or more of the directors. Shareholders in large listed companies rarely do this. The consequences of the entity failing to meet its non-financial objectives are less obvious as they are less clear, but they are unlikely to be much noticed unless a group of stakeholders becomes publicly and vocally critical, for example employees over a redundancy programme. However, even then the consequences are unlikely to be significant.

CCC's failure to meet its objectives could result in the local councillors being voted out of office (or not re-elected). A further consequence might be that central government takes a greater level of control over the region's affairs and/or funding is reduced or withheld.

In conclusion it could be noted that the two entities have a vested interest in each other achieving its objectives.

(b)

Dividend policy is part of an entity's financing policy; a private sector entity can only do one of two things with its profit after tax: pay it back to shareholders or invest it for the future.

In theory, if an entity has sufficient positive NPV projects, each discounted at a specific risk adjusted rate, it should invest 100% of its earnings for the future benefit of the shareholders. If it does not have any positive NPV projects, then it should return 100% of its earnings to shareholders. The argument is only really valid for a public listed entity where shareholders can sell some of their shares to create "home-made" dividends (even then, there are issues of timing and tax liabilities).

Entities rarely operate at these two extremes unless they are either very unusual entities, with a stated policy of not paying cash dividends, or they are in such serious financial difficulties that to pay a dividend would be considered illegal. The two entities will have considerable differences in terms of the number of investment opportunities, the availability of finance and their attitude to dividend policy.

MS's access to funds is likely to be restricted to either debt, secured on assets, or reducing dividends – it is not clear whether shareholders would have sufficient resources to finance a rights issue. However, if financing is with debt of $15 million, the gearing ratio would be around 25%. This does not seem excessive, but MS could still consider whether it would be better off reducing the dividend payout ratio. It has been paying out dividends at 60 cents per share irrespective of its level of profits. The dividend cover has never fallen below 1 or risen above 2, which suggests a generous policy for an entity such as this. There is, therefore, scope for expansion through internal funds if dividend policy were less generous. However, some shareholders may be dependent on dividends for income and they need to be considered in an entity such as MS.

The main shareholders are also the founders and managers of the entity. Given that MS is not at present listed, it is reasonable to assume that the owners/managers are not too concerned with the signalling mechanism of dividends. The employees who have been given shares as bonuses may be upset if they do not receive a dividend, but there is little they can do about it – there is no ready market to sell their shares and they are unlikely to resign in protest.

DDD, on the other hand, has access to a variety of sources of finance and dividend policy is likely to be one of steady growth, most probably influenced more by the signalling mechanism than anything else.